"I can count on Joe to give me the information I need to make good decisions."

—ED BELFOUR, DALLAS STARS

"I have tried other programs to train for hockey. This program is the first that actually carried over to the ice. The in-season program is one that can keep strength all year and is easy to follow."

—MATTIAS NORSTROM, CAPTAIN, LOS ANGELES KINGS

"With a grueling 82-game schedule to endure, it is imperative that I train properly and remain strong before, during, and after each season. Joe Horrigan's professional instruction and extremely thorough guidance enable me to achieve this most important goal every year."

—ROB BLAKE, COLORADO AVALANCHE

"I have been on this program for three years and each year I see better results."

—IAN LAPERRIERE, LOS ANGELES KINGS

"Working with this program I had noticeable improvement in quickness and strength. Not only was I stronger than ever coming into training camp, but my speed and strength actually increased as the season went on. I used the principles throughout the rest of my playing career and now incorporate them as a coach at the NCAA Division I level."

—DAVE SMITH, ASSISTANT HOCKEY COACH,
MERCYHURST COLLEGE

"Joe and Doc have put together a training plan that will accelerate all levels of competition of hockey play."

—GEORGE GWOZDECKY, HEAD HOCKEY COACH,
UNIVERSITY OF DENVER

"I hit a major roadblock in my career in 1999 when I missed almost an entire season because of two foot surgeries. This program has helped me come back bigger, stronger, and quicker than I was before my injuries. This program is a tremendous tool for any hockey player."

—PHILIPPE BOUCHER, DALLAS STARS

"Hockey is a game of speed and strength. No one understands the finer points of speed and strength conditioning better than Doc Kreis."

—Brad Hunt, sports agent

"This strength and conditioning program is the most comprehensive and sport-specific program I have seen. It is ahead of its time."

—Steag Theander, head strength and conditioning coach, Phoenix Coyotes

"Joe Horrigan has designed and implemented the speed, strength, and conditioning program we currently use with the Los Angeles Kings hockey club. Joe's program is specifically tailored for the sport of hockey, emphasizing speed, quickness, strength, and explosive power. The three years that Joe has been affiliated with the Kings team have also been the best three-year run in team history."

—Dave Taylor, vice president and general manager, Los Angeles Kings

"I highly recommend this text for coaches, athletes, and health care providers."

—Mike Reed, D.C., C.S.C.S., chair of sports medicine, USA Weightlifting

"The off-ice conditioning program our team went through played a major role in our success. Our players were faster and stronger, and they played with much more confidence and aggressiveness because of their added strength."

—John Van Boxmeer, assistant coach, Los Angeles Kings; former general manager and head coach, Long Beach Ice Dogs; and former NHL player

"Doc Kreis has put together a book for athletes at all levels. This is a guide for those in hockey who want to excel."

—Frank Costello, strength and conditioning coach, Washington Capitols

"While I was owner of the Los Angeles Kings, Joe was instrumental in the physical care of many of our players. I seriously doubt that we would have made the Stanley Cup Finals in 1993 without his help."

—Bruce McNall, former owner, Los Angeles Kings

"I would not have been able to make a comeback without Joe's help. His assistance with strength and conditioning, injury treatment, and hydration advice was a major role for the Long Beach Ice Dogs."

—MARK HARDY, ASSISTANT COACH, LOS ANGELES KINGS, AND FORMER PLAYER, LOS ANGELES KINGS AND LONG BEACH ICE DOGS

"While playing for the L.A. Kings, I pulled a groin muscle that didn't respond to treatment. Through the great work and expertise of Joe Horrigan and his staff, the problem was corrected. Thank you, Joe, for eliminating my problem and for making the end of my career most enjoyable."

—LARRY ROBINSON, FORMER HEAD COACH, NEW JERSEY DEVILS AND LOS ANGELES KINGS

"I think this program gives players the ability to add and maintain strength throughout the season. . . . It is a great program that all players and teams can use to increase their performance on ice."

—DARRYL WILLIAMS, ASSISTANT COACH, CINCINNATI, AND FORMER HEAD COACH, LONG BEACH ICE DOGS

"Doc has trained athletes at every level of competition, and his results speak for themselves. This book is *the* resource for those who want to maximize their physical ability to play hockey and get the winning edge on their opponent."

—ROB OVIATT, DIRECTOR OF PHYSICAL DEVELOPMENT, WASHINGTON STATE UNIVERSITY

"For well over a decade now, I have advised players to seek Dr. Horrigan's treatment. He gets athletes performing at their highest level in the shortest time just when they feel they have nowhere else to turn."

—RON SALCER, HOCKEY SPORTS AGENT

"I started the program three years ago, after watching the improvements of Luc Robitaille over the course of the season. I was coming off two knee surgeries, and my speed and strength combined with my age had my career in doubt. The power, quickness, and overall body strength achieved by following the program was amazing. I had the best overall year of my career at age 36. I truly owe the extension of my career to Joe and his program!"

—RAY FERRARO, ST. LOUIS BLUES

"Joe Horrigan's facility is the first stop I make if I, or our athletes, get hurt."
— Pat Brisson, vice president, IMG, and hockey sports agent

"This is the most innovative and effective strength and conditioning program in professional hockey. The results are amazing."
— Dave Good, S.S.C., C.S.C.S.,
assistant strength and conditioning coach,
Los Angeles Kings and Long Beach Ice Dogs

"Joe's work has helped bring hockey strength and conditioning into the present and toward the future."
— Ken Vick, C.S.C.S., director of the Performance Edge

"With Dr. Horrigan's program, not only have I kept my strength this season, I feel like I have more power and a quicker first step."
— Dan Bylsma, assistant captain, Anaheim Mighty Ducks, and author of *So, Your Son Wants to Play in the NHL*

"This program was the first time I worked with weights. I always figured that they would slow my reaction; instead they have given me more quickness from side to side, more power. Joe's program really helped."
— Stephane Fiset, Montreal Canadiens

"After training with Joe Horrigan's program, our Long Beach players simply knew we were better conditioned, better hydrated, and stronger."
— Rick Burrill, A.T.C.,
assistant athletic trainer, Los Angeles Kings,
and former head athletic trainer, Long Beach Ice Dogs

"Joe treated me at the Soft Tissue Center when I was playing with the Buffalo Sabres. After one week of treatment my legs felt young again."
— Mike Ramsey, assistant coach, Minnesota Wild

"The training principles provided by Joe Horrigan have revolutionized the game of hockey, raised the level of performance, and decreased the rate of injury."
— Jill Sleight, A.T.C.,
director of the Center for Athletic Medicine,
Manhattan Beach, California

STRENGTH, CONDITIONING, AND INJURY PREVENTION FOR HOCKEY

JOSEPH M. HORRIGAN, D.C., AND E. J. "DOC" KREIS, D.A.

Foreword by Luc Robitaille

Contemporary Books

Chicago   New York   San Francisco   Lisbon   London   Madrid   Mexico City
Milan   New Delhi   San Juan   Seoul   Singapore   Sydney   Toronto

Library of Congress Cataloging-in-Publication Data

Horrigan, Joseph M.
Strength, conditioning, and injury prevention for hockey / Joseph M. Horrigan
and E. J. "Doc" Kreis ; foreword by Luc Robitaille.
p.   cm.
Includes bibliographical references and index.
ISBN 0-07-139925-9
1. Hockey—Training.   2. Muscle strength.   I. Kreis, E. J.   II. Title.

GV848. 3.H66   2002
796.962'071—dc21   2002073516

1 2 3 4 5 6 7 8 9 0   QPD/QPD   1 0 9 8 7 6 5 4 3 2

ISBN 0-07-139925-9

Interior photographs:
Weight room exercises and agility drills by Andre Murray, Bern Agency, Burbank,
California, and Tim Jackson, Boulder, Colorado
Long Beach Ice Dogs photos by Brian Gold, Los Angeles, California. Used with
permission by Don Liebig Photography.
Mike Matteucci hip check photo by Cristina Salvador, Long Beach, California
Greg Schouten weighted sit-up photo by Mike Reed, D.C., Grover Beach, California

Models for all exercise demonstrations:
Deke Anderson, Los Angeles, California
Dave Good, Los Angeles, California
Dave Pletle, Boulder, Colorado
Greg Schouten, Riverside, California

Weight training facilities:
University of Colorado—Boulder, weight room and field
Gold's Gym, Redondo Beach, California
West Coast Sports Performance, Manhattan Beach, California

Graphic design for tables on pages 50 and 166 by Wilson W. Wing, Corona, California

Interior design by Nick Panos
Cover photograph copyright © Shelly Castellano

McGraw-Hill books are available at special quantity discounts to use as premiums and
sales promotions, or for use in corporate training programs. For more information, please
write to the Director of Special Sales, Professional Publishing, McGraw-Hill, Two Penn
Plaza, New York, NY 10121-2298. Or contact your local bookstore.

This book is printed on acid-free paper.

To Janet Horrigan, for understanding what goes into a project like this; to my mother, Eleanor A. Horrigan, for teaching me the clarity and insight of human rights; and to the memory of my father, Colonel William K. Horrigan, for his example and for teaching me to never quit.

—JOSEPH M. HORRIGAN, D.C.

To my wife, Suzi, and my children, E.J., Taylor, Ryan, and Jeremy, for their love and support.

—E. J. "DOC" KREIS, D.A.

CONTENTS

CONTENTS

FOREWORD

I have been playing hockey for more than 30 years, 16 of those as a professional. Over the past 10 years, I have noticed a big change in the game: the size and speed of the players has increased tremendously. Therefore, the need for players to improve their training and preparation is crucial. As a player, I have had to change and improve my game every year. This is the reason I changed my training program and went with the speed, strength, and conditioning program developed by Dr. Horrigan. The summer of 1998, I improved my speed by more than 0.30 second in the goal-line-to-near-blue-line sprint, and I gained much more power.

The authors of this book, Drs. Horrigan and Kreis, have done extensive research in training, treatment, injury prevention, and the psychology of our game. Their effort is appreciated. I have found this book very useful in my own training and injury prevention. Over my past 11 years of professional hockey, I've rarely missed a game due to injury. In eight years, I missed only four games, and that is because of my involvement with Dr. Joe Horrigan and the staff at the Soft Tissue Center. I missed a few weeks in 1998 due to a tear of an abdominal muscle, and I relied on Dr. Horrigan for guidance to return to play. I have always counted on the Soft Tissue Center to give me straight answers and proper treatment. This book gives straight answers regarding training for hockey.

Anybody who loves this game and wants to achieve a different level of play should read this book. It is a good guideline to help you with philosophy of training, injury prevention, and motivation.

—LUC ROBITAILLE,
NINE-TIME NHL ALL-STAR AND
HIGHEST SCORING LEFT WING IN NHL
HISTORY, ALL-TIME AND SINGLE SEASON

PREFACE

I have have had the opportunity to treat hockey players from numerous NHL teams at the Soft Tissue Center over the past 14 years. I also have had the good fortune to serve as the head speed-strength and conditioning coach and team chiropractor for the Long Beach Ice Dogs and as the head speed-strength and conditioning coach for the Los Angeles Kings. The more that I worked with and treated hockey players, the greater my realization that current knowledge of strengthening and conditioning was not being utilized to its fullest extent. This was evident from the poor quality of preseason and the lack of in-season training, as well as from the rate and types of injuries the players suffered.

During the pursuit of available material on strength training and conditioning for hockey, I noticed that a comprehensive and current hockey training book did not exist. The need for this information at the professional level and various league levels was absolutely clear, and the concept for this book began. Five years of research, communication, and writing finally resulted in this book. A few more years passed while seeking the right publisher.

During the writing, another author became involved with this project. I have known Doc Kreis for several years, and I am aware of the improved performance that he has achieved in training Olympic, professional, and NCAA athletes as the assistant athletic director and head speed-strength and conditioning coach for the University of Colorado at Boulder. I asked Doc to join this project to add more input and insight into the conditioning and training aspect so that it could be blended with my own strength-training knowledge and clinical background.

Rounding out the book are chapters about spinal injuries and neurosurgery by Robert Bray, M.D.; dehydration and rehydration in hockey players by Doug Andersen, D.C., C.C.N.; dental injuries, mouth guards, and concussions by Patric Cohen, D.D.S.; and head trauma by Ian Armstrong, M.D. I have had the chance to work with these doctors in various sports medicine events and situations, and I've found their knowledge, work, and results to be of the highest caliber. Their contributions to this project are most welcome and will greatly benefit all those who read this book.

To the best of my knowledge, this the first time that a doctor of chiropractic and a strength coach teamed up on a book or project such as this, with additional contributions by neurosurgeons, a fellow sports chiropractor, and a dentist. The result of this blend is that you, the reader, are able to have not only "the best of both worlds," but also the best of all points of view. Throughout this book, you will notice initials enclosed in parentheses. These initials are those of the doctor who contributed the information. This will enable you to direct any questions you might have to the proper source.

An extensive review of published hockey literature is included for strength coaches, head coaches, athletic trainers, physical therapists, physicians, team physicians, team chiropractors, and anyone else who may wish to read more hockey- and training-related material. Because hockey has not progressed as much as other sports in the field of strength and conditioning, a number of older articles were included in the review of literature to make the review complete.

I hope that readers of all levels of interest will find this book useful for understanding preparation requirements and the practical use of training methods. For those readers who are close to the sport but not necessarily involved in a day-to-day operation, this book should offer an insight into what is required in strengthening and conditioning. Photographs and diagrams are used to make this book as user friendly as possible.

Please read this book in its entirety at least once so that you will understand all of the concepts we wish to address in speed-strength and conditioning, hockey injury patterns, and training with and around injuries. Afterward, this book may serve as a reference tool so that you can apply it to your more specific needs.

Although each chapter could be the subject of an entire book, we felt that the material could be condensed and addressed to be of immediate use to athletes, coaches, doctors, physical therapists, athletic trainers, and strength and conditioning coaches.

Hockey is a wonderful sport, and I have enjoyed being this close to it and involved in it. I think we will all enjoy watching the sport progress to the next level.

—JOSEPH M. HORRIGAN, D.C.

ACKNOWLEDGMENTS

This book is written for the players of the National Hockey League, all professional hockey players around the world, future hockey players, and all the coaches and parents who support them.

Many people are always involved, in one way or another, in any project or career. I would like to thank the following people for their assistance and support not only in the sport of hockey but also in sports medicine:

Nick Adams; David Alper; Dan Altchuler, D.P.M.; Mike Altieri; Doug Andersen, D.C.; Garrett Andersen, D.C.; Ross Arbiter, Esq.; Ian Armstrong, M.D.; John Balik, Mike Neveux, and Steve Holman at *Ironman* magazine; Art Bartolozzi, M.D. (for his professional and clinical interest) and the Philadelphia Flyers organization; Peter Bastone; Ed Belfour; Bill Bergman, Ph.D.; Scott Blatt, D.C., A.T.C.; Hart Bochner; Pat Brisson; Chris Broadhurst, A.T.; Mike Brown; Tim Brown, D.C.; Rosalyn Bryant; Brenda Chan, P.T.; Zena Clark; Bob Clarke; Randall "Tex" Cobb; Patric Cohen, D.D.S.; Mary Collings, D.C.; Lynn Conkwright; Fred Coury; Pat Croce, P.T.; John Cullen; Vinnie Curto; Juliet Cuthbert; Tony Danza; Andrew Deutsch, M.D., and Jerrold Mink, M.D. (for always making room in your schedule to provide diagnostic imaging on the hockey players on short notice); Ron Duguay; Carolyn Durst; Mike Dyer; Cory Everson; Jeff Everson; Mike Fay; Keith Feder, M.D.; Brandt Feldman; Charlie Francis; Harley Frankel; Ted Goldstein, M.D.; Cammi Granato; Tony Granato; Wayne Gretzky; John Hannon, D.C.; Rob Heidger; Pat Helma, D.C.; Ron Hextall; Dustin Hoffman; Mark Hoffman; William Hohl, M.D.; Paul Holland; Sherri Howard; Laurie Hunter, C.P.A.; Nick James; Gea Johnson; Eric Kaufman; Pete Koch; and Steve Kotlowitz.

Thanks to the Long Beach Ice Dogs coaching staff, trainers, and administration: former general manager and head coach John Van Boxmeer for his support of the speed-strength program, the advancement of clinical science in hockey, and his review of this book; former head coach Darryl Williams; assistant coach Rene Chapdelaine; former assistant coaches Mark Hardy, Matt Block, and Brian McCutcheon; former head athletic trainer Rick Burrill, A.T.C., and Van Parfet, A.T.C.; and current head athletic trainer, Bobby

Walls, A.T.C.; head equipment manager Dan Delvechio; Joann Klonowski; Bill Jacobs, Esq.; and owners Barry and Maggie Kemp.

Other members of the Ice Dogs speed-strength and conditioning staff over the past six years are Dave Good, C.S.C.S., S.S.C.; Sean Waxman, C.S.C.S.; Mikio Aoi; Sean Coughlin, D.C., C.S.C.S.; Steve Tunnell, D.C., C.S.C.S.; and Ed Reynolds, D.C., C.S.C.S.

Members of the health care team are Mike Textor, D.C.; David Velasquez, D.C., C.S.C.S.; Ed Scale, D.C.; and Chad Moreau, D.C., C.S.C.S.

Thanks to members of the Los Angeles Kings: general manager Dave Taylor; assistant GM Kevin Gilmore; head coach Andy Murray; assistant coaches Mark Hardy and Ray Bennett; former assistant coach Dave Tippett; assistant speed-strength coach Dave Good; equipment manager Peter Millar; assistant equipment manager Dan Delvechio; Craig Karlan, Esq.; Eric Kaufman; Dean Kennedy; Andy Klein, D.C.; Bruce Markman, M.D.; Todd Lanman, M.D.; Al McGinnis; Bruce McNall; Cass Magda; Bert Mandelbaum, M.D.; Pam Marshall; Al May; Juergen Merz; Jeff Moeller; Bill Moreau, D.C., C.S.C.S.; Brendan Murray, D.C., C.S.C.S.; Carl Mussler; Michael Neumann, M.D.; Jim Nice; and Darrel Oglvie-Harris, M.D. Thanks to the entire Toronto Maple Leafs organization; Keith Oshiro; Pierre Page; Scott Pearson; Gina Perez, A.T.C.; Jorgen Persson, M.A.; Roger Phillips; Jim Ramsay, A.T.; Mike Reed, D.C., C.S.C.S.; Keanu Reeves; Steve Reich, Esq.; Tom Reich, Esq.; Doug Risebrough; Larry Robinson; Luc Robitaille; Gary Ross; Ed Scale, D.C.; John Scaringe, D.C.; Peter Schafer; Rich Semel, D.C.; Castoria Seymore, M.D.; Latanya Sheffield; Rahn Sheffield; Frank Shellock, Ph.D.; Giovanni Silva, D.C.; Jill Sleight, A.T.C.; Gene Smith; Sinjin Smith; Ted Sobel; the Soft Tissue Center staff, especially Ashly Plourde for his tireless effort and Drs. Sean Coughlin and Ed Reynolds for their research assistance on this book; Drs. Steve Tunnell, David Velasquez, and Chad Moreau; Leonard Grainger, for his assistance; Mona Santillanes; C. David Stringfield, former CEO, Baptist Hospital, Nashville, Tennessee; Jamie Talbot; Steag Theander, strength coach, Phoenix Coyotes; Gary Uberstein, Esq.; Pat Verbeek; Rick Waugh; Tom Webster; Joe Weider; Susan Welsh, D.C.; the entire staff at West Coast Sports Performance; William Whiting, Ph.D.; Wilson Wing; John Wolf; Curtis Wong and Dave Cater at *Inside Kung-Fu* magazine; and all of the NHL players, trainers, coaches, general managers, and agents that have consulted with the Soft Tissue Center.

Special thanks goes to John Van Boxmeer; Keith Feder, M.D.; and Dave Taylor for the opportunity.

Very special thanks to Ron Salcer.

I would also like to thank the following track and field coaches, strength coaches, and strength athletes for their invaluable input into my speed, speed-strength, and conditioning experience and knowledge over the years:

For personal input, thanks to Charlie Francis; Chuck Debus; Rahn Sheffield; Dragomir Ciroslan; David Shaw; George Zangas; Derek Hansen; Bob Kersee; Fred Hatfield, Ph.D.; Paul Ward, Ed.D.; Peter Tegen; Mike Reed, D.C.; Mike Burgener; Pat Cullen-Carrol; and John Brenner.

And for their input from published work, thanks to Tudor Bompa, Ph.D.; Bob Ward, P.E.D.; Dragomir Ciroslan; John Garhammer, Ph.D.; Lyn Jones; George Dintiman, Ed.D.; Mike Stone, Ph.D.; Jim Williams; and the late Paul Anderson.

—JOSEPH M. HORRIGAN, D.C.

When you surround yourself with great people, great things happen. I would like to thank a number of great people in my life:

My wife, Suzi, whose passion and love forged new understanding and blessings and gave me a positive direction in my life, and my children, E.J., Taylor, Ryan, and Jeremy, who keep me young and growing.

My staff at the University of Colorado for their support and encouragement: Gavin Ozaki, Scott Asano, Heidi Burgett, "Super" Dave Plettl, Donnie Maib, Jamie Redmond, Big John Freeman, Dave Good, Dave Best, Kylie Feldman, Travis Reust, and Karl Jordan.

The inspiration of Coach Bill McCartney, Reverand James Ryle, Pastor Hansford Van, Don Spicely, Mike Spivey, Milton Carrol, Warren Williams, Dave Rankin, and Sam Talent.

My friends Chip Jackson, Debbie and Leon White, Julie and Roger Berardi, Brad Hunt, Linda and Mike Bynum, Bob Pettyjohn, Lou Rubino, Coach Norman Green, Coach Bill Marolt, Steve Abo and Pasta Jay, Charlie McConnell, Paul McConnell, Pete Pedin, Al Phillips, Keith Phillips, Jeff Cartwright, and my confidante, Gary Lewellyn, and his wife, Tamara.

Strength coaches Frank Costello, Dana LeDuc, Brad Roll, Al Miller, Matt Riley, Ken Coggins, Rob Oviatt, Todd Suttles, Jeff Madden, Johnny Parker, Tom Woods, and Chuck Stiggins.

Josh Ambrose, Thelma Pratt, David Lowry, Coach Ricardo Patten, Dr. Fred Hatfield, Dave Plati, Jim Kelleher, Joe Bozich, Estes and Mary Banks, Bill Harris, and Dr. Dave Pearson for their involvement, support, and expertise.

The many athletes and administrators whom I have been honored to have coached and to work alongside.

And special thanks to my writing partner, Joe Horrigan, for the idea to create and produce something that can better the levels of performance in athletes.

Bless each and every one of you for your part in this endeavor.

—E. J. "Doc" Kreis, D.A.

INTRODUCTION

In the *National Strength and Conditioning Association Journal*, Twist and Rhodes, a strength coach and a physiologist from Vancouver, Canada, defined modern hockey quite accurately:

> It is a one-on-one sport requiring agility, stick handling, passing, shooting at speeds over 90 mph, and interaction with teammates. Other on-ice activity includes body checking, absorbing hits by opponents, and crashing into the boards, posts, and ice. There is no other sport that demands so much. It requires the ability and agility of a figure skater, and the quickness of a speed skater. Physically, it demands the power of a football player to dig in the corners for the puck and absorb full-speed collisions while checking an opponent. Then comes the ability to handle and control a puck, a skill more difficult than finessing a golf ball across a slick green into the cup.

Ice hockey has grown in popularity in the United States at an incredible rate in the past few years. As of 2000–2001, youth hockey (USA Hockey—ages 6–17) in the United States has approximately 354,000 participants. Hockey is no longer exclusively a game of the northern climates, and the increased popularity is no doubt due to the fact that so many of the game's superstars are playing in the United States: Wayne Gretzky was in Los Angeles for seven years before going to St. Louis and then to New York; Luc Robitaille played in Los Angeles for eight years before going to Pittsburgh and New York, back to Los Angeles, and then to Detroit; Mario Lemieux is in Pittsburgh; Jaromir Jagr was in Pittsburgh and is now in Washington; Brett Hull was in St. Louis, then Dallas, and now Detroit; Mark Messier has returned to New York; Temmu Selanne was in Anaheim and is now in San Jose; Paul Kariya is in Anaheim; Eric Lindros was in Philadelphia and is now in New York; and Alexei Yashin and Pavel Bure are in New York. Eight new National Hockey League (NHL) teams have been added over the past several years, and only one was in Canada. The new teams have included San Jose and Anaheim, California; Tampa Bay and Miami, Florida; Nashville, Tennessee; Columbus, Ohio; Minneapolis, Minnesota; and Ottawa, Canada. Additionally, the Minnesota North Stars relocated to Dallas, the Winnipeg Jets moved and became the Phoenix Coyotes, and the Hartford

Whalers have moved to Raleigh, North Carolina. The Quebec Nordiques moved and became the Colorado Avalanche.

This change in hockey can also be seen by the development of college teams where they didn't previously exist. Various leagues have blossomed everywhere, and many ice rinks such as the Iceoplex facilities in California are booked 24 hours per day, several days per week.

Hockey is truly an international event. American fans are realizing what the Canadians, Swedes, Finns, Czechs, Ukrainians, Slovakians, Russians, Danes, Latvians, and Germans already knew: hockey is a quick, exciting, and fun game to play or watch. It is not uncommon to find players from several of the countries mentioned here all on one professional team.

Unfortunately, as in some other sports, much of hockey training has been guided by tradition and not by evolving sports science. Nowhere else has this been as glaringly evident as in the strength and conditioning training and the subsequent difficulty with injury prevention. Discussions with various coaches, players, and strength coaches led to the realization that much of today's hockey training is in a similar position to that of professional football in 1965. The preseason training is lacking in many areas. The in-season training is virtually nonexistent for most teams. The frequency and types of injuries have changed and increased in the past few years. Many veteran hockey coaches have simply not been exposed to strength and conditioning methods that are available today. Many strength coaches do not understand hockey. This combination presents quite a dilemma.

The game has changed so much. The level of speed has steadily increased. Larger players are being drafted and selected. The changes evoke comments from retired players such as: "We used to play with injuries."

Athletes play with injuries today also, but many of the injuries are more significant. With due respect, "old-timers" were champions of their era, but the game is evolving with a new level of skill on the ice today. We have tremendous respect for the old-timers, for they were skilled and certainly tough. However, the nature of today's game has changed, just as all sports and businesses evolve. Today's game centers around speed, size, strength, improved skill levels, and now significant salary contracts. These factors necessitate proper training to yield the bottom line in all professional sports: maximum dollar for maximum performance.

A segment of the television series *NOVA* dealt with the subject of science in sports performance. Biomechanics, physiology, talent identification, training, and coaching were the areas investigated. One example—swimming—stood out as a perfect comparison for hockey. The great Olympian Mark Spitz staged a comeback in 1992, 20 years after his seven-gold-medal Olympic performance. Because sports performances always improve over time, the world records that Spitz set in 1972 no longer stand, and in fact they would not qualify him to go to the U.S. Olympic trials today. When his swimming technique was biomechanically analyzed in 1972, he was found to have the best technique in swimming. He was analyzed again in 1992, and he still had the best technique in the world in swimming. But technique alone is no longer enough. Spitz lacked strength, anaerobic power, and sprint ability. These attributes are obtained by swimmers today through their training outside the pool. Spitz noted that in his day, swimmers spent six to eight hours per day in the pool, and they didn't have strength programs. This is no longer the case. Swimmers spend far less time in the pool today, and they include weight training and cycling in their training.

Mike Matteucci, now with the New Jersey Devils, delivers a big check.

Much of the training that professional hockey players have used to attempt to fill the training void has been copied from the bodybuilding community. Although bodybuilding is a fine activity, it is truly nonspecific for hockey and has little application. Unfortunately, the bodybuilding input has led to training and conditioning programs that have no component other than weight training (and most likely not even a good strength-training program at that). Other components of training such as speed development, plyometric/ballistic training, agility training, and hockey practice must be kept in mind. The body should not be exhausted from the strength training so that all these other components are compromised. It has been appalling to see professional athletes selecting their training routines from lay bodybuilding magazines and local gyms instead of from logical, scientific, effective, and proven methodology. A proper program is a fine art and science (more science). It is not a complicated task to design a proper program of strength and conditioning for an athlete. This book will make the process easier for the reader.

The purpose of a strength and conditioning program is twofold. The first and foremost purpose is to decrease the risk and probability of injury. Maximizing sports performance comes in at a close second. These two points have multiple integral parts, as you will soon see. Remember, one cannot score, win, or set records while sitting on the bench due to an injury or poor performance. The healthier that the athlete is, the more he or she will play and the greater will be the probability of success.

We feel that the supplemental training exercises will soon become a permanent addition to hockey preparation. These exercises cannot be chosen haphazardly. The training must have a plan, goal, and method. No champion is produced by "winging it" in training or performing. Elite athletes do not arrive at the track, field, or weight room and say to themselves, "What will I do today in my workout?" These plans are made well in advance. Canada's track coach Charlie Francis always emphasized the training method questions "When? How much? Why? How much recovery? How do you avoid injuries? How do you avoid problems? How do you recover from injuries?" These are key questions that coaches or managers will be asking on a regular basis. These questions must be answered well in advance—prior to the training period or, even better, prior to the season. The evaluation that the players go through in camp will certainly alter the individual program.

The entire level of hockey will continue to rise as the players become faster and stronger with better conditioning, utilization of better recuperation, and better mental discipline in preparation. The average NHL player in the 1995–96 season was six feet, one inch, and 196 pounds. The average Philadelphia Flyer was six feet, two and a half inches, and 215 pounds. The average size of the Flyers' "Legion of Doom" was six feet, four inches, and 229 pounds. The number one 1997 draft choice, center Joe Thorton, was six feet, four inches, and 200 pounds, and he is playing very well. As coaches and teams select larger players, the proper conditioning and training of the players will become critical.

PART ONE
STRENGTH

STRENGTH TRAINING

The search for improved sports performance continues in all fields. Weight training has become a mainstay in the training of athletes for general conditioning, strength, sport-specific training, and even improved flexibility.

A comparison of various statistics of 1974 and 1984 Division I NCAA universities revealed very interesting data. First, there was little doubt that scientifically based strength and conditioning programs have had an impact on sports. The data also suggest a positive relationship between these programs and won/loss records (McClellan). A recent study of injuries in soccer, both before and after weight training, demonstrated a clear reduction of injuries with the use of weight training. My (JMH) experience with the Long Beach Ice Dogs demonstrated fewer injuries over the course of the 82-game season with weight training. Then–Ice Dogs athletic trainer Rick Burrill commented more than halfway through the 1996–97 season, "I should have seen many more injuries, especially in the low back. It's nice having a quiet training room." Workers' compensation claims were reduced once the strength and conditioning program began.

Professional and college football teams have established standards or guidelines of strength. For some teams, the guidelines are flexible, and for others the guidelines are adhered to quite rigidly. Some coaches feel that strength and conditioning criteria could prevent some athletes from making the team because of their deficiencies in those areas. Criteria other than strength and speed are evaluated and are best determined by the coach. Examples of these other criteria are the focus and determination of the player, the intangible "sixth sense" of awareness of the player's teammates on the field, and the ability to be where the puck or ball is or will be. These types of abilities can certainly make up for deficiencies in other more quantitative measurements such as speed, strength, height, and weight. The same is true for hockey. The tangible measurements are important criteria to keep in mind for general purposes, but they are not absolute indicators of success. Standards of strength and conditioning will not prevent the superstar from rising to the top, as some fear. The superstar will always make it with or without the standards (as long as he or she is not injured). The NHL has

Players angle to get the puck in front of the net.

numerous superstars that are lacking in some field of measurement except the won/loss column. Please note that the superstar compensates for his or her weaknesses. Strength and conditioning should be seen not as a way in which hockey is excessively controlled but rather as a way that it is cultivated.

It is important to realize that we are not trying to turn a bodybuilder, weight lifter, or strong individual into a hockey player. Conversely, the goals are not to turn these hockey players into Olympic weight lifters, powerlifters, or bodybuilders. We are trying to make stronger and better-conditioned hockey players ready for a bigger, better, stronger, and

faster hockey game. This is a very important point. The player already possesses hockey skills. The player already knows how to skate. The player already knows how to make a slap shot. The player understands the strategy of the game. But, if we can make this individual a stronger player and a faster player, then he or she will be a better player. A stronger, better-prepared player will have the desired half-step improvement in quickness, the extra strength in front of the net, a faster slap shot, the strength to dig the puck out from the boards, increased power during the delivery of a check, the ability to withstand the impact of being checked, and the ability to recover faster. The stronger player is simply more durable. Strength and mass are vital to hockey players due to the level of contact between players and boards or ice surfaces.

The myths and misconceptions surrounding weight training are finally, and justly, fading away. We can turn to track and field to see the results of weight training and speed work. We can look at professional football to see the effects of weight training and agility training. *Weight training* and *speed . . . weight training* and *agility*—these terms were not used together 25 years ago. These myths of 25 years ago have been exposed to the light of science and the pragmatic proof of today's maximum performances.

Of course, as with other sports, it is important to note that as the salaries and contracts become continually larger, more players are drawn to the game, and this leads to better recruiting and elevated intensity of play. Multimillion-dollar contracts have a tendency to improve the level of play. There are many examples of this in sports. There was a time when all a professional tennis player did was go to the court and play tennis. As the prize money and endorsement money increased, the level of competition increased, and the nature of training for tennis changed. The days of players like Jimmy Connors and John McEnroe, who did little if any supplemental training, yielded to the multifaceted training programs of players such as Boris Becker, Ivan Lendl, Andre Agassi, Jennifer Capriati, and Venus and Serena Williams. Cardiovascular training, flexibility programs, and strength training have developed in tennis training. It is no longer a matter of going to the tennis court, serving, and seeing what happens. The tennis players of today are prepared, and they will continue to be so. Female tennis players like Venus Williams have served the ball at 126 miles per hour. Male tennis players reached this mark just a few short

years ago. Similar evolution of performance improvement will follow in hockey shortly.

Although strength training applies to all athletes, it is certainly a larger component of training for some than for others. Sometimes players who are not familiar with strength training are resistant to trying it. Often, the unfamiliarity may make the player state something to the effect of, "I am a skill player. I don't need it." The skill player has to begin strength training like any other athlete—by learning technique with an empty bar, PVC pipe, or wooden dowel. Once the technique is learned and the training becomes more familiar, the athlete will be more receptive and the improvements will provide reinforcement.

If we use professional football as an example, we can see that even the players who require less physical development still have some component of weight training in their program. The quarterback position is acknowledged as one of the key skill positions, yet quarterbacks do strength training today. For example, Super Bowl MVP John Elway performed a 350-pound bench press. A recent NCAA Division I quarterback performed a jerk (overhead) with 320 pounds. The 2001 Colorado quarterback, Bobby Pesavento, had a 335-pound bench press and a 545-pound squat. The 2002 number one overall draft pick, David Carr, was reported to have a 300-pound power clean, 390-pound bench press, and 500-pound squat. Skill and strength are not mutually exclusive. While these numbers may seem impressive to some, the offensive and defensive linemen have undergone more extensive training to perform at their positions at optimum levels, and their strength levels are much higher.

As with football, the differences in training for hockey in the future may vary by position. The checking line has traditionally been the intimidating "grinders," "mudders," or "stoppers," known for checking the opposing

When battling for the puck, players need leg, hip, back, and abdominal strength.

line and slowing its momentum. Perhaps the checking line will one day come to be the most physical group of players on the team. If the checking-line players can achieve a new level of strength and conditioning, then they will be able to go on the ice, check, and play their game at a higher level, demonstrating that they are an unrelenting force to be reckoned with. The checks they make in the first and second periods will pay dividends in the third period. The time has come for players who have six to eight minutes per game to stop training aerobically by riding stationary bikes for 30 to 60 minutes and start implementing more anaerobic training. The physical demands of the checking line are purely anaerobic. All players want to have a skill game and play more time each game, but if the athlete doesn't play well for six minutes, he or she won't get eight minutes of game time. Certainly fighters and enforcers will have more physical (i.e., contact) training, and

Play by the boards is always physical.

so will the defensive defensemen. And in the future, even the first-line center, the star forwards, and the offensive defensemen will be unable to ignore the need for strength training if they have to face opponents that have trained in a more efficient and proper manner. For example, a star running back in football cannot beat larger linebackers and defensive linemen who, as a result of participating in a heavy strength program and speed program, are almost as fast as he is. The same applies to hockey. The physical punishment alone warrants proper training, strength, and conditioning as well as the proper mental attitude. Also, improved neck strength may be a significant factor in reducing concussions in hockey.

The strength coach plays a key role in the training process and serves many purposes and wears many hats. One of the responsibilities is to keep the emotional level of the players up and even. The strength coach must be observant. Strength coach John Waters put it quite well:

> Motivation. There is no mathematical formula to calculate it, no lotions or potions to stimulate it, and it cannot be diagrammed on paper or a chalkboard. What stimulates one player may have an opposite effect on another . . . motivation is learned, nurtured, developed, and exemplified by the strength coach and the program. . . . Motivation is more than whistles and T-shirts. It is a positive attitude, a genuine concern, and a humanistic approach.

There is an expression that fits well into this introduction: "The whole is greater than the sum of the parts." This applies to the benefits of training. The parts that benefit from proper training include strength, speed, durability, survival ability, positive psychological edge, and improved confidence. These added together will help produce an athlete who can perform at a higher level. If an entire team elevates these same characteristics, then the players as well as their opponents will feel the strong, positive team synergy. Any coach knows that this feeling is invaluable for the players and can make the difference between those who win and those who lose.

Athletes who have not had much strength-training experience should not be afraid of the weight training as long as they follow these simple safety guidelines:

- Handle the weights properly. The use of correct technique is the most important part of training.
- Do not attempt to move heavier weight than you are capable of lifting or you may strain a muscle or tendon.
- Train properly and handle only the weight that you are scheduled to do. There are no exceptions to the training schedule unless you are being supervised by a qualified strength and conditioning coach.
- Do not attempt to "feel the muscle" as you lift the weight. Instead, learn to move the weight. As your body is exposed to progressively greater training loads, your system will respond; it does not require your conscious awareness of the change in load for you to make gains. You are training your entire body, your system, to move as a unit because you play as a unit. You do not play in body parts, so do not train your body in body parts. Body part training is a bodybuilding concept.

Regrettably, there are training programs that are not scientifically based. When research is not well understood, the training methods may become distorted, sometimes with disastrous results. Bizarre, excessive, and unusual training methods should be avoided.

Training Facility and Equipment

Strength coaches who work successfully at the highest levels are almost unanimous in the selection of free-weight training as the basis of proper strengthening. Machine training alone simply does not provide enough reproducible and carryover effect to be the basis of training. Too much is lost with the lack of balance and stabilizing work around the joint if a machine is used. Also, athletes of different sizes may have difficulty fitting on the machines. The director of strength and conditioning at the Lake Placid U.S. Olympic Training Center feels that strength and conditioning are best centered around multijoint free-weight lifts. The training of elite athletes rarely falls into the realm of machines.

What types of facilities and equipment are necessary? The players do not need to go to the nearest gym or spa. We are not interested in spa training and results. A fair assessment of proper training facilities was published just a few years ago. The previously mentioned survey of Division I NCAA university strength and conditioning programs yielded a fairly concise picture of their training facilities. Ninety-six percent of the universities have a full-time strength and conditioning coach, 32 percent have a full-time assistant, 26 percent have part-time assistants, and 60 percent have graduate assistants. The average size of the training room is 4,002 square feet with a range reported between 15,500 and 1,080 square feet. Thirty-eight percent of the facilities reported that they could accommodate 51 to 75 athletes. The training facilities are equipped with free weights primarily. The most common and popular pieces of equipment and their average numbers in each facility were as follows (a piece of equipment is listed only if the facility has three or more of them).

power rack	5.8
squat rack	5.8
bench press	5.7
incline press	4.2
platforms	3.0
Olympic bars	17.5
curl bars	4.0

The only machines that averaged to more than one per program were the leg curl, leg extension, and four-way neck machine. Fifty-three percent of the facilities report that they did not have single-station machines or full-gym machines.

We recommend adding a few pieces of equipment to this list:

rubber bumper plates
glute-ham-gastroc bench
hyperextension bench
medicine balls (various weights)

The power rack can be used for squats, bench presses, jerks, and other presses.

Standards can be used for squats, jerks, and presses.

A wooden frame with rubber inlays, weight-lifting platforms provide a firm, stable surface to lift from and allow lifters to drop weights if needed.

neck-training harnesses
12-inch to 30-inch boxes
Shuttle

The total amount of weight in the facilities ranged from 4,000 to 25,000 pounds.

Only 36 percent of the universities polled reported their budget for their programs. The budgets ranged from $550 to $70,000 per year with an average of $16,408 annually. The average facility is open 10.5 hours per day, five days per week.

The requirements of an average training facility as we have described are certainly conservative and should be manageable by a professional hockey team. A minor-league team should be able to obtain assistance from the major-league team with which it is affiliated. After all, the minor-league players will be called up to the major leagues someday, and they need to be physically ready to meet the demands of a higher level of play. Junior teams may need to have assistance from the community to raise the money for a basic but effective facility.

Machines of exorbitant cost are not necessary. College teams usually have access to superior training facilities. Lifting platforms can be assembled from two layers of three-quarter-inch plywood for a relatively low cost. For greater expense, teams can obtain platforms that are heavier and more durable; they can even have the team logo on the platform. The bumper plates and proper lifting bars will incur a larger part of the budget for the team.

There is a rise in the popularity of isokinetic equipment today. Isokinetic equipment allows the athlete to perform concentric training only. "Concentric" action is where the muscle is working and shortening. For example, if you perform a curl and lift the bar toward your shoulder, the biceps muscle is shortening. This is concentric action. When you lower the bar, the muscle is still working, but the muscle is lengthening. This is known as "eccentric" action. In the gyms, concentric action movements are called "positives," and eccentric action movements are known as "negatives." Those who try to sell isokinetic training programs and machines often state

Rubber bumper plates are designed to be dropped.

Glute-ham-gastroc benches are usually found in university and pro-team weight rooms.

Plyo boxes of various heights are designed for jumping and hopping.

that the higher speed of training with them is more sport specific. We disagree. The performance of isokinetic training in non-weight-bearing machines is not specific to sport, and the angular velocities that are used in isokinetic training do not replicate velocities in sports performance. For example, the high speed of an athlete's lower extremities during a sprint are unresisted and are followed by an instantaneous halt of velocity as the foot strikes the ground. These movements are not the same as being seated in a machine with resistance through isolated movements in a concentric manner only. We do not advise the

use of isokinetic training except perhaps in a very limited manner, for a very limited amount of time, and only as a supplement to the strength and conditioning program. The improvements we obtain with our athletes in speed, vertical jump, strength, slap-shot velocity, body weight, and body fat have occurred without the use of isokinetic training.

Support and Understanding for the Strength and Conditioning Program

"A strength program should be viewed as a training component required to be developed if performance is expected to improve."

—TUDOR BOMPA, PH.D.

Support of the strength program from the coach is absolutely necessary for its success. This doesn't apply to just the strength and

A big check against the boards.

conditioning coach. The support of the program must come from the top: head coach, general manager, assistant coaches, team physician, head athletic trainer, president, and owner (through financial support). On a smaller level, there may be a need for community financial support for a fundamental training facility for some junior teams or small-town teams.

Troubleshooting

It is important for the management of a hockey team and the players to understand the differences in appropriate training meth-ods. Even a coach with good intentions can choose a training path that will lead to disastrous results. A perfect example of this happened about 10 years ago in the NHL. A head coach hired a bodybuilder/personal trainer from a local well-known gym to set up and design the team's "strength program." Unfortunately, the coach did not realize or comprehend that the bodybuilder/personal trainer did not understand the concepts of strengthening and conditioning. Three or four days before camp was to begin, I received a call from a defenseman on the team. This defenseman was 32 years old at the time and was entering the option year of his contract. He described a situation in which he was advised by the personal trainer to perform an exercise known as "triceps push-downs" using a rope. While doing so, he felt a sudden sharp pain in his elbow. When he called he told me that his elbow had swelled to the size of half of a grapefruit. During my interview with him, I (JMH) discovered that this player did not have any weight-training experience.

Several unnecessary things occurred in this situation. The first is that the personal trainer obviously had no understanding of hockey performance. He was taking professional athletes off the ice and placing them in body-building programs, and thus, in a sense, attempting to turn them into bodybuilders by his training methods and then return them to the ice to play hockey. This is not appropriate strength training or established sport-specific training. The triceps push-down with a rope is not applicable to the sport of hockey. Second, the triceps push-down with a rope is not an appropriate exercise for an athlete who does not have weight-training experience. Third, the trainer's lack of knowledge resulted in a player being injured while performing a supplemental form of exercise three days before summer camp, at 32 years of age, and in the last year of his contract. This type of result can be disastrous for the career of a player. Fortunately, the player was able to come through the injury and continue his career. Clearly, the personal trainer did not have the right to interfere in an elite athlete's training program without due consideration and research. Although this coach thought starting a strength program was a step in the right direction as the team did not have a program previously, the results were poor. Players are not always fortunate enough to remain with a team after such an injury.

This type of situation has happened in other sports where strength and conditioning training is new. There was a very well known National Basketball Association (NBA) team that used a training partner of a famous bodybuilder as the strength coach. The basketball players on the team were performing absurd training routines and often asked other random members in the gym if they knew how to train to increase the vertical jump. Unfortunately, two of the team's top players suffered knee injuries. The most difficult part for us to grasp is that the general manager, head coach, and team physician had no idea that their multimillion-dollar basketball players were using an irrational, ineffective, and perhaps even injurious program. As you have read, misdirection in training can be disastrous. This has to stop in all sports. This book will enable the coach to identify erroneous training practices even if he or she doesn't entirely understand what should be done. Speed-strength and conditioning professionals can be brought in to sort this out.

One NHL coach was quoted in the newspapers as stating, "I would rather have 20 fat, hard-working guys than 20 guys that look like Greek gods." This statement actually demonstrates the point of effectiveness and appropriateness in training quite well. This coach had players that trained, but their training was ineffective, and therefore their performance was not what it should have been. A player that trains as a bodybuilder or simply chooses both inappropriate exercises and aerobic conditioning may look physically impressive but may also not have a proper carryover effect of his or her training to hockey. The player may also be overtrained. We would like to see this coach have 20 players for one season that had been properly conditioned and strengthened and then obtain his response.

As we already noted, the aesthetic appearance of an athlete may or may not be an indication of the athletic power and agility that can generate speed-strength. The real question at camp should be: what is the back strength, hip strength, leg strength, and abdominal strength of this player? This region of the body is where power originates. It is not generated from the biceps and triceps. There is an old weight-training expression that is applicable here: "You cannot fire a cannon from a canoe." In other words, all of the upper-body strength is meaningless without a base of support (legs, hips, and low back).

It is important for the strength coach to explain to the players that the training program will feel different and have different effects from what they have felt before. Some athletes find the change in their training program to be confusing. They may have had success in their early weight training through what appeared to be aggressive bodybuilding training and may not understand why they should change their training methods. There is a good reason for why they feel this way. Verkoshansky gave the reason by stating that in the initial stages of training, the principle of "all means are good" is completely justified. In other words, in the beginning stages of training, almost any type of training is beneficial. The athlete will respond to any new load. Continuation of this same type of training may not produce any further results or take the athlete "any further down the road." Once the results stop, the athlete might then try to simply increase the volume of work (more sets, more exercises). This can lead to overtraining, fatigue, decreased sports performance, and injuries.

It is important to realize that a strength and conditioning coach shouldn't just issue a workout card and walk away from the player. An effective program is more than a piece of paper with numbers on it. The effective strength coach must, in a sense, wade through the players in the weight room to know the results of the overall program, the individual gains and setbacks from on-ice injuries, and the subsequent need for modification in train-

ing. The strength coach must observe subtle signs that tell much about the athlete that day and his or her ability to perform. This means the coach must watch for changes in, or degradation of, lifting technique. This may be an indicator of fatigue and of injury risk. The speed of the pulls may be slowing. The jumps may not have the usual quickness. The athletes may seem like they are dragging; they may look tired and pale after an excessively long or strenuous ice practice. If you have access to their body-weight charts, you may find the athletes to be dehydrated, as indicated by their weight loss. All of these types of observations will allow the strength coach to adapt the speed-strength program to the athletes' needs.

Avoid Overtraining

Olympic lifts and their variations as well as the inclusion of the power lifts are precisely what every sport uses to train. Hockey should not be an exception to this form of training. The training loads must be specific and known. We want to move the athlete away from exercises such as push-downs, curls, laterals, and the like. These are isolation, body part exercises and are a waste of time for an athlete. You must remember that the athlete has a limited amount of energy for training and, more important, limited energy to recover from training. The demands on the athlete's energy come from hockey practices, hockey games, travel, psychological stress (from coaches, parents, relationships, schools, teammates, media, management, finance, injuries), dehydration, and sleep loss with travel. This leaves very little energy for the necessary strength and conditioning. The available energy must be used judiciously.

Subtle changes, either way, in training can make the difference between winning and losing. This includes the unfortunate use of unnecessary exercises that do not contribute to performance. One example occurred a number of years ago in the World Powerlifting Championships. There was a great rivalry between two competitors in the 198-pound class, and everyone was eagerly awaiting another showdown. One competitor arrived and looked more physically impressive than ever. His shoulder and arm development had changed significantly. The other powerlifter, also impressive as any world-class powerlifter would be, did not have the bodybuilding appearance of his competitor. The less physically impressive lifter won the championship. Regarding the more impressive looking lifter, a journalist wrote after the meet, "I don't know how he lost. He must have left it near the preacher curl bench." This comment implies that the time the loser spent on exercises that did not help his competitive cause cost him the championship. Charlie Francis was aware of the same problems in track and field. He wanted his athletes to train the maximum amount of muscle for maximum gain with the least amount of training time and exercises. This was a most successful method. Use the available energy and time on proven exercises, and don't waste it on worthless exercises and long training routines.

The concept of central nervous system (CNS) stimulation and recovery is becoming an area of more significant focus today. If the coach pays very close attention to the signs of CNS fatigue, he or she probably will not cause the athlete to overtrain. Apply the principles you will read about in this book to your program design. Additionally, watch for slowing of the athlete's movements, degradation of technique, slower bar velocity, missed lifts, intermediate weights that appear to be heavy for the athlete, and so on. If these are happening, either adjust the percentages, select low-CNS-stimulation-type exercises, or send the athlete home and resume training the next day.

Another area that is under significant scrutiny is the perpetual mixing of exercises. Exercises that are nearly identical can be varied in a healthy athlete. For example, you may substitute a clean pull for a power clean, a front squat for a back squat, and so on. Do not produce a wide variety of changes on a regular basis. You want the athlete's body to adapt to the increased workload that he or she has applied to it. Adaptation is the goal. A well-known former Mr. Olympia advocated the method of always changing exercises to "shock the muscle" and "keep it from getting used to one movement." Thus far, there is no validity to this theory, and if there is, it may apply to bodybuilding only and not to sport and strength training. This is the difference between well-planned programs and hit-or-miss training. There must be a plan to be successful.

When structuring an athlete's training program, particularly an in-season program, do not train the athlete to exhaustion. Also do not force reps or train with a great deal of eccentric training ("negatives") because fatigue and exhaustion will cause a decrease in performance. The athlete does not have the time and energy reserves to recover and play as well. Properly applied training theories and concepts will produce the results that you seek. Careful planning can balance the demands of hockey practice, speed-strength training, agility drills, plyometric exercises, game schedules, and travel.

Promoting Speed-Strength Training

The coach who plans, formulates, and executes a speed-strength-training program designed to build a stronger and faster hockey team must improve the levels of all of the players, not just a select few. He or she might use several tools to motivate the players and promote the program.

Record Boards

Displaying record boards is an excellent way of encouraging the players to compete against others as well as against themselves. Being recognized as one of "the best" is a motivating reward and will, we hope, encourage others to follow. In addition to displaying team records, record boards can also display personal records—both of which can motivate all the team members to pursue excellence.

Monthly Progress Reports

Monthly progress reports help remind each team member about his or her goals and progress. They also let the athletes know that the coach is overseeing their work—good or bad.

Testing

Testing days should be at the end of each cycle. Coaches can help the athletes by teaching them how to prepare for a testing session. Coaches can use the testing period the same as they would use the game-preparation day—teaching how to be confident and ready to succeed without fear of failure.

Team Contests

Outside of the testing days, the use of team contests is excellent for peaking out of testing periods and also allows the coach to use rewards in the form of T-shirts, trophies, medals, and other school athletic wear. T-shirts can promote the school nickname or team motto as a reward for a certain level met or proficiency in a particular movement. Trophies and medals can be used to reward the best performance. Also, these events provide an opportunity to invite parents, friends, fans, and local junior athletes to come and watch.

Mottoes and Quotes

The use of mottoes, slogans, and quotes in the weight room and/or in the dressing room is another excellent motivation technique. To further instill pride, the weight room itself can be a great motivating factor for all team members. A well-kept, clean, and spirited training facility can make the difference in how athletes interpret the seriousness of the coach. It is amazing what a little paint and cleaning can do. It is not uncommon for parents to become concerned with, and involved in, helping to create a better training site for their sons and daughters. Again, a little enthusiasm and willpower can go a long way in teaching young men and women how to win.

Special Awards

Hockey coaches who keep up-to-date, accurate records of the progress of their hockey players can select the outstanding individuals who complement the speed-strength-training program and acknowledge their accomplishments. The incorporation of special awards, medals, trophies, or certificates to accompany these achievements works as a positive motivating factor for all team members to become more involved and dedicated. Special athletic wear (T-shirts, shorts, hats, and sweats) can take the place of trophies as incentive gifts. The pride that is exemplified by the recipient of such special awards sets an example for others to follow. The special awards allow the hockey coach an opportunity to identify the not-so-talented players who are participating and working to help the team achieve its goals.

Self-Evaluation Training Journal

The hockey strength coach should keep records of all athletes. Just as important is a self-evaluation training journal, which should be kept by each athlete. Coach Gregory Goldstein, formerly of the Soviet Union coaching staff, made the argument in a seminar that an athlete who does not bring his lifting journal to practice should immediately be sent home and not allowed to practice that day. The coach may allow the hockey players to carry the self-evaluation journals home, but it is better to have a filing shelf or designated area in the facility.

By keeping his or her own journal and noting updates with each workout, each athlete can monitor his or her progress and is more motivated to succeed in speed-strength training. The self-evaluation training journal serves to point out the good training days and what made them good and also point out weak days and when they occurred. The self-evaluation training journal also notes one's personal records (PRs) and what new goals he or she is training to achieve. The coach can refer to his or her own records while reviewing each hockey player's journal and make helpful suggestions with this improved insight into the athlete's thinking and motivating factors.

Motivation Techniques in Speed-Strength Training

To teach an athlete how to sustain his or her motivation, the coach may want to incorporate the following steps in the speed-strength-training program:

1. Help the athletes set short-term goals—not just in hockey, but in school, work, and speed-strength training.
2. Work with the athletes for what is and what could be down the road; setting long-term goals may lead to long-range results.
3. Help the athletes learn about the major motivating forces in their lives.
4. Establish a schedule—the success of any program depends on the players' having a well-planned day-to-day, as well as month-to-month, program with goals and objectives.

5. Teach that anything worth working for has a price to be paid; success belongs to those who want it the most. Focus on the end result. Make training-related pain and discomfort a positive factor.
6. Teach what all-out effort is—and instill the enjoyment of the sensation that comes from achieving this effort.
7. Teach the players to understand the challenge in preparing—by learning more and more; construct and reconstruct new speed-strength-training regimens as their knowledge of training develops.
8. Help the players learn to enjoy success.
9. Motivate players to success; success is what you and the coach say it is. Success depends upon the goals of each player and the follow-through.
10. Teach by example—coaches who are enthusiastic and excited about their team always have a better chance of success.

Strength Coach as a Motivator

One task of the coach and trainer involved in a speed-strength program is to consistently motivate the athletes to higher and higher levels. Doyle Kenady, coach of the 1983 United States Powerlifting Team, said that to enjoy success in any sport, "an athlete has to have a lot of drive and motivation. Talent isn't enough. Everybody at the top level has talent." The following motivational principles will help the coach to encourage the hockey players:

1. The coach must motivate the players to get involved in speed-strength training at the very beginning; then he or she should keep encouraging them over the sticking points, those dead periods when strength gains and speed gains come slowly.
2. By being there to help and support, the hockey coach can promote new confidence and build from what the athlete

sees changing in his or her own body—greater strength and body mass.

3. The strength coach should be on hand for every workout, especially in the beginning weeks of any phase. Often at the beginning of training, the coach must downplay the thinking that "if some is good, then more is better."

4. The coach should know that not all athletes respond to the same types of motivational techniques.

Examples of Successful Results of Speed-Strength Training in Hockey

Coaches often ask for specific examples of the successful effects that proper speed-strength training can have on hockey performance. An example of an applied speed-strength program can be illustrated by the International Hockey League (IHL) Long Beach Ice Dogs players in the 1996–97 season. The instruction in lifting technique began in the last month of the 1995–96 season. Because the instruction began late in the season, the weight that was used was minimal—usually an empty bar or a few small plates in addition. The lifts were foreign or new to most of the players. We started the technique instruction so that the players would have enough experience to perform them in their off-season programs.

Examples of the results were evident in the September 1996 training camp. Patrik Augusta arrived with more developed back (paraspinal and trapezius muscles), hip, and leg muscles. He performed a clean pull with 205 pounds, and shortly into the season he stated, "I've checked more players in the first three weeks of this season than all of last year combined." Augusta won the MVP for the team in the 1996–97 season. By February 1997, he could perform four sets of two reps with 205 pounds for the clean pull. This improvement was due to the in-season training program. Dave Smith performed a vertical jump of 32 inches (no steps) and improved his goal-line-to-near-blue-line time by 0.29 second at training camp. All reporting veterans could perform sit-ups with 45 pounds for three sets of 10 reps. More significant, the in-season program began, and all the new players had to learn proper lifting technique as well.

Enforcer Barry Neickar was physically impressive but was a product of high-repetition lifting and had never performed any type of clean or snatch movement. We started Neickar with an empty bar and had him progress quickly to 95 pounds. During the 1997 Turner Cup playoffs, he performed a clean pull with 305 pounds. Prior to his reporting to the Ice Dogs, he had used 225 pounds for reps in the bench press and squat. When questioned about his training methods and reasons, he stated that this was the only training he knew. The speed-strength program lead Neickar to a 345-pound bench press and a 385-pound power squat during the playoffs. At the exit physical, Barry had a 29-inch vertical jump and a 10-foot standing broad jump. The very least that is expected is that the players at least maintain, but should be able to improve, during a season if the program is carefully planned. Neickar continued with the off-season program, and by the time he reported to the 1997 Mighty Ducks training camp, he had reached a 380-pound clean pull, 350-pound bench press, 495-pound squat, and 100 pounds for three sets of 10 reps in the sit-up. This strength aspect of the training was coupled with running, agility and plyometric drills, and medicine-ball drills.

Defenseman Mike Matteucci had performed many plyometric drills and had lifted at Lake Superior College. He responded well during the in-season training, and it showed in his play in the corners. By the 1997 Ice Dogs camp, Matteucci reached personal-best performances in the clean pull with 345 pounds, bench press with 305 pounds, and vertical jump of 29 inches. His vertical jump in June 1997 was 22 inches, and his best in college was 25 inches. He also performed a squat with 440 pounds (free bar). Matteucci's performance on the ice reflected his improved speed-strength status. He shattered our goal-line-to-near-blue-line record by sprinting the distance (20 yards) in 2.62 seconds. His time has dropped by more than 0.7 second over a two-year period.

The overall improvement in the vertical jump for the eight returning Ice Dog veterans was 5.5 inches. This is in keeping with the published data of improved vertical jumps associated with Olympic lifts, track work, and box jumps. Team captain and multiple IHL All-Star and team MVP Dan Lambert had a 19.5-inch vertical jump in March 1996, 24 inches in September 1996, 27 inches in September 1997, and a 31-inch vertical jump in September 1998. Needless to say, head coach John Van Boxmeer stated that he had never seen Lambert have "such jump on the ice."

NHL All-Star Luc Robitaille began this program June 1, 1998. His goal-line-to-near-blue-line time was 3.0 seconds. We introduced him to the program carefully. By September 1, 1998, his goal-line-to-near-blue-line time was 2.67 seconds. He performed a power squat of 275 pounds and a clean pull of 215 pounds. By March 1999, Robitaille performed a 415-pound power squat and a 315-pound clean pull. He also performed sit-ups with 80 pounds for two sets of 10 reps and scored 39 goals (he hadn't scored more than 24 goals in four years). By 1999 training camp, Robitaille's near-blue-line time was 2.62 seconds, his power squat was 485

pounds, and his clean pull was 335 pounds. By the 2000 training camp, he was the fourth fastest out of 52 players to the near-blue line. A few years ago, many people thought his career was coming to an end. Instead, Robitaille has passed the 600-goal mark, passed Bobby Hull as the all-time left wing goal scorer, joined the top 10 all-time goal scoring list, and shows no signs of retiring from hockey.

Many people thought the career of Ray Ferraro was over as well. He applied the same dedication and discipline to this program that Robitaille did, and he rejuvenated his career. He hadn't played more than 40 games in a season for years. The first year on the program, Ferraro played 81 games, and the next year he played 82 games. He had the second highest point season of his career, was made captain of the Atlanta Thrashers the following year, and was obtained by the St. Louis Blues.

Regardless of the team or player, we expect to see increases in the vertical jump, standing broad jump, squat, and clean as well as decreases in sprint time and body fat from this type of program. These players are usually able to sustain a very physical style of play and are strong and fast in the third period. This level of results is the end product of the careful application of data on training, physiology, biomechanics, motor learning, clinical sciences, and great hockey coaching. Any well-applied and monitored program should produce the same successful results.

Strength Evaluation, Assessment, and Physical Measurement

"Coaches rise or fall by the capacity to adjust. One's greatness is demonstrated by one's athletes. The failure to recognize and

adjust to the superior output will end (limit) the athlete's capacity to exceed or even equal the same level of output again."
—CHARLIE FRANCIS

Assuring success in training requires many factors to be in concert to produce the desired, predicted effect. Training is a science, especially at today's level of elite sports. There are numerous theories about training. Unfortunately, some of the theories have been fabricated by people who haven't studied physiology, biomechanics, or pathology and who lack certification in strength and conditioning or weight lifting. Some of these theories have no scientific basis whatsoever and usually produce poor results. Even strength-training authorities differ in their opinions, and certain methods work better for one sport than they do for another. There are numerous textbooks addressing basic anaerobic physiology and training. These books are readily available for anyone who wants to obtain a basic knowledge of the training effect.

There are methods of analyzing the needs and demands of any sport. Many disciplines contribute to the final analysis. Theories have been raised about what the Soviet training approach to football would be. The editor of *Soviet Sports Review* (Yessis) had this to say:

> The Soviets would use specialty coaches with the team and these coaches would include a biomechanist, conditioning-exercise specialist, part-time physiologist, psychologist and a doctor trained in technique to work directly with the athletes. The biomechanist would analyze player skills at each position and this would be on a year-round basis. Additionally, the biomechanist could be used in a scout-like manner to analyze skill weaknesses in opposing teams [this could be used with division rivals and play-offs]. The conditioning-exercise specialist would be responsible for the all-round and spe-

cialized physical training of the players. The physiologist would be responsible for the periodic testing [of] athletes and would work closely with the conditioning-exercise specialist and doctor. The doctors there spend 1-3 years in a physical education institute. The sports psychologist [would] work with the players during the season and pre-competition. The specialized programs would closely resemble the necessary skills needed for the sport. The Soviets do not believe that an athlete can develop his/her full skills by merely playing the sport. In fact, the coaches try to limit the actual amount of time spent playing the sport, especially at the higher levels, due to the psychological and physiological factors. The Olympic lifts are the cornerstone of their training. If the proper technique has not been mastered in these lifts, then similar lifts can be substituted such as the power clean and clean pulls. Players will have high enough intensity (not volume) to maintain their strength and if significant strength losses are found, the player would be placed on a program to compensate for the loss ("a remedial program"). The overall training program would be broken down into yearly, monthly and weekly cycles.

This process has occurred already in many sports. Scientific data is available on hockey, and we are trying to pull much of this information together in this book.

J. R. Olson and G. R. Hunter performed a study of NCAA Division I football players over a 10-year period (1974 to 1984). The points that were studied were height, weight, 40-yard sprint, bench press, parallel squat, and power clean. Changes in stature and performance were divided into player position categories. The results were most interesting. Because most NHL players are not the size of football's offensive and defensive linemen, when making comparisons, you should focus primarily on the linebackers, offensive backs, receivers, and defensive secondary due to their closer physical comparison with hockey player stature. All positions demonstrated improvement in strength in all lifts and speed. This echoes the words of Luc Robitaille in the Foreword in which he noted the change in size and speed of hockey players of the past few years. The improvements by the football players are listed in the chart below.

We can conclude from this study by Olson and Hunter that 10-year improvements in speed and strength demonstrated by these football players strongly suggest that proper strength and conditioning programs have a positive effect on explosive strength activities.

This information clearly expresses what can be done with a proper program. Hockey player selection has produced athletes that are taller and larger, similar to the increases in football. However, the ideal strength and conditioning program has not followed. An athlete that gains size can also be stronger, quicker, and faster. We have all seen improved football performance. We know football players are stronger. We know they are faster. These changes did not happen by simply practicing longer on the field or by riding stationary bikes for 45 to 60 minutes. Programs similar to those outlined in this book provided the improved sports performance.

The testing of today's teams varies in method. Some teams use push-ups, sit-ups, body-weight bench press, max VO_2 (maximal oxygen uptake), max bike effort, and sit and reach to evaluate the players. While some evaluation of muscular endurance may be gained by having an athlete perform a test of maximum number of push-ups and sit-ups, it will do little to evaluate strength, overall anaerobic power, or explosive ability. Few NHL teams use hockey skills as a basis for the evaluation of players. The evaluation of hockey skills usually comes from scouting or watching videotapes.

The U.S. Olympic Training Center has used the following criteria for the measurement of training change in the athlete:

body weight
flexibility with Wells sit-and-reach test
vertical jump
power clean (one rep max)
bench press (one rep max)
parallel squat (one rep max)
200-meter repeated sprints for anaerobic endurance

Improvement by Category

Position	40-Yard Sprint (in seconds)	Bench Press (in pounds)	Squat (in pounds)	Power Clean (in pounds)	Height Increase (in inches)	Weight Increase (in pounds)
Offensive Line	0.19	61	69	40	1.14	21.12
Defensive Line	0.17	52	85	35	1.87	35.95
Linebackers	0.15	49	67	34	1.37	4.40
Offensive Backs	0.15	54	70	31	1.00	14.90
Defensive Backs	0.15	54	59	37	0.93	1.22
Receivers	0.11	46	56	33	1.26	3.30

Mental awareness is essential when looking to make a pass.

A word of caution is needed here. It is unwise to suddenly introduce a test of a power clean or parallel squat for a one-repetition maximum for players that are unaccustomed to performing the lift or athletes that train consistently with light weights. The players need to be introduced to proper lifting and be given an opportunity to adapt to the strength changes.

There are several interesting published articles on the testing of hockey players. A professional hockey team used a variety of tests to evaluate and predict parameters of the players (Minkoff). All tests were performed in training camp in September and repeated in late December and early March. A treadmill and various equipment were used to determine cardiovascular factors (max VO_2). A battery of eye tests were performed to determine visual speed and span. Muscular

testing was performed on the Cybex II system to determine values for knee extension and flexion, hip flexion, and hip abduction. Game time (shifts) of home games was tracked. Players were divided into playing positions. Also, if the players had been selected as All-Stars within the five years preceding the study, they were specially noted. Other statistics (penalty minutes, goals, assists, total points, faceoff successes, plus-minus) were also recorded. The head coach and general manager were asked to rate players (excluding goalies) for their skating skills, playing intensity, and shot accuracy. Skating skills were assigned 15 points (5 each for speed, smoothness, and agility). Player intensity was rated on 0 to 5 points and shot accuracy on a 0- to 7-point basis.

The results of this study indicated that the forwards had higher max VO_2 than defensemen, and in late season, right wingers predominated. The visual results were the most interesting. All 21 players were tested, and 6 players scored 6 (maximum) in either speed (tunnel-like vision) or span (peripheral vision). Three of these players were goalies, and the other three were All-Stars. Only three scored a 6 in both speed and span: two were goalies and the third was the team's leading goal and point scorer for the season. The player that was rated by management as the least accurate shot also had the lowest total eye score. All other All-Stars had perfect scores on their stereoscopic testing. The shot accuracy and faceoff success were found to correlate very highly with the visual span test. It is even more interesting to compare these visual scores with those of a professional baseball team. None of the baseball players scored above 5 in either speed or span. Among all groups tested by the optometrist supervising the study, the best overall scores were found in fighter pilots. The peripheral vision is felt to be important for the hockey shooter in order to perceive the goal, the net, the player passing the puck, movement of the puck, the faceoff, and the referee's hand. Of great interest also is that some visual skills may be improved in some instances.

The muscular strength results revealed three positive associations with skating speed and three with skating smoothness. In both categories, the significance pertained only to the left lower extremity. Further tests were performed once this was found, and the results of these tests revealed that left-handers were stronger on the right side and right-handers were stronger on the left side. The aerobic ability was noted to be only as important as the anaerobic ability in hockey due to the nature of the sport—rapid bursts interspersed with periods of rest. The anaerobic threshold is more important than max VO_2 for evaluating hockey. A difference between running and

skating was found to be that running can accelerate quickly, whereas skaters needed nearly half the rink to reach peak speed. The hip flexor muscles are of importance to speed and for preventing a loss of balance moving backward. The team average for hamstring-to-quadriceps ratio was 0.6 (more on this later). The knee-extensor-to-hip-flexor ratios for the team were 0.79 and 0.89 for the All-Stars. Twenty-three men on a professional baseball team had an average knee-extensor-to-hip-flexor ratio of 0.62. The hip adductors help maintain balance during the glide phase and maintain a narrow base under the skater, thus adding maneuverability. The abductors help stabilize the gliding leg, which is opposite to the driving leg. This may explain why right-handed players have skating skill correlations to the left hip-abductor-to-knee-extensor ratio.

The iron levels of Canadian Winter Olympic athletes preparing for the 1988 Olympic Games were evaluated. Iron deficiency can lead to anemia and would impede sports with an aerobic capacity or demand. Twenty ice hockey players were evaluated, and none were found to be anemic. Other athletes were evaluated, including 37 Nordic skiers, 20 Alpine skiers, 7 figure skaters, and 8 speed skaters. For accurate statistical evaluation, data from male and female athletes were separated. Among male athletes, the ice hockey players were found to have statistically significantly higher hemoglobin and blood iron levels than athletes in the other sports. It is also of interest to note that iron can be lost during heavy sweating. In fact, one milligram can be lost during a hard training session. This doubles the daily iron loss for men and usually needs to be replaced.

Twist and Rhodes evaluated 31 NHL players on another team prior to the 1992–93 season to develop a physiological profile of professional hockey players. Defensemen were on the ice for almost 50 percent of the game, and forwards averaged 35 percent. Defensemen had a shorter recovery phase and a higher off-ice heart rate than forwards did. On the average, defensemen skated slower than forwards throughout the game with high intensity efforts and periods of submaximal activity. Defensemen have more playing time and shifts because intensity and duration have an inverse relationship. In other words you can have a high volume of skating or you can skate very fast, but you cannot skate very fast with a high volume. Heart rate and oxygen uptake are related up to a point with skating and on-ice energy expenditure. In addition to skating velocity, the player expends energy with skating style efficiency, changing acceleration and deceleration, battling for the puck, checking, and possibly fighting. Forwards have a higher rate of energy expenditure than defensemen because forwards tend to cover more ice (which is more intensity). The interruptions in on-ice play count toward immediate muscle recovery (anaerobic). Defensemen in the recent past have been taller and heavier than forwards. Now, forwards and defensemen are more similar in size due to player selection and strength training.

Other studies have been performed regarding the energy systems involved in ice hockey (Green). Preseason tests of two Ontario junior ice hockey teams were compared with tests five months later near the end of the season. The tests performed included measurements of body weight, body-fat percentage determined by skinfold thickness, maximum aerobic capacity, maximum heart rate, and anaerobic capacity. The results were that the forwards gained 1.7 percent body weight and body fat remained constant. The body-weight and body-fat percentage remained the same for the defensemen. The maximum heart rate and absolute maximum oxygen uptake did not change. Significant improvement occurred in anaerobic capacity. No adaptation of aerobic power occurred. This lack of aerobic change could be accounted for in one of three ways: inability of the system to respond to training, lack of stress necessary to realize change, or inability of a treadmill running test to detect improvements from ice skating. Other studies have found a significant correlation between ice skating and treadmill running, however.

Green and Houston's analysis of playing time proved most interesting:

- Actual playing time is approximately 20 to 24 minutes, varying with position.
- This is divided into 17 shifts.
- Each shift averages 75 to 85 seconds.
- Each shift is separated by 3.5- to 4-minute recovery periods.
- During each shift there may be two or three play stoppages, thus allowing only 35 to 40 seconds of continuous activity with 25- to 30-second stoppages.
- Heart rate frequently exceeds 90 percent of maximal response.
- The frequency of games (three per week) has discouraged unduly intense practices.

Evaluation and Testing of Speed-Strength Training

There is no appropriate substitute for evaluation and testing. Coaches can implement knowledge gained from testing results, and this outweighs a haphazard approach of "let's wait and see what happens" in training. A legitimate plan of action leads to reduction of errors in a training program.

It will be important for hockey coaches, general managers, and owners to have a common language about the physical attributes of hockey players. This will ensure that everyone is on the same page when discussing trades, talent prospects, free agents, and draft picks.

For example, if a football general manager or coach wants a linebacker and talks to another team or college's coach, the data from the 40-yard-dash time, height, weight, power clean, bench press, and vertical jump are usually discussed. There is a universal understanding of what these parameters mean and how they translate to the football field. For example, if one agent calls a coach and says, "I have a linebacker who is six-four, weighs 253 pounds, runs the 40-yard dash in 4.48 seconds, performs a power clean with 365 pounds, squats 600 pounds, bench presses 425 pounds, and has a vertical jump of 28 inches," the coach understands the performance ability of this athlete and will most likely take a look at him. The same needs to occur in hockey as well. At present, we too often hear a scouting report or talent report note that the player "handles the stick well and sees the ice well." This is not enough definitive data. In a few years, coaches will be able to inquire about the goal-line-to-near-blue-line time, vertical jump, power clean or clean pull, squat, height, and weight. This data will mean something about the athlete's ability to physically perform and about his or her physical preparedness. This data is in addition to the coach's opinion about the player's ability to see the ice, pass, shoot, read the defense, and so on. This chapter will assist in the implementation of measurement tools and skills.

When to Evaluate

The annual training cycle for high school hockey players in speed-strength training has three evaluation and testing times. Running, reaction speed, strength, jumping, and throwing should be the main movements evaluated and tested. Professional and junior hockey players can be tested at training camp, during the season (to determine speed-strength

and conditioning status), and at the end of the season.

The midseason testing can be minimal, such as measuring a 20-yard sprint, vertical jump, and slap-shot velocity. The changes between the end of one season and the training camp of the next will reveal the player's off-season progress.

Races

The purpose of evaluation and testing in the races is to help the coach, trainer, or athlete distinguish among quick speed, running speed, and strength speed, all of which are recorded to the nearest hundredth of a second. The following are examples of the four kinds of races that should be evaluated and tested:

Race 1: 40-yard dash—quick start and acceleration of speed; run one each
Race 2: 60-yard dash—running speed to maintain the starting point and pickup of acceleration in a longer sprint; run one each
Race 3: 100-yard or 100-meter dash—speed generated and maintained over quick speed and speed-strength; run one each
Race 4 (on ice): goal-line-to-near-blue-line sprint from a standing start, not a gliding start—explosiveness, as in a game setting; skate two

The Los Angeles Kings and Long Beach Ice Dogs use the goal-line-to-near-blue-line and goal-line-to-far-blue-line sprints to evaluate explosive speed and sustained speed.

By evaluating and testing the hockey players in these races, the hockey coach or strength coach can better evaluate the running talent of his or her players. For some of the players, the times will represent a beginning reference point. Regardless of how big or small the athlete may be, the recorded facts concerning him or her (how quick, fast, strong, and tough in running) may give a little more insight concerning the best possible position for the young hockey player. This approach also represents a good way to evaluate both running and attitude.

Races 1, 2, and 3: 40-, 60-, and 100-Yard Dashes

Starting Position
Allow the hockey players to use a starting position that will give them the greatest amount of force off the starting line. This can be either a one-arm or two-arm track starting stance. The same kind of stance is used for each of the three races.

Action of the Movement
The hockey players want to generate quick and fast speed that will allow them to cover the desired distance in the least amount of time.

Speed-Strength Coaching Tips
Remind the athletes to run through the finish line. Also, remind them not to worry for the present about form or technique but to run all out. Record the time for each of the players as they run their races. The timers will start their clocks when the athletes make their "first movement." Record times to the nearest hundredth of a second. Make sure the athletes have a thorough warm-up; this is a good time to demonstrate proper warm-up routines before racing.

Race 4: Goal-Line-to-Near-Blue-Line Sprint

Starting Position
Have the hockey players position themselves on the ice for a quick start from a stationary position. Players will not have a gliding start.

Action of the Movement
Players are to quickly sprint through the near-blue line.

Speed-Strength Coaching Tips
The purpose of the goal-line-to-near-blue-line sprint is to more accurately assess the players' sprint speed. This distance is constantly skated in game conditions. The commonly used skating test of one lap around the rink is not applicable to normal game conditions. Note: tell the players that they should skate past the blue line rather than skate up to it and slow down. Also, it is important for the players to not rock back before the forward motion during the test.

Reaction-Speed Drills

Evaluation and testing of reaction-speed drills will assist the trainer or hockey coach in determining speed-strength of the hockey player. The ability to display "quick feet" is of utmost importance. Following are the procedures and methods to be used for evaluating reaction-speed drills:

Drill 1: Line Touch

Starting Position
Have the hockey players position themselves at the midway point between the two lines that will be touched. The lines should be 10 yards apart. The starting direction to be followed by the player should be determined before the drill begins.

Action of the Movement
The time starts with the first movement of the players. They are told to stay low and move as fast as possible. They should touch one line and then the other line one time each. The reaction speed from the final touch is a 10-yard sprint past the finishing point.

Line touch A. When doing the line touch, start with the knees bent and the legs about shoulder-width apart.

Line touch B. After touching the marker, run back to the other side.

Speed-Strength Coaching Tips

If you do not have enough personnel to see that each player touches each line, you may have the player pick up and deliver two-by-four-inch wooden blocks instead of touching the lines. Remind the athletes to not cross their feet, to stay low, and to drive off each line touch. Record two completed efforts (side-to-side reaction two times).

Drill 2: Figure Eight

Starting Position
The hockey players are positioned at the starting line. They can choose any kind of starting stance.

Action of the Movement
The race requires the players to cover the set distance in the least amount of time. The players must pivot and turn around each of the two cones placed 10 yards apart. They drive off the starting line and sprint to the first cone, turn and pivot, and drive to the starting cone. Again, they pivot and turn (they may place their hands down) and drive

back to the first cone, repeat, and then sprint past the starting line, which is now the finish line.

Speed-Strength Coaching Tips

This is a more difficult reaction-speed drill. It is a good idea to have the athletes perform a practice run for this drill. The equipment used includes plastic traffic cones. Remind the athletes to place their hands down and pivot around each turn as quickly as possible. Record two completed cycles. Look for explosive starts, good acceleration, balance, and coordination in this race.

Drill 3: Four Corner

Starting Position
The hockey players take a standing position at the starting line. The stance used is the players' choice.

Action of the Movement
The ultimate reaction-speed test is the four-corner drill. Athletes assume their starting position and move toward the cone markers.

Hex drill A. Start the two-leg hex drill on your toes with both feet inside the hexagon.

Hex drill B. Jump over one side of the hexagon, then jump back inside and work around the hexagon.

The cones are placed in the four corners of a square that is approximately 10 yards on each side. The starting movement is a straight run. At the point of approaching the first cone, the pivot is made inward, and the movement is now a crossing-leg movement called carioca. Approaching the second cone, the player again pivots to the inside and then runs backward to the third corner. The pivot at the third cone is again approached with an inward movement and drive. The movement after the inside pivot at the third cone is a sprint through the fourth and final cone.

Speed-Strength Coaching Tips

The four-corner drill has it all. You should discuss the importance of reaction speed and the way the skills from the four-corner drill carry over to sport performance. Record two complete cycles for each player. Remind the players to always pivot when making the turns at the first three cones.

Drill 4: Hex Drill

Starting Position

The athletes start in the middle of a hexagon ("hex") that can be made out of tape. The length of each side can be 18 or 24 inches.

Action of the Movement

The athletes hop out of the hexagon and back in, but not to the center point. They then hop over each side of the hex, working their way around making three round trips. Then the athletes repeat three times going the opposite direction (one set clockwise, one set counterclockwise).

Speed-Strength Coaching Tips

This drill is becoming a common test. Time the athletes for three revolutions around the hex. When this is a new drill, athletes often feel very awkward, but they quickly improve. This drill can also be done using one leg.

Dice drill A. To start the dice drill, place each foot on one corner of the hexagon.

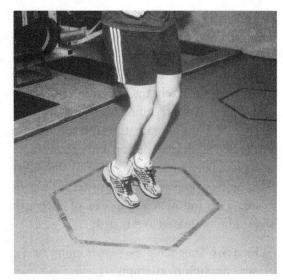

Dice drill B. Jump into the center of the hexagon and across to the other side, landing on the two corners.

Drill 5: Dice Drill

Starting Position

Place five points on the floor to look like the face of a die with five dots (four points as if in the corners of a square and one point in the center). The athletes can start in the center of the five points with the feet together. A center and four points of a hexagon can be used as well (as in the photos).

Action of the Movement

The athletes move from a feet-together position and jump back, splitting the feet so they touch the two back points. Then they bring the feet back together on the center dot, and then forward and apart to the front two dots. They then jump back to the center dot. This process continues for 10 seconds.

Speed-Strength Coaching Tips

Like the hex drill, the dice drill is commonly used and is great for foot quickness and agility. Observe the athletes to see how many times they go back and forth during 10 sec-

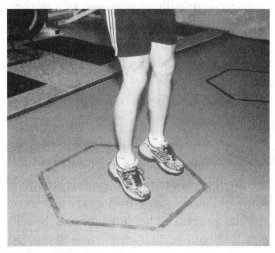

Dice drill C. Now jump backward into the center of the hexagon.

onds. The dice drill can also be performed using one leg.

Strength

The purpose of evaluating and testing strength is to help the hockey coach to identify players' strength level, starting point, and strength condition and to incorporate an individualized speed-strength-training program to benefit all of the hockey players. The proper speed-strength program will help develop the basic techniques of hockey.

After the initial evaluation and testing, the hockey coach has an opportunity to evaluate what has been accomplished from the starting point of the speed-strength-training program. The following exercises of strength should be evaluated and tested:

> **Exercise 1:** bench press—maximum or near maximum attempts
> **Exercise 2:** back squat—maximum or near maximum attempts
> **Exercise 3:** power clean—maximum or near maximum attempts
> **Exercise 4:** military press—maximum or near maximum attempts (standing position); OK to substitute the push press if the player does not have any wrist injuries or pain
> **Exercise 5 (optional):** chin-ups—as many as possible

Maximum attempts should reflect a good effort but not one that is an all-out, gut-busting attempt where the athlete forsakes good form and technique. This is a very important testing process. The introduction by the coach should include discussion about the attitude necessary for lifters just starting out who have never been exposed to a speed-strength lifting program. The coach needs to make it loud and clear that no lift should be attempted where the technique and method are ignored. This keeps the young athletes from foolishly attempting more than they really can lift; plus the coach should restate that the evaluation and testing are for the purpose of establishing a starting point for new athletes and a reevaluation of the players already in the program.

The testing procedures should follow the exercise descriptions as presented in this book concerning the use of proper technique, form, and method.

Jumping

The purpose of the jumping evaluation and testing is to help the strength coach, athletic trainer, or hockey coach evaluate the explosive leg strength of the hockey players as well as their ability to incorporate and transfer the skills developed in hockey. The three different jumps help measure vertical jump, quick jumping reaction; standing long jump, strength and jumping reaction; and triple long jump, the distance and jumping reaction. This gives some measure of vertical and horizontal jumping explosiveness and starting strength. Take two attempts at each jump. There is a technique factor involved in the triple jump. The evaluation and testing allow for a review of the hockey players' improvements in jumping.

Listed here are the procedures for evaluating and testing the jumps. For further information on the training jumps, refer to Chapter 6 on plyometrics.

Drill 1: Vertical Jump

Starting Position

Before jumping, the athletes approach the marking board, raise their arm to full extension, and place their fingers against the board so that a mark can be left as a starting point for measuring.

Action of the Movement

The athletes position themselves to jump as high as possible, leaving their mark to be measured and recorded. They start with both feet in the jumping position most comfortable

Vertical jump A. Starting position for the vertical jump.

Vertical jump B. Jump for maximum height using a Vertec.

to them. No movement of either foot (and no stepping back) is allowed before the jump is completed. Record the highest of two jumps. There is another method that allows a few-step approach prior to the jump. The few-step method involves more technique than pure explosive jumping ability. Remain consistent with your testing methods.

Speed-Strength Coaching Tips

The chalk used for marking can be the same chalk used in lifting. A variety of vertical jumps can be used: static jump (from a dead start), countermovement jump (slight dip and then jump), or depth jump (jump down off a small box and jump up again from the floor). The changes in the jumps should be closely monitored and documented. The vertical jump is an indicator of explosive power and

is closely related to skating speed. A Vertec (pictured) or similar equipment can be used instead of a marking board if available.

Drill 2: Standing Long Jump

Starting Position

Athletes take a position close to the starting line.

Action of the Movement

This jump is forward for distance rather than straight up. Once the athletes jump and land feet first, neither of their feet can move. For the long jump to be recorded, the athletes must "stick" the jump. This test allows two jumps. The jump is measured from the heel of the back foot, that is, the foot closest to the starting point.

Speed-Strength Coaching Tips

This drill encourages hockey players to increase flexibility and dexterity. Remind the athletes that they must "stick" the jump— they cannot move either of their feet upon landing.

Drill 3: Standing Triple Jump

Starting Position

The same rules apply as in the long jump, except the athletes must do three consecutive jumps.

Action of the Movement

This test measures the length of the starting to finishing jump achieved with three consecutive jumps. (The test is two triple jumps.) Have athletes use the same techniques and form that are displayed in the standing long jump. Also, they can use the arms coordinated with the legs to improve the forward momentum of the entire body. This used to be called the "hop, skip, and jump" in track and field.

Speed-Strength Coaching Tips

Remind the hockey players to jump as far as possible on each of the three jumps. The total distance is then recorded. Stress that each jump is as important as the others. This test is a combination of the vertical and standing long jump and measures endurance jumping and speed-strength. It may not work well for players with unstable knees, patellofemoral pain (pain behind the kneecap), or reconstructed anterior cruciate ligaments (ACLs).

Medicine-Ball Throws

The purpose of medicine-ball-throwing tests is to help measure upper-body explosive strength in the hockey player. The evaluation and testing of throwing consist of the fol-

Seated long throw A. The knees should be bent and the feet apart when beginning the seated long throw.

lowing medicine-ball drills: (1) seated long throw for distance, (2) standing long throw for distance, (3) standing backward long throw for distance, and (4) sit-up and throw. An eight-pound (or four-kilogram) medicine ball is used. Posttesting allows the coach to evaluate the amount of upper-body explosive, starting, and absolute strength that has been transferred to the skill of throwing.

Following are three samples of throwing drills. For further information on throwing, refer to Chapter 6 on ballistic training.

Drill 1: Seated Long Throw

Starting Position

The athletes position themselves in a seated position on the throwing surface, keeping heels and feet behind the line.

Action of the Movement

Placing the medicine ball in front of the chest, the athletes attempt to project the ball forward in an explosive manner as far as possible. The longest of two attempts is recorded.

Speed-Strength Coaching Tips

This allows you to measure movement of the upper body's ballistic speed-strength. Incorporate a warm-up routine of four to eight

Seated long throw B. For the most explosive power, lean back, keeping the shoulders off the ground.

Seated long throw C. To finish the throw, sit up and launch the ball.

practice throws in preparation of a measured attempt.

Drill 2: Standing Long Throw

Starting Position
The athletes position themselves in a standing position on the throwing surface, keeping heels and feet behind the line.

Action of the Movement
Starting with the medicine ball behind the head, the athletes project the ball forward in an explosive manner to achieve the greatest distance. The longer of two attempts is recorded.

Speed-Strength Coaching Tips
This is an excellent exercise to evaluate the transfer of coordination of speed-strength. Make sure the medicine balls are dry and the players use both hands on the ball for the throw.

Drill 3: Standing Back Overhead Long Throw

Starting Position
The athletes position themselves as close to the starting line as possible without stepping on or over it.

Action of the Movement
Standing on the throwing surface, the athletes throw the medicine ball backward and over the body. The longest of two attempts is recorded.

Speed-Strength Coaching Tips
This is a more difficult throwing drill than the previous drills; it requires a higher degree of balance and athletic skill. Remind the players to not step over the line.

Drill 4: Side Throw

Starting Position
The athletes start facing somewhat sideways to the direction they will throw the medicine ball (much like batting in baseball).

Action of the Movement
The athletes will take an over-the-top hand placement on the ball, with the arm closest to the direction the ball will be thrown placed on the top. They will wind up and throw the ball using the rotary power of the hips, legs, back, abdomen, and shoulders.

Speed-Strength Coaching Tips
This is an excellent test and exercise for rotary-power generation of the body. Make sure the athletes avoid using the arm closest

Standing long throw A. Step forward and allow the ball to drop behind the head.

Standing long throw B. The torso and arms contribute to the power in the long throw.

Standing back overhead long throw A. Stand with feet as close to the line as possible without being on it.

Standing back overhead long throw B. The ball is projected over and behind the head. Note the athlete's commitment to the throw.

Side throw A. In this photo of the side throw, the athlete has already wound up and is ready to throw.

Side throw B. Note the changes in the hip, shoulder, and foot positions.

to the throw in the underhand position; this becomes a biceps and shoulder test more than a rotary-power test.

Structuring the Testing

All of this material is presented to assist the coach, speed-strength coach, athletic trainer, doctor, general manager, and even the player with methods of testing.

It is certainly not necessary to use every test that we listed in this section. Our intent is not to provide one "cookbook" that will fit every high school, college, junior, and professional team. Rather, we chose to present the appropriate methods of evaluation and allow you the ability to select the tests from each category that will fit the number of players, coaches, doctors, and trainers who are available for the testing.

An example of a training camp testing program could be as follows:

Speed-Strength	Speed/Speed Endurance
power clean	goal-line-to-near-blue-line sprint
back squat	40-yard sprint (land)
bench press	100-yard sprint (land)

Explosiveness	Agility/Coordination
vertical jump	four-corner drill
standing long jump	line touch
standing back overhead long throw	

You may add another lift or two in the speed-strength section, other runs in the speed/speed endurance section, the triple

Coach John Van Boxmeer behind the Long Beach Ice Dogs bench. Van Boxmeer is now with the Los Angeles Kings.

jump in explosiveness, or additional agility drills to further evaluate the coordination of the prospective athletes.

After such testing, especially if the athletes lifted in the 95 percent to 100 percent effort range, it is advisable that the next day be very limited in physical activity. In other words, it is not a good idea to tax the athletes' central nervous system and muscles to such a limit during the testing and then have hard workouts the next day. One suggestion would be to follow the hard workout days with team meetings and discussions of the direction the team will go, and then regular workouts can resume the second day after testing. The skating in camp will serve as the transition after the peak and before entering the limited in-season program.

2

PROGRAM PLANNING AND PERIODIZATION

"In training nothing happens by accident, but rather by design."

—TUDOR BOMPA, PH.D.

Training, particularly for elite sports, requires specific and careful planning. This is done to increase strength and conditioning and to allow for a peak, or multiple peaks, of performance. Most sports follow the method of implementing and cycling various forms of training to enhance performance. This method is known as periodization. Unfortunately, too few coaches and athletes structure a plan to achieve such performance.

The purpose of periodization is to achieve maximal performance results and minimize fatigue and exhaustion. Periodization allows for a peak performance at a predicted time (e.g., playoffs, etc.). We touch on this topic several times in this book, but this chapter will allow a more in-depth look to assist the reader with this concept.

An athlete cannot perform at a maximal level at all times. You would not expect Oscar de la Hoya to step into the ring on any given day and defend his title. Nor would you

expect athletes like Michael Johnson, Maurice Green, Carl Lewis, or Jackie Joyner-Kersee to achieve their best sprints or jumps on any given day. Their training programs are carefully planned and structured well in advance of the training day. If other sports have carefully planned training programs, then hockey teams must follow suit or the individual players who will have access to these types of training methods will separate from the rest of the players.

There are many factors that need to be cycled, or periodized. These factors in hockey are strength training, speed training, agility training, balance work, plyometric/ballistic training, and of course hockey practice. While all of these factors are addressed in this book, this chapter is primarily about strength training.

Many coaches and players feel that when the season begins, the strength training should end. This places the athlete in the unfortunate position of being in the competitive season while experiencing a detraining effect. Some aspects of detraining can be detected within five to six days without training and skills requiring strength, speed, and power. Noticeable deterioration of strength and speed can occur in two weeks' time according to Bompa's sources. Detraining also results in protein degradation and decreased testosterone levels.

I (JMH) have discussed the advantages of periodization, Olympic lifts, agility training, and balance work with a number of hockey coaches. Sometimes I receive a quizzical look, sometimes complete cooperation and support, and sometimes overt resistance to change. The good training results usually eliminate any doubt. The sport of hockey has changed, and training methods and concepts have changed. The use of the stationary bike once permeated hockey training thought due to the fact that when the bike was first used, it was the only method of supplemental training, and usually some training is better than none. Some differences were noted, and the bike became part of hockey. Regrettably, other sports passed hockey by. The following excerpt from *Soviet Training and Recovery Methods* by Rick Brunner and Ben Tabachnik refers to methods of high-level training and its ongoing changes:

> Today, many American coaches are asking questions about Soviet periodization, planning, and plyometrics (a form of explosive exercises). We have read many recent articles and books from the USA which discuss macro and microcycles, even though the Soviet scientist Dr. A. Matveev invented these training methods in the late 1960s. With great delay, they are just now being discussed in the USA. In the past ten years, many of A. Matveev's ideas about volume, intensity, and waves of training have been changed in the USSR, especially for top athletes. American coaches have been 10–15 years behind in learning enough about the Soviet system to make it effective.

It is important to remember that the hockey season is very long, and it is unrealistic to expect that one will maintain one's peak strength and proper conditioning for an eight-month season without a careful plan. A program can be structured that will allow a player to at the very least minimize strength loss and in many cases increase strength levels.

Low levels of general strength may become a limiting factor in the performance of an athlete. We have all seen cases of athletes with superior skill levels who depend exclusively on these playing skills. They have done so because their talent carried them so far without any other training assistance. These athletes don't realize that changing their training can take them to the next level. Frequently, these athletes don't even realize there is another level to achieve. Too often, we have seen many of these athletes with lower strength levels suffer from injuries. We may see that their overall lack of strength does not allow them to succeed against talented opponents who do have strength. Perhaps if they had increased their own strength, they would have had a greater ability to survive in their sport. A proper program plan can develop and maintain strength during the off-season and throughout the season.

Unfortunately, because the strength and conditioning program has not been fully understood and utilized, the training program has frequently been postponed until after the games by some coaches. It is my (JMH) opinion that after a game the athlete is physically, psychologically, and emotionally spent. Significant postgame workouts are not advisable because energy and the ability to focus are prime ingredients for efficient training and improvement. Training in an exhausted state may lead to injury. Time must be set aside for a proper strength program. Poor training programs cannot be used as examples or standards by which the effectiveness of training is judged. Excessive time and energy demands on the athletes will produce poor results. Therefore, it is imperative that you utilize a program that is designed for effectiveness and efficiency of energy.

Occasionally, a player who did not play much in a game, or a player that is still wound up from the game, can perform a few reps of an exercise with light to medium intensity after a game. This can serve to settle the player a bit.

Periodization of Training

Periodization allows for the predictable peaking of athletic performance and is used in all forms of athletic training. This method of program planning used to be known as cycling, but the complexity of the cycling program intimidated too many athletes, so they avoided it. Periodization has been made more "user friendly" today. Anywhere from two to four peaks per year can be used. However, it is important to realize that the nonpeak time is useful as well.

Periodization works by varying training loads. (Unfortunately, injuries may change the training plan; ways to train around injuries are presented later in this book.) Here are the main components of periodization:

1. Volume—This is the number of total repetitions being performed in a set, exercise, workout, week, month, or cycle.
2. Intensity—This is the amount of weight that is used. It is usually referred to as a percentage of a one-repetition-maximum (1RM) effort. For example, if a player can bench press a maximum of 225 pounds for one repetition (1RM), then 80 percent of his 1RM is 180 pounds. The 1RM can be determined by either a known maximum effort or by knowing what the player has lifted for three to six reps.
3. Frequency—This is the number of workouts in a period of time (week or month) and also the number of times a particular lift is trained in a period of time (week or month).
4. Sequence of exercises
5. Duration—This is the length of time that the training program will go on (e.g., six, eight, or twelve weeks) before a break or active rest is taken from training.
6. Recovery—This is determined by components 1 through 5.

An older method of tracking training is to monitor the tonnage lifted for a single workout, week, or cycle. Although tonnage is no longer extensively used to track the players' training, it can still add insight into the players' program if questions arise.

Thus far, this information applies to the strength-training component of training. However, periodization applies to all the components of training. There will be more on this later in the book.

There are numerous types of periodization cycles. For example, the most common, simple structure for periodization includes several stages. The first stage is now known as a hypertrophy stage, which is characterized by high-volume/low-intensity work (e.g., three sets of 10 reps on a particular lift), and this phase may last up to four weeks. (The rep range of pulls is five or less). The purpose is to build a preparation base for the rest of the cycle and to increase anaerobic endurance. This stage usually incorporates lifts in the 60 to 70 percent range. Usually, the target total rep range on a particular lift is 36 reps (± 5 reps) during an off-season program and 24 reps during an in-season program (more on in-season training later) for an advanced lifter.

The next stage or phase is sometimes known as the basic strength stage. This phase is one of moderate volume/higher intensity. It is usually in the 75 to 85 percent range, and five to eight reps are used. The maximum repetitions that can be performed with 80 percent is commonly accepted as six during a maximal effort.

The next stage is the strength or competitive phase. The heaviest weights are used. The percentages are in the 90 to 100 percent range, and one to three reps are used.

The next phase is known as active rest. This phase can last from three days to two weeks depending upon the time of the season and the demand of the previous periodization. We do not wish for athletes to lose all of their conditioning, even though their bodies and minds may need a rest. Therefore, active rest incorporates other sports such as swimming, cycling, running, basketball, and so on. Even light lifting can be used during this time. The athlete will return to the periodization with new, higher training loads, and the same principle of increasing workloads will repeat. Another method is to keep varying the load, and this is presented later in this chapter.

The Soviet strength coach Zaitchuk is reported to believe that once the base work is achieved, that base cycle will work only once and only with beginners. Once the consistent gains reach a peak or plateau, they will remain for a brief period of time and then regress. We disagree with this. A change in the percentage lifted and the repetitions can yield excellent results. The drop in performance usually stems from the athlete becoming overtrained or losing interest. Because the athlete and coach expect performance in the present as well as in the future, the training that produced the plateau must be changed. This can be done by a variety of methods.

Physical and technical work must be performed together during the preparation phase. Do not separate the two categories. This is a key point.

The Russian programs were targeted to reach three peaks per year, which is what the coaches believed the athletes could do. Bompa labeled this "triple periodization." The training diary will allow for perfect hindsight of peak performances so that predictable clues will alert you for future peaks. Rest after each peak is critical. Once the peak is approached, the Russian coaches would alter the training by 15 to 20 percent. The altered factor would be intensity, exercises, or volume. The main point would be to keep the peak as long as possible. A word of caution: different athletes respond differently to changes in training. We feel that many hockey players fall into a beginner category because of a lack of proper initial base and/or muscle imbalances that have been created by the sport. The training load must be progressed rather quickly in professional hockey players, because of their age and physical maturity. College, junior, and high school players need not progress so quickly because they don't have as great a demand on them to perform.

Because the championships are at the end of a season, the competitive season must become part of the periodization plan. We must plan the training so that one of the peaks will occur at playoff time. The coach must accept the fact that the athletes cannot be at 100 percent performance for long periods of time; they can be in great performance capacity but not 100 percent. How often have teams come up from the ranks to win or place well in the Stanley Cup playoffs? Just as in any sport, it is not necessarily the best team that wins; rather, it is the best-prepared team. Many NHL teams did not perform well during the first half or first two-thirds of the season, but they "turned it on" for the last third and carried it into the playoffs. This may have been their own crude form of periodization. They were less physically beaten down and better mentally prepared at season's end.

Hockey can have three or four peaks during a season:

1. beginning of the season (October)
2. midseason (late December)
3. midseason (February)
4. playoffs (mid-April)

or

1. beginning of season (October)
2. midseason (January)
3. playoffs (mid-April)

Volume

As we mentioned earlier in this section, volume can be measured in daily, weekly, monthly, or yearly total repetitions. As you can see from the following example of Soviet Olympic weight lifters, the measurements are quite precise. Goldstein's general recommendations for the first three years of training are broken down into total number of lifts:

first year: 6,000 to 7,000 lifts annually broken down to 500 to 1,100 lifts per month, ranging from 60 to 70 percent

second year: 7,000 to 8,500 lifts annually broken down to 550 to 1,300 lifts per month, ranging from 65 to 80 percent

third year: 8,500 to 10,000 lifts annually broken down to 600 to 1,500 lifts per month, ranging from 70 to 85 percent

This general type of plan could apply to high school and junior hockey players.

USA men's Olympic weight-lifting coach Dragomir Ciroslan informed me (JMH) that his elite Olympic weight lifters are performing 22,000 to 25,000 lifts annually.

Al Vermeil's weekly workout load definitions include these:

heavy: 340-plus reps
medium: 150 to 340 reps
light: 70 to 150 reps

Note that this scheme does not apply to the period in which high volume and low intensity is performed.

Coach Vermeil divides workouts for football players into categories based upon volume of training load. His daily workout definitions include these:

hard: 100-plus-rep workout, only once per week
medium: 50- to 100-rep workout, maintenance workout
light: 50 reps or fewer, to recover after a hard workout

Vermeil, as most strength coaches, counts only the key exercises such as pulls, snatches, cleans, squats, and bench presses. Light or low-intensity movements such as sit-ups, leg extensions, and leg curls are not counted. Heavy workouts are always followed by light workouts. Vermeil believes in using a recovery week every three to four weeks, and this should not include any lift over 80 percent; the total week's reps should be between 150 and 175. I (EJK) feel that unloading days are more efficient in the training program as opposed to an entire unloading week. Garhammer emphasizes that an unloading day must have decreased both volume and intensity. Of interest, tracking of the total number of repetitions was initially used by the Bulgarian and Soviet training systems to monitor the total exposure of the body to the training load.

Vermeil's training philosophy is to perform speed and technique work (e.g., hops, jumps, bounding, and speed work) first before fatigue sets in. This should be followed by speed lifts such as cleans, pulls, and so on. Last in the workout would be squats, presses, and so on. There are, of course, differing opinions on this order, but Vorobyev, Kreis, Bompa, Francis, and others follow this method, and it has proved its efficiency. As you can see, the monitoring of training is quite specific. There is nothing haphazard about the training plan of athletes.

As previously mentioned, the preparatory phase and precompetitive period has a maximum number of repetitions per exercise in the 18 to 36 range, and in the main competitive period, the total number of repetitions per exercise falls to the 12 to 28 range. Having limits on the amount of repetitions allowed during a training time safeguards against overtraining. In planning a routine of speed-strength training, a natural time factor should be built in so that each exercise has a limited number of total repetitions as well as a maximum number of exercises. The sequence of exercises does not include warm-up sets; each exercise moves the athlete in a progressive direction that prepares him or her for the next exercise. The listed percentages, sets, and repetitions are the workout program and have no additional or extra lifting. Another factor is the limit of repetitions per set. Again, the training zone will illustrate the number of repetitions that can be cycled during that set or series of exercises. Keep in mind that exercises repeated more than eight repetitions become more endurance productive. Five to six repetitions are speed-strength productive, and three to four repetitions

develop more explosive strength. If one or two repetitions are the maximum, usually the exercises are executed with a high and a heavy percentile weight. The most productive number of repetitions for speed-strength (mass) is five to six.

Intensity

The coach should be aware of the intensity (the amount of weight being lifted), which determines how strong the athlete is and what exercise performances are within his or her limits of correct performance. Only after initial testing and supervision should the athlete be allowed to perform movements in the high percentile ranges of weight. The information collected during initial testing and posttesting allows for new personal records and new absolute speed-strength (1RM).

The example used in the preparatory phase of the power snatch could be 50/5, 55/5, 65/5/2. Here are what these three sets of numbers indicate: the 5s (5 reps) show the volume levels of these three increments. The first set of numbers (50/5) means 50 percent of the 1RM in the power snatch. The second set (55/5) means 55 percent of the 1RM in the power snatch. The third set (65/5/2) means 65 percent of the 1RM in the power snatch for two sets. Assuming this athlete had a previous personal record of 135 pounds for a 1RM lift for the power snatch, the new goal is 150 pounds, or 110 percent of the original; this number can be looked up on a percentage chart or figured with a calculator. Fifty percent of 150 pounds is 75 pounds for five repetitions (corresponding with the first set of numbers), 55 percent of 150 pounds is approximately 80 pounds (second set of numbers), and 65 percent of 150 pounds is approximately 95 pounds for two sets of five repetitions (third set of numbers). The challenge of the coach is to be well versed concerning the intensity and number of repetitions needed to correlate correctly for that particular percentage of weight.

Frequency of Workouts

Anything that is good can be overdone, and this can happen when the speed-strength program is not planned and carried out properly. During the preparatory phase, the use of four lifting days is excellent for the hockey program. Coaches can oversee a better distribution of the exercises and better use of the developing athlete's time in the weight room and on ice or dry land. Some coaches still adhere to a three-day lifting schedule. However, the four-day training schedule has a greater advantage because of higher weekly total volume and intensity of exercises that can be duplicated from workouts. Remember that the frequency of workouts is also held in check by the volume (number of repetitions that can be performed per exercise).

Combinations of workout days are left to the discretion of the coach or trainer. Each team has a different personality; it is up to the coach to know what will best prepare his or her hockey team. The following table shows possible schedules of frequency of workouts in the preparatory phase:

Sample Workout Schedules for Preparatory Phase

Four-Day	Four-Day	Three-Day	Three-Day
Monday	Monday	Monday	Monday
Tuesday	Tuesday	Wednesday	Tuesday
Thursday	Wednesday	Friday	Friday
Friday	Friday		

Here is an example of frequency of workouts in the main competition period:

Sample Workout Schedules for Main Competition Phase

Four-Day	Three-Day	Three-Day
Saturday	Sunday	Saturday
Monday	Monday	Monday
Wednesday	Friday	Wednesday
Friday		

If you are involved in a hockey game schedule of 70 to 82 games per season, then nearly every off day must be a training day. The load will vary, and there will be occasional complete days off. College players can train Sunday or Monday through Thursday.

Structuring a Basic Periodization

It is relatively easy for someone who is unfamiliar with periodization to construct a simple traditional periodization program. One of the most basic and simple training periodization methods is to gradually increase your lifts based upon a percentage of your 1RM. If the athlete has never trained heavily, then this is a good transition schedule. If the athlete has never performed a maximum lift, don't worry. There are easy guidelines to follow to determine an approximate 1RM. If you know what you can lift for 10 reps, then this weight is approximately 70 percent of your 1RM; if you know what you can lift for 6 reps, then this weight is approximately 80 percent of your 1RM; if you know what you can lift for 3 reps, then this weight is approximately 90 percent of your 1RM.

For example, if you lift 150 pounds in a bench press for 10 repetitions, a simple math equation will give an estimate of your 1RM. A calculator or percentage chart will greatly assist in determining your training schedule.

$$\text{percentage} \times 1RM = \text{weight used}$$

$$.70 \times 1RM = 150 \text{ pounds}$$

$$1RM = 150 \text{ pounds} \div .70$$

$$1RM = 214 \text{ pounds}$$

This athlete has an approximate 215-pound 1RM bench press. We can now use this 1RM to calculate the percentages. A simple method for calculating the percentages is to have a weight chart, which lists beginning weight (in this example, 215 pounds) and the corresponding weight at each percentage. Look up the appropriate poundage for each workout and note them in your training log/diary.

Note: you must be completely honest with yourself when determining these lifts. Do not select a poundage that you think *should be* your maximum effort. If you do this, then all of your workouts will be incorrect. It doesn't matter where you are starting. All that matters is where you will end up. It is better to build the base properly than to be struggling and straining from the word *go*.

The most simple, basic periodization program (and probably the wisest and safest for those unaccustomed to training properly) is to follow an eight-week off-season program as follows (all percentages are from the 1RM):

Week	Percentage
One	65
Two	70
Three	75
Four	80
Five	85
Six	90
Seven	95
Eight	100

Keeping with the 215-pound estimated 1RM bench press, we simply multiply these percentages by the 1RM. Here is the bench press weight periodization training chart for this athlete (all poundages are rounded off):

Week	Percentage	Poundage
One	65	140
Two	70	150
Three	75	160
Four	80	170
Five	85	180
Six	90	195
Seven	95	205
Eight	100	215

The repetitions can be from 8 to 12 for weeks one through three. At week four (80 percent), the reps will drop to 6 reps. By week six, the reps will have dropped to 3. A maximum attempt can be made in week eight. Note: higher reps do not usually apply well to the pulling movements. Low-back fatigue is easily induced. This can require a long recovery and may lead to injuries. Keep the pulling movements between three and five reps regardless of the percentage.

The progression accomplishes several key points. First, the athlete is exposed to progressive resistance and therefore gains strength. Second, this progression allows the muscles, tendons, joints, and nervous system a chance to adapt to the increasing demand. Too often, athletes will "try to see what I can do" on a maximum effort even when they have never had the slightest exposure to it. There can be pain and injury after such an irrational attempt. The example we have given will allow athletes to actually perform the poundage they should have already been able to perform if they had trained properly.

The next cycle will begin at a higher 1RM and then take the percentages of the new

1RM. For example, if the athlete did, in fact, bench press the estimated 1RM, then we will add anywhere from 5 to 15 percent of his 1RM and establish a new 1RM. If the athlete bench pressed 215 pounds, then we can add 10 percent to this lift and make a new target 1RM of 235 pounds. Now week one will begin with 65 percent of 235 pounds, or 155 pounds. We feel that a simple program like this is the most effective way for a relative beginner or for someone who is relatively inexperienced to start training periodization with the lowest injury potential. The most difficult part for the athlete is to get through the first three or four training cycles. Once that point is reached, the beginning weights will require more focus because of the gradual increase in weight that has occurred. The early periodization programs will be fairly easy for the first half (first four weeks). The athlete may not feel like he or she is working hard enough until the fifth or sixth week. This is OK for the early phase. Most beginners need to continue to improve technique and also become used to handling heavier weight. The athlete does not have to be aware of the change in workload in order for change to occur. If the workload is increased, the body will adapt. The significant early fluctuation can also give the mind a break from hard training. This classic periodization may work well for some sports and not as well for others. Elite powerlifters usually need the physical and mental break in their training during the weeks of lighter loads.

Periodization is that simple. Be patient enough to get through the first three or four training periods.

The example we have given is the most simple level of periodization. There are many ways to vary training periodizations, especially in the off-season. Once an athlete is accustomed to proper training (at least one year of proper training), then more advanced programs can be utilized. Similar volumes can exist with different combinations of sets and reps. Other concepts of varying training were utilized by the Soviets, Bulgarians, and Romanians in their training programs shortly before the collapse of the Iron Curtain. Then their focus shifted. The new ideas focused on the fluctuation of volume instead of intensity. The intensity (weight) remained relatively high all year. The volume (total sets and reps) diminished during "lighter" training and increased during "heavier" training. The squat program of Charlie Francis's sprinters used this type of training, which is presented later in this chapter.

Sequence

The sequence of the lifts is critical. Vorobyev, in an excerpt from his book *Weight Lifting*, outlined the order of exercises in each training phase with the fastest movement first. The following are 12 speed-strength categories of lifting exercises and the sequences. Some of these exercises may be carefully selected to meet the needs of each hockey player:

First Exercises: Snatch
1. power snatch
2. split snatch
3. muscle snatch
4. snatch—Olympic style
5. snatch pull
6. dumbbell snatch
7. one-arm dumbbell snatch
8. snatch pull—high pull

Second Exercises: Clean
1. power clean
2. split clean
3. muscle clean
4. clean—Olympic style

5. clean pull (can be determined by intensity of load)
6. hang clean—not a complete movement
7. dumbbell power clean
8. clean pull—high pull

Third Exercises: Press
1. bench press
2. incline bench press
3. dumbbell bench press
4. dumbbell incline press
5. behind-the-neck press
6. front press or military press
7. push press
8. narrow-grip bench press

Fourth Exercises: Squat
1. back squat
2. front squat
3. split squat
4. one-legged squat
5. lunge
6. step-up with dumbbells
7. step-up with barbells

Fifth Exercises: Good Morning
1. squat style
2. straight legged
3. seated (straight legged and bent leg)

Sixth Exercises: Combination Lifts
1. clean and jerk
2. snatch and squat
3. squat and jerk

Seventh Exercises: Jerk
1. from the rack
2. from the clean
3. push jerk

Eighth Exercise: Hyperextensions
1. hyperextension

Ninth Exercise: Glute-Ham-Gastroc Raise
1. glute-ham-gastroc raise

Tenth Exercises: Gymnastics
1. chin-up
2. dip
3. ballistic push-up (except for those athletes have been diagnosed with shoulder instability)

Eleventh Exercises: Abdominal
1. sit-up with weight
2. pulley crunch
3. crunch
4. Janda sit-up
5. Ab mat

Twelfth Exercises: Neck
1. wrestler's bridge
2. pulling movement
3. neck harness
4. neck machine

The athlete or strength coach can choose from these 12 different categories of lifting exercises as well as select from plyometric and ballistic training drills. Each exercise is listed in the order of speed to strength, incorporating the four components of speed-strength training for the preparatory phase. Thus, by using the same exercise worked in a different motion, the duplication of snatching, cleaning, pressing, and squatting every day is possible.

There should be a prescribed limit to the number of exercises in one training session. In the preparatory phase, the number of exercises would be no fewer than five and no more than eight. In an exercise, volume and intensity are cycled from small to medium to big, which are derived from a maximum (absolute effort) number of lifting movements of speed-strength. Examples are: (1) power clean, (2) bench press, (3) back squat, and (4) jerk from stand. A cycle of training can be derived from a maximum number of these exercises. Another example is that (nonspecific) general, plyometric, ballistic, neck, abdominal, and gymnastic movements are not included, but they are aspects of the total program. Total programming involves no fewer than eight and no more than fourteen speed-strength exercises. In the competitive phase, the speed-strength lifting movements would be no fewer than three and no more than five.

The total speed-strength program would be no fewer than six and no more than ten exercises. Note that in the precompetitive period, the number can vary from one lift a day to three lifts a day, with one or two exercise (nonspecific) movements added. The coach should constantly monitor the amount of practice the athletes are subject to.

Variability of Load in Training

Variability of load means the intensity (weight) and volume (sets and reps) are changed during a training cycle. This does not mean that the weight and sets are always going up but, rather, are varied during training. Variability of load allows for a greater adaptability during training. This helps to avoid fatigue and overtraining. While some coaches utilize unloading, or light, weeks, Kreis and Bompa feel that unloading days throughout the program are entirely sufficient for recovery, so they incorporate these unloading days. In *Speed-Strength Training for Football*, Kreis stated, "A workout of four sets of four reps with 60 percent, if performed ballistically, can be a great workout and serve as an unloading day." The next workout may be at an intensity that is significantly higher, and the unloading day provides a minor stimulus and allows the athlete to be more recovered for the heavier day.

The last workout may have used 90 percent for two sets of two to three reps during the last sets. The current workout may have 80 percent for two sets of four reps. This is an example of variability. The weight should not and cannot always increase. The variability of load helps to prevent a peak from occurring too soon, avoids overtraining, avoids sticking points in gains, and still allows for effective speed-strength training. If the plan is for the lifts to go up continually, the athlete may state that the amount he or she lifts reaches a plateau and then actually diminishes, perhaps significantly.

The classifications of the athletes will give volume boundaries (number of repetitions) geared to the level of each player's ability:

	Prephase and Precompetitive	Main Competitive Period
Beginning Number of Reps	18	12
Intermediate Number of Reps	24	18
Advanced Number of Reps	30	24
Elite Number of Reps	36	28

By limiting the number of repetitions (volume), the athlete gains speed-strength throughout the year. The key to developing greater athletic success is to get the most out of each training session. By incorporating the "training load cycle" and the labeling systems of S = small, M = medium, and B = big zones, the planner will progress with the desired training-zone load. These labels are relative to the total number of reps in each exercise session. Regardless of the number of workouts per week, the change to the training goal allows the exercise to not have a plateau or leveling-off effect. With the labeling system, the zones become easy to arrange so that maximum results will be made and each workout receives a value. For example, workout days Monday and Thursday can be structured with Monday as small and Thursday as medium. More variability can of course be used.

The idea is to not put any three zones back to back, thus allowing for speed-strength restoration to occur. By using the S-M-B training-zone-load cycle, the creative athlete, coach, and trainer can put many interesting and different combinations together and provide maximum gains in speed-strength training. Here is an example.

If two training zones are the same, the next workout zone will vary. For example:

S-M
M-B
M-M
B-S

This variation allows the training routine to be creative for the individual as well as the team during the different training periods. The plan designer should watch for and protect against overtraining. Adjustments and flexibility can allow for maximum speed-strength gains.

According to Grigory Goldstein, a Soviet weight-lifting coach, the training loads must be varied simply because of how quickly the athlete's body adapts to a specific movement and specific exercise. The use of percentages and repetitions will help the coach adjust the training program to properly progress. By understanding the big, medium, and small percentages, coaches' athletes are less likely to fail to progress. Here is another example of excellent planning:

Week 1—first workout with power clean: 50/5, 60/5

Week 1—second workout with power clean: 55/5, 65/5, 75/5, 80/2/2

During neuromuscular training and coordination, recruitment of motor units, or groups of muscle fibers, is enhanced by training more often, and a greater training load is obtained during the training cycle. The lower and varied volume avoids short- and long-term fatigue, exhaustion, and overtraining.

This concept of variability of load cannot be overlooked or underestimated. Anyone who has been a strength coach will know the frustration of seeing an athlete's performance decrease with overtraining or a too-early peak, while other athletes rise to the occasion by having their training peak at the right time. Variability of load is of particular importance to advanced lifters or participants in sports like hockey that have a long season. The coach or strength coach needs to be aware of the status of the players and may need to adjust the training session based on the fatigue of individual athletes. The principle of variability of load is ideally suited for such situations.

Basic Notation

It may assist the speed-strength coach to use a common notation for workloads when assigning training sessions. This is particularly useful when giving workouts to entire teams. Here is an example of the notation we use:

$$\frac{\text{load (percentage)}}{\text{reps}} \text{ sets}$$

Multiply by one set if nothing is indicated for reps. A typical example would be

$$\frac{80 \text{ percent}}{6} 2$$

which means use 80 percent of your 1RM for two sets of six repetitions (reps). If your 1RM in this particular lift is 180 pounds, you would turn to a percentage chart and find 80 percent of 180 pounds, or you would multiply 0.80 by 180. This weight of 144 is rounded to 145 pounds. You then perform two sets of six reps with 145 pounds.

Warm-Up

The purpose of a general warm-up is to elevate body temperature, which makes the muscle, tendons, and ligaments more pliable and flexible. It also improves circulation to the muscles (to provide oxygen and energy sources and to remove waste products like lactic acid) and improves nerve function. An easy sign of adequate warm-up is when you begin to sweat. This shows that the body temperature has elevated enough to cause the thermal regulators in the brain to try to cool the body by sweating. A specific warm-up should follow the general warm-up, and this can be using an empty bar or very light weight to perform some of the movements that you will be performing in the workout. The specific warm-up should last approximately three to five minutes. Do not exhaust yourself with an extensive warm-up. It is unnecessary and an exhausted muscle is not capable of quick and powerful contractions. The cooldown is also an important step. Numerous studies demonstrate that easy, continuous work at the end of a training session helps to rid the muscles of lactic acid and other by-products at a much quicker rate, and this helps reduce fatigue and the perception of fatigue. In addition, stretching after training has been documented to reduce the delayed-onset muscle soreness that can follow training you are unaccustomed to performing.

In-Season Training

Players cannot perform at peak for eight to nine months and 82 games. There will be normal physiological and psychological fluctuation regardless of the desire of the players, coach, and management. The in-season training volume limit is critical. The concept is to keep the volume low and the intensity relatively high so we can maintain as much strength as possible. An example of this in track and field is Charlie Francis's weight-training program for sprint athletes: assume a sprinter could perform the bench squat with 600 pounds for two sets of six repetitions during the preseason. Instead of lowering the weight (intensity) during the season, which would have caused the athlete to lose strength toward the end of the season, at the time of the biggest meets, Francis and Bompa chose to lower the repetitions (volume) and keep the weight (intensity) high. So the in-season bench squats were 600 pounds for two sets of two repetitions. Several months later, the sprinter still had the strength that was gained during the preseason training while the reduced demand on the body from four fewer reps per set (two-thirds' reduction in volume) provided additional recovery for other training drills and methods.

It is also possible to have players simply maintain a peak level of physical performance once they have achieved a peak. This cannot occur with just one year of training. The athlete must have trained for several years to have obtained a relative peak. Usually novices to training keep improving in strength all season. This can also occur with the training loads as described previously by Francis. For example, a player could perform one repetition with a weight he or she could handle three times. If a player could squat 405 pounds for three sets of three reps in August, the player could easily perform two sets of one rep with 405 pounds during the season in October. A total of two reps is performed with 405 pounds instead of nine reps. There will be little fatigue for the player from the 78 percent reduction in load. The potential difference of a trained versus an untrained team in the playoffs could be staggering. The graph below is designed to illustrate this point. If one team has had a significant overall drop in the players' strength curve and the opposing team has not and all other factors (skill, overall age of the players, number of key players, travel, home-ice advantage, dehydration) are equal, then the stronger team will have a distinct advantage.

There are a number of reasons the in-season training is a different situation altogether.

Games are usually played three days per week. Travel schedules can have 11 games in 20 days. Games, fatigue, poor sleep habits, early flights, hockey practice, questionable diets, dehydration, pressure to perform again and again, jet lag, and travel time paint a pretty clear picture. These are the reasons that hockey players usually drop their training program during the season. This is coupled with the fact that the athlete doesn't understand what proper training is and how to manipulate training loads and choose the correct exercises for performance. If hockey players are still performing the exercises they read about in a bodybuilding magazine and in the higher set and rep scheme, then the sheer fatigue will cause the athlete to stop the

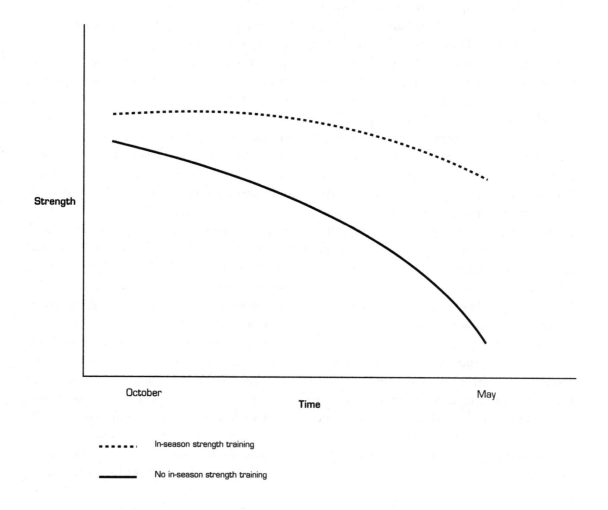

Strength

Time

October

May

.... In-season strength training

—— No in-season strength training

training altogether. This type of past experience is often the exact reason a hockey player is reluctant to start a new, properly designed program.

One NFL team modified the in-season training program so that the basics were used and fatigue would not be an issue. It is true that professional hockey players play two to three times per week and have an 82-game season and professional football players have 1 game per week and 16 games per season. However, this particular NFL in-season training program can be borrowed and modified:

Day	Lift
Monday	rest
Tuesday	squat*
Wednesday	bench press*
Thursday	power clean*
Friday	rehab exercises only**
Saturday	rest
Sunday	game day

*Neck and abdominal training should be performed during the week also.
**Rehab exercises are performed as needed Monday through Friday.

Do not be surprised by this type of program. Limited programs are of enormous value, and great gains can be made. An example is the training program of an elite American shot-putter, John Brenner. Brenner used only four lifts in his training program: the power clean, power snatch, bench press, and squat. Each lift was performed only once per week and performed by itself. He followed this program both during the season and in the off-season. Brenner's lifts included a 550-pound bench press, an 800-pound squat, a 460-pound power clean, and a 290-pound power snatch. He was six feet, three inches, and 295 pounds and was very quick and explosive, as you would expect an elite shot-

putter to be. The point is that an athlete can gain terrifically on a limited program. A professional hockey player could use this type of brief but effective program during the season. Page 52 shows a one-month sample program.

This is not an ideal off-season training program, but it will certainly do the job quite nicely during the season. It is important to ask yourself how often you are currently performing any lift, much less these key lifts, during the season. The volume (sets and reps) of an in-season program would be limited, and the intensity would be relatively high. The goal is to get into the weight room, get the job done properly, and get out as relatively soon as possible without causing unnecessary fatigue or depletion of the body's ability to recover. The stimulus of the higher intensity and the use of important lifts will keep your strength up. We could theorize that hockey players should have a more comprehensive in-season training program, but for all of the travel and fatigue reasons cited previously in this chapter, it does not seem likely.

If the coach can reduce the on-ice practice time, the strength coaches can "rob Peter to pay Paul." The body has a finite ability to recover. We cannot keep adding training components to the athletes' program without expecting the athletes to break down. It would be ideal to take away from on-ice practice time to allow for increased time, physical energy, and mental energy for the in-season speed-strength program to be able to enhance overall performance. Remember that these athletes are playing in games at the highest level of intensity (physically and psychologically) three times per week. The games require recovery, and so do practices. It is not possible to continue to perform practices at high intensity all season. Sometimes the overall fatigue is not recognized. Unfortunately, the fatigue that is caused by excessive practice is sometimes noted only when players

Sample In-Season Hockey Schedule with One Key Lift

Week One

Monday	clean pull, neck training
Tuesday	game
Wednesday	bench press, shoulder-stabilization exercises
Thursday	game
Friday	squat, neck training
Saturday	game
Sunday	military press or push press, abdominal training

Week Two

Monday	snatch pull, neck training
Tuesday	game
Wednesday	bench press, shoulder-stabilization exercises
Thursday	game
Friday	squat, abdominal training
Saturday	game
Sunday	clean pull, hypers, neck training

Week Three

Monday	bench press, shoulder-stabilization exercises
Tuesday	game
Wednesday	power clean or pull, abdominal training
Thursday	game
Friday	push press, neck training
Saturday	game
Sunday	squat, abdominal training

Week Four

Monday	game
Tuesday	bench press, shoulder-stabilization exercises
Wednesday	game
Thursday	game
Friday	pull, abdominal training or rest day
Saturday	squat, neck training
Sunday	military press

"don't have the jump on the ice." If the players are fatigued from the game (and practice), and if the team loses, they are sometimes subjected to a hard practice the next day. This practice is designed to punish them. We can predict that this team will be further fatigued and further from recovery and will perform poorly the next night. One top NHL goalie called me (JMH) to inform me that his back pain returned after the team lost a few games in a row. The coach skated the players very hard and had the goalie perform many drills. I asked the player if a goalie really needed to perform these drills, and he stated: "I have no choice. The coach wanted us to do them." The result was that the goalie couldn't play because of his low-back pain being aggravated by the punishment drills, and he was sent home from the road trip. This occurred two weeks before the playoffs. The physical punishment of players must come to an end. If a tennis player loses a few games, we don't make him or her serve 600 times and blow out his or her shoulder as punishment. If a racehorse loses a race, we don't take the horse to the track the next day and race the horse to fatigue and then put the horse back into another race. The same should hold true in hockey. There are other methods of punishment and enforcement.

The physical demands of the game should not be underestimated. The same NHL goalie recently told me that he can lose up to 12 pounds during a game. That quantity of fluid loss necessitates an adequate recovery and fluid replacement (see Chapter 9 on dehydration and rehydration). Frequently, poor play is because of too much practice, not because "the players need to work harder." If the workload is lessened but the efficiency and quality of training are increased, then physical performance will improve and the players can be kept more fresh and recovered (see Chapter 7 on recovery).

It is important to understand the significance of low-volume, high-intensity training. This type of training concept has been utilized in track and field in the United States, Canada, and the Eastern Bloc countries with excellent results for decades. Track and field coach Chuck Debus believes that because hockey games are actually training of the most specific type, the off days should be used to hone or enhance specific skills, not for on-ice conditioning. One recent Stanley Cup Championship team had six practices over a five-week period. Please note that this was not the extent of their work. There were three games per week during that time. So the actual workload was 15 games and six practices over five weeks. Coaching great Scotty Bowman often gave players a day off from practice and games and eliminated many morning skates on game days. This was his pattern on many teams. Of course, Coach Bowman made 13 trips to the Stanley Cup Finals and won nine championships.

If enough practice time is reduced, it is possible to have two key exercises per training session. The table on page 54 gives a sample training schedule.

One plyometric drill can be performed in each workout as well, and this may include hopping over cones, jumps up on a box (and stepping down), side hops, or various medicine-ball throws. Two sets of five to six reps are sufficient considering the overall training load.

Many of the exercises do not demand a facility for the visiting team to use. However, the visiting team could be allowed to use the professional team, minor-league, and junior-league facilities. If a facility cannot be provided, perhaps other exercises can be done on the road without much difficulty. A roommate or teammate can provide manual resistance for neck training. The team athletic trainer or equipment manager can bring a few

Sample In-Season Hockey Schedule with Two Key Lifts

Week One

Monday	clean pull, squat, neck training
Tuesday	game
Wednesday	snatch pull, bench press, sit-up with weight
Thursday	game
Friday	clean pull, squat, neck training
Saturday	game
Sunday	snatch pull, push press, sit-up with weight

Week Two

Monday	snatch pull, hyper with weight, neck training
Tuesday	game
Wednesday	clean pull, bench press, rotator cuff exercises
Thursday	game
Friday	snatch pull, squat, sit-up with weight
Saturday	game
Sunday	clean pull, push press, neck training

Week Three

Monday	snatch pull, hyper with weight, rotator cuff exercises
Tuesday	game
Wednesday	clean pull, squat, sit-up with weight
Thursday	game
Friday	hang snatch pull, bench press, neck training
Saturday	game
Sunday	clean pull, squat, sit-up with weight

Week Four

Monday	game
Tuesday	snatch pull, push press, rotator cuff exercises
Wednesday	game
Thursday	game
Friday	clean pull, hyper with weight or rest day
Saturday	snatch pull, squat, neck training
Sunday	hang clean pull

small weights (plates) for resisted sit-ups. A nearby gym (not just a "spa" or hotel "fitness center") may provide enough equipment for one key exercise for the players; one key exercise could be used during a road trip, and this would require less recovery, which fits with the demands of travel.

Some sources recommend weight-training sessions twice weekly during the season with 60 to 70 percent of maximum loads. This type of training may not provide enough stimulus to promote strength and speed; 60 to 70 percent is a very light load. Remember, we can keep the intensity high (85 percent and up) during the season if the volume is kept low and fatigue is minimized.

Track coach Francis had a great deal to say about the subject of proper training loads, overtraining, and recovery:

> If the previous workout has been spectacular, I will pull back and force an easier workout as a matter of principle. The athlete will usually want to build on a spectacular workout and train even harder because they are so highly motivated. As this can lead to overtraining and injury, it is always better to err on the light side—do too little rather than too much. If an athlete performs a personal best on the third repetition I've prescribed for five repetitions (i.e., 30-meter starts) then the last two repetitions are not performed.

Francis believes in moving on to the next training element in the workout. He says, "90 percent of my time is spent holding athletes back to prevent overtraining and only 10 percent is spent motivating them to do more work."

Francis also believes in combining different types of training (bounding, heavy weight training, speed training, tempo training) and incorporating all aspects of training at all times. It is the ending and reintroduction of exercises that causes stiffness and soreness. Because the athletes will never perform one type of training and then leave it and move into another type of training, stiffness and delayed-onset muscle soreness are reduced—a critical point.

There are several ways that training can be sabotaged inadvertently. Bompa noted that single-repetition work with inadequate preparation in strength training yields a very high injury potential, and the single-repetition work should be prescribed for relatively mature athletes. Francis points out that more training leads to less performance gain or injury. This fits in very precisely with our philosophy on training as well. The work that is performed must be quality work, and each repetition must count. Higher volume of training is commonly mistaken for higher quality of training. There cannot be wasted sets and repetitions—wasted workouts. In the recent past, an NHL assistant coach, now head coach, took the players out of the weight room because they seemed visibly fatigued on the ice after weight training. This is evidence of inferior planning and poor training methods. A well-planned speed-strength program would not have produced this effect.

The in-season program should be short—for example, 30 to 40 minutes. This will allow the athlete to get in and out of the weight room fairly quickly and still be able to stimulate the central nervous system with one or two key lifts. This short workout works both physiologically and psychologically.

Rest Intervals

The primary energy pathway during strength training must be allowed to be restored as much as reasonably possible. This requires rests of at least two minutes between sets and even longer (five minutes or more) if very high intensity sets (90 percent or more) are being performed. The rest interval between workouts is critical as well. Francis stated: "There is application (training) and recovery from application. That is why we train." This recovery is the basis for the variability of load in training. Many factors are used in determining the rest interval: volume and intensity of the speed-strength and conditioning program, overall condition of the athlete, existing fatigue levels, travel schedule, dehydration, psychological stress, and injuries.

Many athletes and coaches have previously trained in a bodybuilding manner with moderate intensity (weight), high volume (12 to 20 sets per "body part"), and short rests between sets (30 seconds to 1 minute). They probably thought they had a good workout and felt a "good burn." This "burn" is a lactic acid buildup and local oxygen deficit (ischemia). The lactic acid buildup prevents the muscle from performing further work. This is the last event we want to have happen in a strength program. We want the muscle to be recovered so that the planned intensity can be performed and the planned speed-strength gains can occur. Undue fatigue leads to exhaustion. "Exhaustion to overtraining is just a short step" noted Bompa. You will never gain the targeted strength and speed if you train the muscle to exhaustion.

Bompa added, "For sports where speed and power are the dominant abilities, bodybuilding methods defeat their purpose." There exists much controversy over the idea of order of muscle-fiber recruitment. It is believed that as the fast-twitch muscle fibers—those fibers that are explosive and powerful—fatigue,

slow-twitch muscle fibers—those fibers used in endurance exercise—contribute to the work being performed. If this happens, then fatigue is interfering with the proposed speed-strength plan, in which power is the goal, not endurance. There aren't too many (if any) bodybuilding programs, which generally emphasize high volume and low intensity, that have ever produced a desired speed and speed-strength gain in a national- or international-class athlete.

Transition Phase

The transition phase, also known as active rest, concludes the training period or cycle. The length of a transition phase can be a few days to two weeks, and the purpose of this phase is to allow for neuromuscular and psychological recovery from training. The active rest does not mean that the player should sit on a couch and watch television. Rather, the player should be active but at a less intense level: playing racquetball, playing basketball, swimming, and/or participating in very low intensity weight training (40 to 50 percent of training intensity at low volume) two to three times per week. Golf is an enjoyable recreational break from training but is insufficient by itself during the active rest period. The players can enjoy the mental break that golf provides and the social fun that goes with it, but other forms of exercise will be needed too. A mild demand on the body is desired to prevent a detraining effect.

The following are examples of activities that can be done during the active rest period:

Sample Active Rest Exercise Schedule

Monday

440-yard run at medium speed
stretches to loosen up
one-legged squat
standing long jump
snatch pull
back squat
behind-the-neck press
gymnastic movement—chin-up
sit-up
12-minute run

Tuesday

sport activity (basketball, racquetball, swimming) for 45 minutes to one hour

Wednesday

12-minute slow run

Thursday

440-yard run at medium speed
stretches to loosen up
one-legged squat
box jump
power clean
bench press
front squat
gymnastic movement—dip
sit-up
12-minute run

Friday

sport activity (basketball, racquetball, swimming) for 45 minutes to one hour

3

SPEED-STRENGTH

The term *speed-strength* was coined more than 30 years ago in the Soviet Union; it clearly identifies the two significant training factors that athletes must have to compete effectively, and it reinforces an understanding of each factor's importance. The definition of *power* is nearly identical, but somehow the common understanding of power has been lost. One renowned instructor is Yuri Verkoshansky, who believes that the primary objective of strength and speed training is the development of speed, which is largely dependent upon the muscle's power of contraction (maximal force in a minimum period).

There is much literature on the speed of training (meaning how fast lifts are performed), and that could be the subject of a book by itself. There is also much debate on the issue. As a clinician, I (JMH) feel that the increased torque that quick movements would place on a joint would substantially increase the likelihood of injury. However, there are some lifts that have evolved over time and demonstrated an ability to withstand the quick acceleration of this increased speed. These lifts are the Olympic lifts and their variations. The Olympic lifts are also known as the "quick lifts." They are the clean and jerk and the snatch. The variations of the Olympic lifts include the power clean, clean pull, hang clean, snatch pull, power snatch, push press, push jerk, jerk from rack, high pull, and a few others. David Rigert, nine-time world champion in the 198-pound class of Olympic lifting and former Russian weight-lifting coach, defined Olympic weight lifting as "standing over the bar, getting set for the lift, and then exploding." This of course applies to a very experienced Olympic lifter. Other movements such as stiff-legged dead lifts, Romanian dead lifts, leg curls, and so on should not be performed so quickly, nor is it necessary to perform the lift very slowly. A normal speed of movement is appropriate for these other exercises.

Verkoshansky in 1970 stated that application of the athletes' training to their sport is part of their entire profile and presentation. This applies to their speed-strength program as well. This is demonstrated in two sprinters; they are roughly equal in muscular strength, yet one runs the 100-meter sprint in 12.1 seconds, and the other runs it in 12.4 seconds. The difference is in the ability to quickly develop maximum working force or "ratio of maximal strength to time of its display for explosive-isometric muscular tension." Today this is collectively known as "speed-strength." Other nontraining factors come into play as well; genetic characteristics are the biggest nontraining component.

Noted track coach Charlie Francis stated:

> We know that the amount of work is equal to the weight × distance × time. You can vary any component. I never believed in maximum velocity with weights due to the injury factor. You can improve the maximum velocity in another major component. Ben Johnson's heel was found to travel from 0 to 80 km/hr and back to 0 in 0.10 seconds. That is equal to 22.2 meters per second. The squat is approximately 0.5 meters per second velocity. If the squat speed is increased to 0.6 meters per second, which is really quite an increase, the injury risk is raised substantially and the overall speed has changed very little.

The subject of speed of movement is still one of much debate; however, Francis's point is echoed strongly throughout much of the strength community. Proper technique, execution, and selection of exercises to perform quickly are critical.

Because speed-strength training is defined as the combination of maximum strength and speed, it produces the greatest amount of power. A speed-strength-training program should first be constructed in accordance with the principle of a gradually increasing work intensity. Second, it should be combined with technique training to help the athlete develop the capacity to execute his or her position at full exertion.

Other forms of power include explosive strength, starting strength, absolute strength, and reactive strength. Performance improvement of players at the professional hockey level, representing the highest state of speed-strength mastery, is determined primarily by increasing each individual's special-specific work capacity. This is also an essential operating condition for improving the athlete's ability in the competitive situation—game or practice.

Four Components of Speed-Strength Training

The combining of speed and strength into a training program can be divided into four components:

1. explosive strength—the greatest amount of force developed in a given time frame
2. starting strength—how fast and forceful the athletic motion is at the beginning
3. absolute strength—the maximum one can lift, regardless of the time chosen to perform the lift
4. reaction strength—the speed in which the initial body movement causes an opposite and increased reaction from the second movement that occurs to the follow-through

Verkhoshansky lists the first three components as the foundation of speed-strength training and essential for peak athletic performance. The fourth is what we believe to be the final component that incorporates the total development of the speed-strength-training model for hockey.

All of the components are important for maximum athletic performance. An athlete who improves in all four components will progress in speed and in strength. If one area is allowed to lapse, then it is just a matter of time before athletic performance suffers. Successful performance and survival in competition events require all four components.

Explosive Strength Component

Of the four components of speed-strength training, the most important is explosive strength. Explosive strength is the maximum amount of power developed in a certain time frame. A key to explosive strength is to explode in the beginning or where the force is maximum for acceleration to finish or repeat an exercise or athletic movement. Explosive strength is developed by using weight-lifting exercises and jumping and throwing exercise drills of an explosive nature, which are now known in the sports world as plyometrics and ballistics.

Lower-Body Explosiveness

Today, speed is even more high priced than ever before. We are no longer faced with the good, fast, little guy; now we see the good, fast, big guy who does it all. The key to hockey training is the lower-body explosive strength dealing with plyometric explosion of the legs, hips, and back. The lower body is refined and strengthened by jump exercises. These jumps are described as jumping on top of, jumping over, jumping around, jumping up, and jumping out. The depth jumps, whether with one leg, both legs, single, or double, are best described as jumping off, step-offs, and altitude jumps. The depth jumps are the best and most effective method for developing this quick, explosive strength along with the proper speed-strength training program. The hops and bounds bring to the athlete the skill-transferable factors of balance, coordination, and dexterity of plyometrics.

Upper-Body Explosiveness

The more popular lift today in hockey weight training seems to be the bench press. Too many hockey players who train with this particular lift seem to do very little to assist the development of speed. In speed-strength training, the upper-body ballistics and the principles of explosive strength are enhanced. Too many hockey players become one-dimensional. In their training they have no option other than just loading the bar and letting it go. Upper-body explosiveness can help attain absolute strength and add speed to improve the explosiveness of movement. For the hockey player, upper-body explosive strength is vital in the hockey activities that require the use of the arms, shoulders, chest, and back.

Starting Strength Component

Starting strength is the second component of speed-strength training. Starting strength and explosive strength work together very closely, yet their values are different. Starting strength is a measure of how fast and forceful the movement is at the beginning. What quickly comes to mind as an example of starting strength is the tremendous sprinting start of Ben Johnson of Canada in the 100-meter finals of the world championships in Rome, Italy, in 1987. His start was one of the greatest ever witnessed in track and field history, and his time proved this fact. With little more than body-weight resistance, the running or sprinting start is a foundation for starting strength. Fred Hatfield and Michael Yessis state in the book *Plyometric Training* that the lighter the implement the athlete moves and the shorter the distance, the more starting strength he or she acquires; the heavier the resistance and the longer the distance, the more important his or her explosive strength becomes.

Starting is the individual's instantaneous ability to recruit as many muscle cells as possible. The first key of starting strength is the ability to concentrate and gather for the initial effort. An example that exemplifies starting strength in the lifts is the starting position of the Olympic snatch lift. The individual athlete should be able to gather for the intended movement and then allow the second chain reaction of explosion to reaction strength to occur. Starting strength should be built on a foundation of great absolute strength. The takeoff and the quick-strength are other names for the starting strength component. An example is an offensive lineman firing off the line of scrimmage and making contact with a defensive player. This is a picture of starting and explosive strength made visible by working together and following through with the starting and explosive speed-strength. Starting strength and acceleration are dependent upon each other. A hockey player may find that the starting strength will allow a sprint to begin down the ice or will allow him or her the power to move a player away from the front of the net. One of the best ways to develop the starting strength component is by coaching the athlete to make the maximum effort at the beginning of any speed-strength training exercise or drill.

Absolute Strength Component

The third component of speed-strength is absolute strength. Ever since Milo, a Greek athlete of much fame and Olympic magnitude, lifted his first baby calf, man has been infatuated with how much he can lift. Milo would carry this newborn calf upon his shoulders daily. At first, there was the task of lifting and positioning the animal; then Milo had to walk the prescribed distance for this training regime. As the calf grew, the weight also increased, but as the story goes, Milo's strength grew along with the growing calf. Milo's search for strength led in the direction of absolute strength training.

This principle is based on how much one can lift in a single repetition or a given exercise. It is a measure of maximum strength. For the beginning weight trainer, how much weight is lifted in a single try is not important. What is important is the proper technique and method. The beginner often tries to lift too much too soon. Many young athletes associate strength and speed gains as the important results of pounds lifted. This leads the intermediate athlete to try too much or to try to keep up with someone who is further along in his or her training. Without proper coaching of technique and method to guarantee that the exercise is performed correctly, the idea of absolute strength only stands to hinder the hockey player's training and incur a risk of injury.

Absolute strength training for the advanced athlete comes at a period of time when scheduled practice and development of speed-strength movements are totally involved with the training program. This is the time when absolute strength is to be reached and peak athletic performance is developed—the new understanding of when to attempt 90, 95, and 100 percent or a new personal record. Absolute strength is the total effort, not just the attempted but the accomplished. That is what one strives to project in peak performance.

These are the most common questions from advanced athletes regarding absolute strength:

- When should these peaks be tried and how often?
- What effect will the attempt of absolute strength have on the body, and what will the period of recovery and restoration be?

Answers to these questions will vary from individual to individual—based on how one's body best functions and what limitations one must face. Again, as with the beginner and the intermediate athlete, too much too often will not only lead to possible enthusiasm failure but will also injure muscles, tendons, and ligaments and dampen the spirit.

Reaction Strength Component

The fourth component of speed-strength is reaction strength. Reaction strength is defined as the speed in which the initial body movement causes an opposite and increased reaction from the second movement that occurs to the follow-through. An example is when a hockey player is moving to gain an advantage of position before delivering a check. The player's reaction strength increases from the second movement to the follow-through that is required in most playing skills.

Many athletes use reaction strength in defining quickness. Friction and acceleration are key elements of reaction strength. The development of force in pushing off or pulling aids in the total attitude of reaction. A few years ago, in working with assistant basketball coach John Bostick at Vanderbilt University, I (EJK) observed that he used a drill that he named action-reaction. The drill consisted of one player moving and the other player facing the individual and reacting to his movement. The drill lasted a few seconds, but the amount of force and concentration exerted by the players points to the base of reaction strength—that the component of speed-strength occurring in an athlete's training exemplifies the importance of "the greater the strength, the greater the speed" of an athlete. The reaction strength component (meaning two movements in one) can best be developed by use of combination lifts. By changing movement to movement, the muscles are given greater direction for growth and speed-strength development.

Coupled Effect of Speed-Strength Training

The four components of speed-strength training—explosive, starting, absolute, and reaction strength—are only as good as "the coupled effect" of the combined skills needed for the overall development of the hockey player. The skills of skating, checking, defending against a check, and gaining position in front of the net are all methods and techniques to be improved as the player's skill level improves.

The use of speed-strength training helps maintain the delicate balance of the four components of speed-strength. Author John P. Jesse states:

> Because strength is easier to develop than other qualities, athletes spend more time in developing great strength than in developing speed, timing, and balance that would put their strength to greater use in performance. By understanding the difference between bodybuilding, powerlifting, and weight lifting, you understand the process of developing a faster and stronger athlete.

Still, hockey comes down to skating, shooting, passing, checking, and receiving a check. If you execute these skills more effectively, you improve and so does your team. This leaves us with the statement that "with speed-strength training, the best athletic performances are yet to come."

The program should also entail gymnastic movements—dips, chin-ups, pull-ups, and push-ups (as injuries allow)—as well as specific running and reaction development drills—knee lifts, bounds, strides, and frequency drills. For the intermediate athlete, absolute strength starts to become a factor in the training program. Intermediate athletes should build into their program a method of checks and balances so they can periodically see what progress has been made. Standards are important, but only from the standpoint of records of individual accomplishment. More important is the supervision of the athlete by a successful and well-instructed coach or trainer who can advise him or her of what can be accomplished with intelligence, hard work, and time. Too much programming for absolute strength is the same as too many timed races for running and sprinting. The athlete never gets to learn how to develop strength or speed because he or she is never allowed to train. The concept of training cannot be lost. An important factor to keep in mind with the intermediate lifter is in practicing a specific movement that encompasses the transfer from one area of sport to another; the intermediate athlete demands more sets and repetitions with more training time.

Nine Components to Implementing a Program

When implementing a speed-strength training program, the essential elements are the lifting exercises and the plyometrics and ballistics. These are the nine components in which a speed-strength-training program is implemented:

1. period of the cycle
2. sequence of the lifting exercises
3. number of repetitions
4. intensity
5. frequency of workouts
6. warm-up routine
7. relaxation and flexibility routine
8. variability of the load
9. number of exercises

Utilization of these nine components will allow the athlete, trainer, or coach to incorporate the four components of speed-strength

(explosive, starting, absolute, and reaction), thus providing the key elements and foundation for a winning edge.

Warm-Up Routine

The days of having an athlete just walk into the weight room and start lifting should be over. The safety of the athlete is a top priority, and the warm-up routine minimizes injury due to carelessness. The warm-up routine is a safeguard against lack of preparation before starting the speed-strength program.

Here is an example of a preparatory-phase warm-up routine:

1. 440-yard jog—medium speed
2. one-legged squat—three sets, eight reps
3. upper-shoulder flexors—three sets, eight reps
4. glute-ham raises—three sets, eight reps
5. 10 long jumps or 10 vertical jumps

The 440-yard jog is done any time the athletes have not been running or skating before they enter the weight room. As in the competitive phase, if an athlete lifts after practice, the 440-yard jog would not be necessary. In the transitional phase, the warm-up is similar to the warm-up in the preparatory phase, except that the number of sets is changed to two sets instead of three sets. Also, a variety of lifts with the empty bar make a good transition in the warm-up as well. The players can perform five reps of each of the following in succession without placing the bar down: cleans, snatches, snatch squats, front squats, back squats, and Romanian dead lifts.

Relaxation and Flexibility Routine

Regardless of the training phase, the coach should implement the relaxation and flexibility routine (cooldown). This aspect of the speed-strength-training program helps in the athlete's recovery and restoration from hockey practice or conditioning practice in the preparatory phase. Mental fatigue and soreness are remedied, and physical conditioning can be improved by incorporating a relaxation and flexibility routine at the end of each workout.

Here is an example of a preparatory-phase relaxation and flexibility routine:

1. chin-up hangs with pull-down—three sets, six seconds (avoid if you have or had a shoulder injury)
2. side-to-side stretch—three sets, eight reps
3. snatch-split stretch—three sets, eight reps
4. Russian shower: before leaving the shower, gradually turn the cold water up and the hot water off. Using the cold-water shower is a way to massage and stimulate the body, particularly in areas that have experienced trauma or injury and feel like they will be sore. Take a five- to ten-minute shower.

Following the steps for the implementation of a speed-strength-training program will allow the hockey coach, trainer, or athlete an opportunity to incorporate the four components of speed-strength, thus providing the foundation and key elements for a successful competitive edge.

Checkpoints in Implementing a Speed-Strength-Training Program

1. periods—time of annual plan (precompetitive, competitive, and transitional)
2. task—what exercise or exercises are chosen; what the coach wants during this period (the main goal)
3. preparation—the condition of the athlete considered when planning the athletic program
4. length of sport career—high school, college, junior, or professional
5. age of athlete
6. body weight
7. training loads—amount of volume plus intensity recorded (records and charts)
8. volume of the program—number of reps used per exercise per day
9. intensity—amount of weight being used
10. quality of the exercise—kind of movement skill being used
11. character of exercise—for speed, for strength, for flexibility, etc.
12. loading—what reps and weight are being used in training cycle
13. order—arrangement of exercises, speed to strength
14. tempo—execution of speed-strength in the exercise movement
15. volume plus intensity of training period—having a plan, daily, weekly, monthly, yearly

Coach Darryl Williams. Williams is with Cincinnati in the AHL.

4

EXERCISES

"American athletes should look toward the preparation of track and field athletes and Olympic-style weightlifters to learn more about how to increase power and speed."

—RICK BRUNNER AND BEN TABACHNIK

There is not a hockey coach anywhere who does not want to find a young athlete with potential talent and skill and start him or her on the pathway to college and professional ranks. To do this, much depends upon which training principles the coach will rely on during this formative time. When working with the hockey player, proper selection of exercises is an essential key to the successful development of speed-strength. This chapter describes the snatch and clean lifting exercises as well as other key lifts and discusses starting positions and grips, action of the lifts, and coaching tips. The lifting exercises are designed to enhance the athletes' speed-strength development. All forms of these exercises are presented to provide a complete information base. All exercises will not be chosen for every athlete.

Lifting Exercises: Full-Range Movements

Speed-strength lifting exercises should emphasize a full range of movements. It has been hypothesized that full-range movements build more strength in the muscles, tendons, and ligaments because more muscle fibers become involved in the exercise movement.

The Starting Position

The initial movement of all lifting exercises from the floor is referred to as the starting position. It is also the position players should return to when completing each exercise. These are the main points of the starting position:

Snatch. In the starting position for the snatch, the grip should be wide, the back flat, and the chest out. This movement requires more bend in the hips.

Clean. When starting the clean, the grip should be medium width, with the back flat and the shoulders in front of the bar.

1. Feet should be hip-width apart with the weight of the body evenly distributed over the base from toe to heel. The insteps are underneath the bar so that you are close to it.
2. Knees should be bent to approximately 90 degrees with the seat a little higher than the knee joint.
3. Back should be maintained in a flat, strong position. Remember that "flat" can be at any angle and does not mean vertical. This is a key point.
4. Hands should be positioned to give the desired leverage. Keep the arms straight.
5. Shoulders should be above and slightly in front of the barbell.
6. Head should be in a comfortable position with the eyes looking slightly up.

Arms will be wide apart in the snatch grip, and they will be medium or slightly wider than shoulder-width in the clean grip. The reference to starting position in the rest of the clean and snatch exercises in this chapter are like these photos unless indicated otherwise.

The Grip

The position taken while holding the bar or grip should be taught from the very beginning. The standard grip is the hook style. In the hook grip, the thumb is placed under the bar with the fingers placed firmly over the top of the thumb. After learning this basic grip, the athlete can then learn to use the three widths of the grip: wide (near sleeves), medium (shoulder-width), and narrow (toward the center). Grip width in the snatch is very important. The greatest advantage of the wide grip is that it enables the athlete to retain his or her position under the bar. The use of the medium grip is more prevalent in the pressing, pushing, and cleaning exercises. The narrow grip is used more in the specialty movements

Players use their hips, back, and legs to fight for position.

of an exercise and in certain specialty situations. If there have been any thumb injuries, you may have to substitute a standard grip (without the hook). Some hockey players may be uncomfortable with the hook grip.

Snatch Exercises

The snatch exercise is one of the two classic Olympic lifts, with the other being the clean and jerk. The snatch is the movement of lifting the bar overhead onto straight arms in one movement. The two-hand snatch is performed in an uninterrupted movement of the bar from the floor to a fully straight arm position overhead. The snatch is the fastest and most explosive movement. Recent published research found an association between the snatch movement and increased vertical jump. Another article found a correlation between vertical jump and hockey skating speed. Those hockey players with the greatest vertical jump were the fastest skaters. The

Snatch A. In this photo of the snatch, the athlete is not quite at full extension. From this position his hips will move forward, his knees will straighten, the heels will come to the floor, and he will shrug.

Snatch B. In the catch position of the snatch, drop under the bar with elbows locked.

connection between proper training and performance are quite clear. Our own research supported this same finding. Several co-researchers and I (JMH) had a paper supporting this same fact accepted by the sixth IOC (International Olympic Committee) Congress on Sports Science.

The snatch has three consecutively performed parts:

1. starting position
2. the lift upward toward full extension
3. the drop under the bar and recovery to a standing position

There are four different styles of performing the snatch exercises: (1) power snatch, (2) split snatch, (3) muscle snatch, and (4) squat or Olympic-style snatch. Each style has two starting positions: (1) the static start, which

Snatch C. To finish the snatch, stand up with arms locked to support the bar.

Power snatch A. This photo shows the middle position of the power snatch. The athlete is not yet at full extension.

Power snatch B. Catch the bar overhead, but do not drop into the deep squat.

is also called the start without preparatory movement, and (2) the dynamic start. The static start is rarely used because of the technique of tearing or ripping the barbell from the platform instead of lifting. The most widely used start is the dynamic start. The majority of hockey players should adopt a variation of the dynamic start. First, make sure the knee and ankle joints are in line. Second, before lifting the bar from the platform, raise the hips, thus increasing the angles of the knee and ankle joints. This keeps the back position parallel to the starting position and improves the leverage in the knee and hip joints. This position taken in the preparatory action the moment the bar breaks from the platform is called the dynamic start.

Power Snatch

Starting Position

Using the basic stance or starting position, place the hands on the barbell using the wide grip width.

Action of the Movement

Initiate the upward pull when the barbell leaves the floor and is past the upper thighs. Keep extension through the hips, knees, and ankles in preparation for dropping under the bar. The bar will be almost above the waist. Continue the drive to lockout (full body extension) at the same time, forcing the hips in and upward while pulling strongly with the arms and shoulders until you achieve final extension with the bar in the overhead position and the high squat finish of the feet. The power snatch final position is not as low as the squat-style snatch. This exercise will be more in line with what athletes will master in form, method, and technique.

Speed-Strength Coaching Tips

This is a great movement for speed development and strength. Check to make sure the athlete is balanced on his or her feet from toe to heel in the starting position. Remember that this is a dynamic starting motion that can have great benefits that transfer to the field.

The power snatch is an excellent explosive strength movement.

Split Snatch

Starting Position
Repeat the correct starting-position stance as used in the power snatch. Place hands in the wide grip width.

Action of the Movement
This action begins the same as in the power snatch when the first movement onto the toes is completed and the bar is about at the level of the tops of the thighs. Make sure the weight is supported on both feet while lifting the bar to the level of the waist. But, beginning at this level in the split snatch, move your center of gravity onto one leg, and move that leg forward half a step. Maintain your balance while you move the other leg about two to three times that distance backward. Continue to move the bar upward using the action of the arm and shoulder muscles. From this point of the split extension, the recovery is achieved by extending the forward leg and then the other (back) leg. The distance that the bar is pulled in the split snatch is much higher than in the power snatch.

Speed-Strength Coaching Tips
The additional distance that the bar must travel makes the split snatch excellent for training to develop more coordination and quicker foot movement. It also helps the young hockey player develop hip and leg flexibility and balance agility in an athletic motion. The additional height that occurs from the pull makes for more and faster muscle use being coordinated into the pulling. The split snatch is an excellent explosive exercise. This is a somewhat complex movement and may not fit into all routines.

Split snatch. In the split snatch, the legs are split during the drop under the bar.

Muscle Snatch

Starting Position
Repeat the starting-position stance as used in the power snatch. Place hands in the wide grip width.

Action of the Movement
The action of the lift is the same as the power snatch. The only difference is that there should be very little or no flexing of the knees—as if you are trying to keep the hips and legs from dropping at all.

Speed-Strength Coaching Tips
The muscle snatch involves just what its name says—muscle. The amount of weight will be less than is used in the split snatch and power snatch.

Snatch pull. From this stance the athlete will extend the hips, knees, and ankles and then shrug. He will then drop the bar to the platform.

Snatch Pull

Starting Position
Repeat the correct starting-position stance as used in previous snatch-style lifts. Place the hands in the wide grip width.

Action of the Movement
This is the same as in the other snatch exercises, except the movement is taken only to the point right past the top of the thighs or right above the groin. After you force the hips in and upward, raise the arms and shoulders upward to pinch the base of the neck, utilizing the trapezius muscles in the finishing pull. Then return the bar to the floor.

Speed-Strength Coaching Tips
The amount of weight will be much greater than what is used in the power, split, muscle, or Olympic-style snatches. The use of lifting straps can help when additional weight is used when performing this movement. Remind athletes to let the grip stay wide and to pinch the shoulders to the neck. This is a good choice of the snatch exercises for hockey players because they don't have to catch the bar at the top of the snatch. This eliminates the compression force to the wrist.

Hang Snatch

Starting Position
This movement does not start from the floor. Place the hands in a wide grip position, and start standing erect or hanging or from various heights where the bar is set on boxes or racks.

Action of the Movement Starting with Barbell Hanging
The action of the hang snatch begins with the bar resting at midthigh level and the arms straight. This is where the label "hang" comes from. The method and technique of completing the hang snatch are the same as in the power, split, muscle, and Olympic-style snatches.

Speed-Strength Coaching Tips
This would be a good movement to do as the last snatch lift before resting prior to a once-a-week hockey game (for those in high school, colleges, or leagues that play once per week). It involves less work on the back and is extremely explosive. The hang snatch also can be used from the blocks or racks.

One-Arm Dumbbell Snatch

Starting Position
Place the feet a little more than shoulder-width apart, with the toes turned outward slightly. Position the dumbbell between your two legs on the floor. Take a squatlike posi-

Hang snatch A. At the start of the hang snatch, the bar should be just above the knees.

Hang snatch B. In the finished position the legs should be straight and the elbows locked.

tion over the dumbbell. Start with the right hand gripping the dumbbell and the left hand in a balancing position on the left thigh.

Action of the Movement
Pull the dumbbell in an upward movement. The hip and shoulder muscles continue to support the dumbbell until the desired extension is obtained. Once the number of repetitions is completed with one arm, switch to the other arm and repeat. The dynamic starting movement requires that the free arm (not holding the dumbbell) act as a balancing aid on the thigh in the successful completion of the lift.

Speed-Strength Coaching Tips
This is an excellent lift to be used in preparation for an athletic event. It involves less work from the lower back, and the demand is less a factor in fatiguing the athlete. This movement is used with a light weight and can frequently be used with the opposite arm to an injured arm.

Snatch High Pull

Starting Position
Repeat the starting position as used in the snatch-pull movement. Use the wide-grip hand position as is customary in the snatch exercises.

Action of the Movement
First pull: pull bar from floor to knees. Second pull: pull from knees to full extension. After you complete the first and second pulls with the bar, the elbows will make the breaking pull from extension of the hips to the toes raising to the top, allowing the completion of the lift. This is what makes the snatch high pull different from the snatch and the snatch pull.

After you complete the first and second pulls with the bar, make the breaking pull by bending the elbows. The hips should already be extended and the toes raised to the top, allowing the completion of the lift. This is what makes the snatch high pull different from the snatch and the snatch pull.

Snatch high pull A. The bar has just come off the floor; the back is flat but inclined forward.

Snatch high pull B. At the point of full extension, the arms will bend and pull the bar higher.

Speed-Strength Coaching Tips

The amount of weight will be lighter than weight used in the snatch-pull exercise because of the elbow-breaking move. Remind the athlete to drive with the hips to the tips of the toes. This is a super exercise for lower- and upper-back development and coordination for sports transfer. There is a possibility of shoulder pain developing from the high pull. If this occurs, have the athlete see a physician. The shoulder position at the top of the pull may cause a problem known as subacromial impingement syndrome.

Clean Exercises

The clean exercise is just the first half of the Olympic classical lift, the clean and jerk. Again, the position used is basic to all pulling exercises and to all movements when the weight is lifted from the floor. It will also be the position to which the athlete will return when the lift is completed. The principles that apply to the snatch also apply to the clean. The difference is that the athlete uses a medium grip and a different finishing movement. This position provides for an additional level of strength that can be exerted. Strength coach Bill Starr calls the clean the athlete's exercise simply because of the amount of speed used from start to finish.

Power Clean

The power clean is a significant exercise for strength, timing, coordination, and explosiveness. It strengthens the trapezius and erector spinae muscles of the back, the gluteal muscle of the hip, and the quadriceps and hamstring muscles of the thigh. Numerous other muscles are recruited to stabilize the body during this lift. It is a lift that requires practice and coordination. This exercise is best performed in lower reps (three to five). The movement of the power clean is one of proper lifting mechanics. Its performance is identical to the methods of proper lifting that one can see in any work environment. The

Hockey players are always moving around—and sometimes through—the competition to get the puck.

back (spine) is kept flat or slightly arched (not rounded) throughout the lift. The abdominal muscles remain in isometric contraction. This adds to torso stability, or "lumbar stabilization," which is a buzzword in rehabilitation today.

The power clean will require practice to learn proper lifting technique before you can pursue this lift with significant weight. Do not rush the learning process. It is all right if you are not quite ready to push your limit a little harder. Become more efficient first. The power clean has been utilized in more sports than any other weight-training exercise except the squat. Top-level track coaches have stated: "More sprint-specific weight training can bring consistent improvements in strength and power which would have a direct effect on an athlete's ability to perform work and run fast" (Durck). The power clean has numerous advantages for the healthy athlete. (Training modifications for those who currently have injuries will be discussed later in this book.) It allows the body to be trained in a synergistic manner, and this allows many muscle groups to be incorporated in a manner that will carry over greatly to sports. Hockey performance will benefit from the clean in checking another player, struggling for body position on the boards, battling for position in front of the net, and recruiting muscles during a sudden change in direction. The clean movement is similar to so many athletic movements, it has near universal appeal.

Starting Position

Place the feet flat on the floor with your weight evenly distributed. Grasp the bar with hands slightly wider than shoulder width. Keep the bar close to the body (at your legs) and make sure the shoulders are in front of the bar. Keep the back straight and the chest out, looking straight ahead.

Action of the Movement

The action of the power clean technique is best summarized by one of the leading authorities in weight-lifting biomechanics, John Garhammer, Ph.D. (terminology has been simplified):

- The arms are inclined backward from a vertical line connecting the shoulders with the floor. This creates a "shoulders in front of the bar" position for liftoff.
- The barbell is lifted from the floor to just above knee level by simultaneously straightening the knees and hips.
- During the first portion of the pull, the shoulder and hip joints should rise at the same rate, so that a line from the shoulder to the hip at the end of the first pull is parallel to the same line drawn at liftoff.
- At the end of the first pull, a transition in body position occurs. This transition is often called the scoop, second-knee bend, or double pull. The hips move forward and slightly downward as the knees rebend under the bar and the torso shifts to an almost vertical position. However, the shoulders should remain slightly in front of, or directly over, the bar. The transition begins with a shift of balance on the feet from near the heels to the toes.
- At liftoff, balance should be around the balls of the feet and gradually shift backward toward the heels as the first pull progresses.
- The upward speed of the bar should gradually increase during the first pull, but may level or decrease. This is caused by the temporary reduction in force applied to the barbell as the body interrupts its general straightening, or uncoiling, in order to shift into a much stronger leverage position for the second pull.

Power clean A. In the first pull of the power clean, the bar is lifted to midthigh.

Power clean B. During the catch phase, the knees are bent, or flexed, to drop under the bar.

- Immediately after the transition, the second pull begins. The reason for the second pull is the leverage system has improved and the quadriceps (muscle in front of the thigh) are now in a position to be rerecruited from the increased knee bend. The second pull is a very explosive movement that resembles a vertical jump with the barbell.

- At the top of the pull, the bar decelerates. The athlete then moves under the bar to catch it. The arms continue to pull on the bar while knees, hips, and ankles bend. The athletes actually pull themselves under the bar. The torso remains vertical (not leaning forward), and the elbows rotate upward in assisting with catching or cleaning the bar.

Speed-Strength Coaching Tips

The motion of the power clean is used when football players are coming off the line of

Power clean C. To finish the exercise, stand up. The elbows are held high for bar position and for balance.

scrimmage in the execution of blocking and tackling. It also applies to checking and initiating explosive speed and quickness in hockey. When you are teaching this movement, make sure athletes keep the bar close to the body in order to achieve maximum performance. Speed is the most important factor of the power clean. If the bar is scraping the knees of your athletes, the knees are not moving backward fast enough. So, make sure the knees are traveling backward early in the pull. If the bar is scraping their shins, the athletes may be too upright in the deep position, making it difficult to move their knees back fast enough.

Split Clean

Starting Position

Begin in the same starting position as in the power clean, using the medium grip.

Action of the Movement

The difference between the clean and the split clean will be in leg position and not having to lift the bar past the chest and into the drop. Begin the action as described for the power clean. Once you start the second pull, shift the center of gravity onto the leg that is to be moved forward. The distance of the other leg will vary from the center of the starting position. Balance and coordination are key factors in completing the split clean exercise.

Speed-Strength Coaching Tips

The split clean is a difficult movement to teach because of the split method and technique. The athlete must exert more force because of the additional height the bar must be pulled compared to the power and squat-style clean. The athlete should follow the down movement of the bar in correct fashion back onto the floor. Because of the technical difficulty of this exercise, a qualified strength coach should teach this movement to athletes.

Muscle Clean

Starting Position

Repeat the starting position of the previous clean-style lifts using the medium grip.

Action of the Movement

Begin the action as described for the power clean. As in the muscle snatch, there is little or no flexion. Try not to bend or drop the hips and legs. The muscle clean does not have much knee bend. The bar is pulled up quickly.

Speed-Strength Coaching Tips

The muscle clean involves what the name says—muscle. Make sure the amount of weight is lighter due to the height to which the weight is being pulled.

Olympic-Style Clean (Squat Clean)

Starting Position

Repeat the starting position used in previous clean-style lifts using the medium grip.

Action of the Movement

Begin the action as described for the power clean. The unique aspect of the Olympic-style, or squat, clean is the position in which the bar is caught. In the power clean the athlete catches the bar in a shallow, or half, squat position; in an Olympic-style clean the athlete catches the bar in a very low, full squat position. After you drop the hips, keep the low position of the hips and torso.

Speed-Strength Coaching Tips

The two biggest mistakes made in the Olympic-style clean are (1) not keeping the back flat, which will hinder the amount of power that can be generated by the hip muscles and thighs, and (2) trying to pull the

Olympic-style clean A. This photo shows the midpull position of the Olympic-style clean; the bar has been pulled from the floor.

Olympic-style clean B. Drop under the bar in a full squat for the catch position.

weight off the floor with the arms instead of using the arms as guide wires until the final pull. The success the athletes have will depend on the coordination of these movements into one explosive strength move.

Clean Pull

The racking of the bar position during a clean can place stress on the wrist for some athletes. Due to the high level of wrist injuries in hockey, a substitute for the clean can be made without losing all of its value. This substitute lift is known as a "clean pull." All of the lifting and pulling muscles are used, but the bar is not caught at the shoulders. The athlete pulls the bar high, but instead of catching it, the athlete drops/lowers the bar at the top of the pull. This is why special weights known as rubber bumper plates are used in this type of training and lifting. The rubber bumper plates are designed to be dropped onto a lifting platform without breaking the weights or the floor. If a clean pull rather than the complete clean is performed, the pulling tech-

Olympic-style clean C. To finish, the athlete stands up, keeping the bar at shoulder height.

niques are identical until the top of the pull position. The bar is then returned to the floor. Because heavier weights can be used in a clean pull, the bar may not rise as high. We advise against a lightweight, very high pull

Hang clean A. Start the hang clean with the bar hanging at midthigh. From this position, move to full extension and drop under the bar to the catch position.

Hang clean B. The finish position of the hanging clean

due to the fact that the arm position at the top of a high pull can cause what is known as a subacromial impingement syndrome in the shoulder. Remember, we do not wish to incur new injuries in the supplemental training program. It is the pull without catching the bar at the shoulder that is recommended for hockey players.

Starting Position
Repeat the correct starting position as in previous clean-style lifts using medium grip.

Action of the Movement
Start with the bar on the floor and the action of the lift similar to the power clean exercise. Do not do the drop from full extension to the squat position. At full extension, keep the follow-through of the arms nearly straight with the shoulders pinching the trapezius muscles to the neck, and rise up on the balls of the feet (weight-lifting shoes are advisable).

Speed-Strength Coaching Tips
This is an excellent exercise for the overloading of weight as well as the strengthening of the pulling movements. The use of straps may also be of great benefit in helping the athlete maintain the grip in order to keep the bar from coming loose in his or her hands. Remind your athletes not to bounce the weights off the platform. Make sure that they use good form and good technique.

Hang Clean

Starting Position
There are two possible starting positions. Either stand erect with the weight hanging, or stand with the barbell in blocks or on the rack. Use the medium grip.

Action of the Movement
The position of the second pull of the power clean is the starting point of the hang clean

Clean high pull A. The bar has been pulled from the floor, and the athlete is nearing full extension.

Clean high pull B. After reaching full extension, use the arms to pull the bar higher.

(bar hanging at midthigh or a little lower). Making the clean from this position requires more back and hip movement because the weight is already in the second-pull position. The movements from the second pull to the rack position are the same as in the power, split, muscle, and Olympic-style cleans. Remember to keep your elbows up.

Speed-Strength Coaching Tips

The easiest way for athletes to learn the starting position would be to practice with the bar from the hang position. Have them learn the feel of the lift before attempting to put the total clean movement together.

Clean High Pull

Starting Position

Repeat the starting position used in the clean pull or power clean exercise. Use the medium grip.

Action of the Movement

Take the same action as in the clean pull to the point where you have completed the first and second pulls and you are moving into the finishing position. The additional part of this exercise is the high pull. Upon completion of the pull, move the hips in and upward as the bar is just above the groin; then draw the elbows up, which allows the bar to travel to the position at midchest. Raise the arms and shoulders upward to pinch at the base of the neck, utilizing the back and trapezius muscle in the finishing pull.

Speed-Strength Coaching Tips

Raising the toes and pulling the bar to the chest will develop more body control. The use of lifting straps can aid in successfully completing this exercise because of the improved grip. Again, if the athletes develop shoulder pain, have them stop performing this movement, as some people can develop a problem known as subacromial impingement syndrome.

Clean and Jerk Exercise

The clean and jerk is the second lift of the classic Olympic lifts. It combines strength and speed into one exercise. For the player, mastering the technique of this lift will pay off in the coordination of speed and strength. There is much that carries over from weight-resistance training to the ice rink. The clean and jerk improves the feet coordination and the placement of the feet for recovery quickness.

Starting Position

Repeat the starting position used in the power clean. The second movement to the position is racking the bar across the chest and shoulders, as illustrated in the clean exercises. Use the medium grip.

Action of the Movement

After completing the clean phase of the clean and jerk, move to the second phase—the completion of the jerk. Keep the back straight with the elbows and head up. Dip the knees approximately six inches, and in one explosive jump, drive the weight overhead with the legs. Use the arms mainly as a guide for the weight, even though you explosively press with the arms as the entire body comes off the ground. The split movement will have one leg forward and one leg back—usually the dominant leg goes forward. This lowers the body under the bar.

Clean and jerk A. Hands are slightly wider than shoulder-width apart.

Clean and jerk B. The bar has just cleared the knees. From this position the pull accelerates.

Clean and jerk C. At full extension, the hips and knees are straight and in line with the back. Lift the heels off the ground and shrug.

Clean and jerk D. As the athlete pulls himself under the bar, the arms begin to bend.

Clean and jerk E. In the catch position, the feet and back are flat, and the elbows are high.

Clean and jerk F. The recovery position.

Clean and jerk G. Dip to prepare for the jerk overhead. Be careful not to let the knees move too far forward.

Clean and jerk H. The bar is pushed overhead and the body drops under the bar as the legs split.

Clean and jerk I. To finish, the legs are brought together and the bar remains locked overhead. This move requires a great deal of "core" strength.

To return to an upright, erect position, push back with the front leg and begin to take the needed steps back to where both feet are hip-width apart and the barbell is supported overhead. Hold for a count of two seconds, and upon completion, lower the bar to the starting position on the floor.

Speed-Strength Coaching Tips

One mistake that is commonly made while performing the split movement of the jerk is stepping back with the back foot and not splitting the front foot forward. Splitting the feet and keeping the hips collected will keep the athlete positioned under the bar and also help in the development of explosiveness, balance, and speed—total qualities of speed-strength training.

Press Exercises

Bench Press

It is difficult to discuss shoulder strength without someone mentioning the bench press. In fact, the bench press is so popular that when someone asks, "How much do you lift?" it is almost universally known that the bench press is the lift in question.

The bench press is the lift for the upper body that will allow the most weight to be handled. The main muscles that are targeted include the pectoralis major, serratus anterior, deltoid, and triceps. The importance of these four muscles during checking, controlling the stick and puck in front of a crowded net, and controlling your opponent cannot be underestimated.

There are injuries that are attributed to the bench press, but most of these are the result of poor lifting technique, poor training plans, existing or preexisting shoulder injuries that the athlete may not know about, and general inexperience.

Bench press A. When starting the bench press, feet are flat, the back is tight, and the hips stay on the bench at all times.

One of the first points of concern with the bench press is technique. Many have learned to perform the bench press in a linear manner by placing the bar high on the chest with the elbows flared out (shoulder abduction) in the bottom position. This position places a great deal of stress on the shoulder. Do not perform the bench press this way. Instead, allow the bar to travel in more of an arc. Let the bar touch low on the chest, nearly to the area that is commonly known as the solar plexus. Let the elbows travel closer to the body (not tightly against the body). From this new bottom position, press the bar back upward and toward your shoulders. This is the powerlifting style of bench pressing. If you already perform the bench press on a regular basis, reduce your poundage until you adapt to this new style. It usually doesn't take long for the poundages to increase, and, because of the reduced shoulder stress, the weight can be increased with less discomfort. All bench-press world records are set with the

Bench press B. Lower the bar to the chest until the forearm is perpendicular to the floor. Drive the bar in an arc over the shoulders.

muscles are sometimes injured by a single trauma or force, or they may be overused and become weak. Some athletes have never developed adequate rotator cuff strength.

It is interesting to note that there are differences in technique among the varying weight classes of competitive powerlifters. There are also differences between novices and champions. Champion powerlifters use slower bar descent speed than novices use. Lifters with heavier body weight have twice as much torque at the shoulder as lighter lifters even though the heavier lifters lift only 30 percent more weight. This difference may be explained partially by the 32-inch grip limit allowed in competitive powerlifting. Heavier champions also required 0.3 second less to press the bar up than lighter champions, indicating that more torque and power are involved.

bar placed lower on the chest in the bottom position. For any athlete to achieve greater strength in this movement, he or she should use this technique.

A problem that causes shoulder pain is shoulder instability, which is common in hockey. One particular type is known as anterior glenohumeral instability. This problem usually occurs after trauma of various types. The bottom line is that the supporting ligaments in the front of the shoulder cannot support the shoulder as they should because they have been overstretched or partially torn. As the barbell is lowered during the bench press, the shoulder can no longer be stabilized adequately and pain is produced. Changing the bench-press technique to the one just described can reduce the pain for those with very mild cases of instability.

A rotator cuff injury or weakness can also cause shoulder pain during the bench press. The rotator cuff is a group of muscles that actively support the shoulder joint. These

Starting Position

The position of the feet provides the foundation of support on which the bench-press force is generated. The feet should be placed at a comfortable width. It is important once the foot position is in place that the feet stay firmly planted. The feet should not be on the bench or held off the ground.

Action of the Movement

As you receive the barbell from the spotter or remove it from the rack, lower it to the center of the chest, at the end of the sternum. This is more appropriately called the groove point or power zone. Then, touch the chest to ensure a full range of motion, and extend the bar back in a quick motion. Some athletes may find that touching the bar lower on the chest may eliminate shoulder pains and increase the weight that can be handled.

Keep the hips and back on the bench throughout the exercise. That means no arching or lifting of the hips off the bench. It is important to get the natural arch to allow the maximum use of strength. As you move the bar upward, try to move it in a slight arc back over the eyes. The bar then does not move in a straight line but from the center touchdown spot on the chest to the center of the head.

Speed-Strength Coaching Tips

Make certain that the athlete's body is balanced and positioned properly on the bench before he or she starts the lift. The use of spotters to aid and assist is a rule of the game. Having a big bench press is only important to the athletes if they transfer that strength to the hockey rink. Do not overvalue a movement that is performed lying down.

The quick upward drive builds speed-strength directly into the muscles, training the muscles to react quickly. The athlete may not be able to handle maximum weights with explosion. Good rotator cuff muscle strength is required for this type of training.

Reverse-Grip Bench Press

One alternative to the bench press exists, and that is the reverse-grip bench press. There are subtle differences in technique between this and the traditional bench press, but the athlete can still benefit from developing upper-body power. The most attractive point of this lift is that many who cannot bench-press because of shoulder pain can perform this lift relatively pain free.

I (JMH) have one main theory about why some athletes do not experience pain during the reverse-grip bench press but do with the regular-grip bench press: the shoulder is in more external rotation during the reverse-grip bench press, and perhaps this assists the rotator cuff in stabilizing the shoulder. Regardless of the reasons, this may be an invaluable substitute. World-record bench presses have been set by powerlifters using the reverse grip.

Reverse-grip bench press A. Note the difference in hand position compared to a traditional bench press.

Starting Position

The position of the feet provides the foundation of support on which the bench-press force is generated. Heavy bench presses require a stable body. The feet press into the floor to support the body. It is important once the foot position is in place that the feet stay firmly planted. Feet should be placed at a comfortable width. Use an underhand (reverse) grip.

Action of the Movement

The leverage of the reverse grip does not allow for you to take the bar off standard bench-press racks. Use a power rack so that the bar can be set high enough (close to a lockout position) to take the bar off and perform the lift. The other possibility is to have a teammate or training partner assist you with a liftoff to get the bar out of the supporting rack. As you remove the bar from the rack or receive it from the spotter, lower the barbell to the center of the chest, at a point below the end of the sternum. This is more appropriately called the groove point or power zone. Then, touch the chest to again ensure a full range of motion, and press the bar in an arc back up over the shoulders in a quick, explosive motion. Do not press the bar over your face during this lift. If you lose the balance of the

Reverse-grip bench press B. When lowered, the bar will come to the low chest. Press the bar in an arc over the shoulders.

Reverse-grip bench press C. This view of the bottom position of the reverse-grip bench press shows the forearm perpendicular to the floor and the bar at the low-chest position.

bar, the weight can (and will) crash down on your face. At the top position, the triceps are supporting the weight, and these small muscles cannot be expected to stop a heavy bar that is out of balance.

Speed-Strength Coaching Tips

Make it clear to athletes that they should not attempt to "force out an extra rep" if they are alone in the weight room. They should not attempt a maximum effort if they are alone. They should not attempt to do more than their program has scheduled that day. The grip will vary from player to player. Athletes should not use a wide grip. A wide grip places too much stress on the shoulder glenohumeral ligaments and rotator cuff.

Incline Bench Press

Starting Position

Repeat the starting position that is used on the bench press. The feet should be in a comfortable, natural position.

Action of the Movement

Lower the position of the bar to the chest and place it right under the chin. The action of returning to lockout follows the same guide-

lines used in the bench press. Remember to push the bar slightly back as it is going up.

Speed-Strength Coaching Tips

This is a good alternative exercise for hockey players because of the degree of angle of the incline pressing motion. Some players may find that the incline causes more shoulder pain than the standard bench press does. If so, they should not perform this exercise.

Dumbbell Bench Press

Starting Position

Repeat the starting position used in the barbell bench press. Because you must balance two implements of weight instead of one, you may place the feet a little farther apart than what is normally used in performing the barbell bench press. The path of the dumbbells depends on the balancing position of the dumbbell.

Action of the Movement

Lower the dumbbells sideways from the starting position gradually, allowing the arms to torque to the position of the shoulder and armpit section. Upon making the full range of motion, return to the starting position.

Standing behind-the-neck press A. To start the standing behind-the-neck press, the bar should rest behind the neck on the shoulders.

Standing behind-the-neck press B. Raise the bar over the head to finish the exercise.

Speed-Strength Coaching Tips

All dumbbell exercises require a great degree of control, and as a consequence, the muscle groups that are used in the movements have additional resistance placed upon them. Keep a watchful eye out for athletes having trouble controlling the exercise movement if the athletes have unstable shoulders. If an athlete has already had the shoulder ligaments reconstructed or tightened, then he or she should not perform the dumbbell bench press. There is a risk of restretching the reconstructed ligaments or further stretching or tearing already damaged ligaments.

Dumbbell Incline Bench Press

Starting Position

Repeat the starting position used in the dumbbell bench press. The path of the dumbbells depends on the balancing position. The bench can be placed at an angle anywhere between 30 degrees and 70 degrees, with 45 degrees being the most common.

Action of the Movement

Lower the dumbbells sideways from the starting position, progressively allowing the arms to bend throughout the movement until you feel the touching position. Once you make the touch, reverse the movement and press back to the starting position.

Speed-Strength Coaching Tips

In using the dumbbells, as with a leverage movement, ease into the full-range movement through the initial repetitions. The lowering of the dumbbells should be controlled, and they should be brought back to the starting position in a dynamic fashion. Again, if the athlete's shoulder is unstable or reconstructed, he or she should not perform this exercise.

Behind-the-Neck Press (Standing)

Starting Position

Before you start the lift, the body should be in a strong, well-braced, and balanced position. Rest the bar on the shoulders behind the

Seated military press A. The abs should be tight to support the back.

Seated military press B. The bar should move in a vertical line to a point above the head.

neck. Set the head slightly forward so the bar may travel in a vertical line from the shoulders. The grip position can be wide, medium, or narrow. Place the feet approximately hip-width apart.

Action of the Movement

Press the barbell with dynamic force overhead to arm's length in a vertical line. Then lower the barbell back down until it is in the starting position.

Speed-Strength Coaching Tips

Note that control must be used lowering the bar back to the starting position on the shoulders. Full range of motion of the shoulder, particularly in external rotation, is necessary for this exercise. If the athlete's shoulder range of motion is limited, this exercise will probably cause shoulder and neck pain.

Front Press or Military Press (Seated or Standing)

The overhead lifts, including the military press, are important in a strength-training program. The muscle that can be considered the foundation of the shoulder is the serratus anterior, which rotates the shoulder blade upward and allows overhead movement to take place. This muscle is a major scapular stabilizer. The military press is a most effective means of strengthening the serratus anterior.

There are mixed opinions as to whether or not the military press causes a shoulder impingement syndrome. Most athletes include the military press without ever having an incidence of pain. However, there may be an explanation for the few who do have pain. The first reason is anatomical. The roof of the shoulder (acromion) is not always flat (normal or type I). Sometimes the roof is downsloping (type II) or actually hook shaped. Those that have a hook-shaped acromion (type III) may need to avoid the military press as this hook may irritate the rotator cuff. The roof shape (acromion morphology) is determined by an x-ray known as the scapular outlet view. You can ask your doctor to order this view to assist you if you have shoulder pain when performing the military press. Another theory for pain during the military press for athletes with stable shoulders is that the hypertrophy of the supraspinatus exceeds the space for the muscle in the bony tunnel known as the scapular outlet.

Starting Position

In the seated position, rest the barbell on the top of the chest and shoulders with the grip in the desired position. When standing the feet should be at a comfortable width to provide balance. For most people this will be approximately shoulder-width apart.

Action of the Movement

Repeat the same movement as in the behind-the-neck press. Press the barbell in dynamic movement from the chest to a point above the head, and then lower it back down into the starting position.

Speed-Strength Coaching Tips

Set the head slightly forward so the bar may travel in a vertical line from the shoulders. Remind the players that the trunk should remain still and that the bar's path travels in a vertical pattern.

Push Press or Push Jerk

Another exercise for shoulder power is the push press, which is modified from the clean and jerk. The clean has already been discussed, but briefly it is the lift of bringing the bar off the floor to the shoulders by a combination of pulling and dropping the body under the bar and then quickly standing up from a squatting position. The jerk is when the bar is already at the shoulders and the lifter bends the knees a little and then straightens the knees fairly quickly, thus driving the bar upward. Also, the weight should be felt over the heels an°d the balls of the feet. The lifter then splits the legs apart (one forward and one back) and drops under the

Push press A. In this photo the knees and hips have already begun to dip. Quickly straighten the knees and hips to accelerate the bar over the head.

bar and then stands erect with the bar overhead.

The push press begins the same way. The athlete bends the knees and then drives the bar upward and continues to finish the pressing motion by taking advantage of the momentum from the leg drive. This allows the athlete to move the weight in a coordinated manner and exposes the shoulders to more weight than they could handle during a strict press overhead. The push jerk is similar except that once the athlete drives the bar upward with the leg drive, he or she bends the knees again and drops the body under the bar while the arms are still pushing up. Be careful here because too quick a drop may cause knee pain. Once the bar is overhead and the arms are locked out, the athlete then straightens the knees. Athletes usually like the quickness and coordination of this movement.

Push press B. Once the bar is driven upward with the legs, finish by pressing it to lockout.

There is a major caution for this lift. If the athlete has any significant wrist injuries from hockey, he or she should not perform this lift. Instability of the wrist from a previous significant injury may not allow the athlete to perform this lift. If an athlete has shoulder instability, or if trauma has recently caused a flare-up of the pain from instability, he or she may need to avoid this exercise also.

Starting Position
Take a medium-grip position. Stand erect with the bar at the shoulders-chest position.

Action of the Movement
Dip the knees about six inches, and drive upward with the legs as you press the weight overhead. The push jerk will have you drop under the bar to catch it overhead while the weight is moving up. Stand erect before the bar is lowered. The sequence of the action is dip-drive-dip. Lock the weight overhead and stand erect.

Speed-Strength Coaching Tips
This is a good exercise for athletes who may be injured or who cannot do the split jerk due to some other circumstance. Remind the athlete to hold for a two-second count once the weight is positioned overhead. This is a good exercise to learn to recruit and coordinate more power.

Squats and Lower-Back Exercises

The squat has been called "the king of the exercises" by weight-training enthusiasts for decades. Like the dead lift and power clean, the squat uses a tremendous amount of muscle during the lift. The squat emphasizes the quadriceps (muscle in front of the thigh), hamstring muscles (back of the thigh), adductor muscles (inner thigh), gluteal muscles (hips), erector spinae muscles (muscles that run up both sides of the spine), and a number of other supporting muscles—the calf muscles providing balance, the trapezius muscles supporting the bar, the forearm and hand muscles gripping the bar, the muscles of respiration (breathing) used during exertion, and the abdominal muscles remaining contracted to support the low back. As you can see, this is an important exercise.

Thirty years ago, the squat had a bad reputation. Many alleged "authorities" who allowed their personal biases to interfere with their scientific thinking process, stated that the squat was harmful to the knee. The leg-extension exercise was considered the "ideal" knee exercise, and everyone used the leg extension. However, the weight-training community never stopped using the squat exercise, because they knew it wasn't inherently harmful. Certainly, if you bounce at the bottom of a squat you may cause harm. Some individuals have an uncommon shape to their patella (kneecap) or have significant patellar tracking problems. These are areas of caution but they occur in only a minority of people who train.

Knee specialists today (orthopedic surgeons, sports and orthopedic chiropractors, athletic trainers, and physical therapists) are using a one-third to one-half squat in the rehabilitation of the knee today. It is now called "closed-chain terminal extension" or "proprioceptive training." The weight-training community simply refers to this movement as a partial squat. The leg-extension machine has fallen out of favor because of the tremendous stress it places on the patellofemoral joint (region of the knee where the kneecap glides over the femur or thigh bone). This mechanical stress from the leg extension produces degenerative or arthritic changes in the knee. The leg-extension exercise also produces an undesirable stretch on the anterior cruciate ligament (ACL) in the knee. It is amazing how opinions change over a few years—once proper analysis is utilized and personal biases are removed. O'Shea noted that enhanced strength of the muscles surrounding the knee make the knee much less susceptible to injury in sports such as ice hockey, football, and basketball.

Without strong legs and hips, speed and strength development is minimal. As the squat strength increases, so does the speed-strength in other lifts. The squat requires hard work and gut-busting effort. This is why few conditioning programs succeed in this particular lift. There is no doubt that the bench press is far more enjoyable, but athletes' futures may depend upon the results of training with squats.

Alvin Roy, "First Father of Strength and Conditioning" and former strength coach for the San Diego Chargers, felt that if squatting exercises were incorporated into a proper running program in the early high school years, the athlete's speed would increase as his strength from squats increased. Coach Roy used to say, "The stronger I get, the faster I run." The squat is definitely one of the foundation movements of speed-strength training for hockey players. It has elements of all of the components included in the speed-strength concept.

Some players I (JMH) have dealt with used to perform squats on an apparatus known as a Smith Machine, but now they excel with the free-bar squat. The Smith Machine is popular in many gyms because it is easy to do lifts without a spotter. There are two uprights that the bar is attached to, and there are two hooks that can be rotated toward or away from the uprights to stop the movement of the bar. These uprights make the bar travel in a direct, vertical line. Different body types move differently, and for this main reason, I (JMH) do not recommend the use of the Smith Machine. Additionally, the balance that is required when performing a free-bar squat is much more applicable to sports. If there is difficulty with back pain and squatting, there may be a few problems such as weak back muscles, leaning too far forward, or looking up during the squat. "Looking up," which is a popular cue in gyms to teach novices to squat, causes the neck and low back to extend, and this can lead to jamming of the small joints of the low back (facet joints) and cause more pain.

Back Squat

Starting Position
Start with the feet a little more than shoulder-width apart, with the toes turned slightly out-

Back squat A. In the back squat starting position, the bar is placed high on the back with the chest out.

Back squat B. To begin the descent, unlock the hips and then the knees.

ward. Rest the barbell across the trapezius and back of the shoulders, and keep the arms in a comfortable position for balance. You may vary the stance to achieve balance.

Action of the Movement

Keep the head in a slightly raised position, with the eyes focusing straight ahead, the back tight, and the shoulders back. With the barbell centered over the hips, begin to squat down until the tops of the thighs are as low as possible. From this low position, drive upward and return to the starting position. Keep the chest up and the back tight through the entire movement.

Speed-Strength Coaching Tips

If the athletes lean forward as they come out of the bottom position, have them force the hips under the bar more while keeping the head up and chest expanded. The back in the squat is kept flat, but not vertical. Also, the back squat develops hip and leg power as well as back strength and aids in the development

Back squat C. In this sideview of the back squat at midpoint, note that the knees are behind the toes and the athlete is sitting back into the squat.

Back squat D. At the bottom of the squat, the back is flat but not vertical and the chest is out.

Back squat E. This sideview of the bottom position of the squat shows the forward inclination of the back, which is held flat.

of running speed, power, and strength. If the athletes develop back pain while squatting, have them change their head position. They should look down slightly, at the point where the wall and floor join, to reduce the stress on the low back. Small joints in the back (facets) become more weight bearing when the low back is arched. When athletes look up, reflexes involving the neck, head, and eyes will increase the curve in the lower back as the curve in the neck increases. This increases the load on the small joints in the low back and will produce pain if the joints have already undergone mild or moderate arthritic changes (facet arthropathy). When I (JMH) published an article about this subject in the *Ironman* sports medicine column, an enormous amount of mail and telephone calls came in from weight-training athletes who claimed that their back pain had stopped once they stopped looking up while performing squats. Also, make sure the knees don't travel too far forward during the squat. This is a common mistake. Have the athlete move the knees backward while he or she is straight-

ening and maintaining the proper position with the rest of his or her body.

Power Squat

The squat can be performed many different ways. For the purpose of hockey training, a power squat can also be used for strength purposes. A power squat has a few minor variations from a standard back squat.

Starting Position

Position the bar a little lower on the upper back than during a standard squat. This is called a "low-bar position" and allows for a better lever arm to lift the weight. Position the feet farther apart during the power squat than you do during a standard squat.

Action of the Movement

"Sit back into the squat" with a forward lean of the upper body (while keeping the back flat but not vertical). Reach the thighs parallel or a little above parallel to the floor (in power-lifting competition, the hip joints must drop below the knee joints—slightly below paral-

Power squat A. Note the low placement of the bar on the upper back during the starting position of the power squat.

Power squat B. Note the wide stance in this front view of the starting position.

lel). This tends to recruit the gluteal muscles and adductor muscles of the inner thigh a little more than standard back squats. This movement produces significant reduction of groin injuries.

Speed-Strength Coaching Tips

Another variation is the bench squat, or box squat. In this variation, athletes straddle a bench as they squat, and they barely touch it with their butt before standing up again. This provides a safety factor for some trainees. The bench squat was popularized in the early 1970s by hammer thrower George Frenn. The bench squat received some criticism years ago as a result of trainees slamming down hard on the bench and bouncing back up. This type of movement obviously places severe stress on the spine. Do not allow athletes to perform the bench squat that way.

Power squat C. Unlock the hips first to maintain proper position.

Power squat D. The bottom position of the power squat is not as deep as it is in the back squat. Stop the squat when the pelvis tilts backward.

Power squat E. Front view of the bottom position of the power squat. It is important that the knees do not cave in (move inward).

When parallel squats are performed using heavier weight, the use of knee wraps may give added stability, as research by Harman and Frykman demonstrated. However, the use of knee wraps on a regular training basis is not advised as it can cause too much pressure between the patella (kneecap) and the femur (thigh bone), causing cartilage damage. This can lead to what is called a patellofemoral pain syndrome.

Approximation of poundages relative to the other major lifts can be determined. The squat poundage can approximate 134 percent of the power clean (W. Young).

Front Squat

Starting Position

Rest the barbell across the front of the shoulders and on top of the chest. Place the feet a little more than shoulder-width apart, with the toes turned outward slightly. Keep the trunk upright, and hold the barbell with the grip in a comfortable position of balance with the elbows held high.

Action of the Movement

Keep the back as straight as possible. With the head up and back tight, squat down until the tops of the thighs are as low as possible. From this low position, explode in a driving upward force, returning to the starting position. Keep the elbows up, the shoulders square, and the back tight throughout the entire front squat movement.

Speed-Strength Coaching Tips

Review the coaching tips for the back squat. In the front squat, the weight is more in the front thigh area rather than the hips. This squat is tremendously important in increasing

Front squat A. For the front squat, hold the bar across the shoulders near the throat, with the elbows held high.

Front squat B. Drop into a full squat, keeping an upright position with elbows high.

hip flexibility if performed with proper form and technique.

For athletes who cannot keep their heels on the floor, use a shaved wooden board or a five- to ten-pound plate under each heel. This can be done for back squats also. Remember to encourage athletes to hold their elbows high. USA Weightlifting coach Mike Burgener cues his athletes to "lead with your elbows" when rising out of the low position of a front squat. This cue works well. I (JMH) also tell athletes to try to push the floor down with their heels. These two cues help keep the body in proper alignment during the squat.

The joint on top of the shoulder (AC joint) is commonly injured in hockey players. If an athlete has this injury and placement of the bar across the shoulders is painful, then this exercise is not for this athlete.

Split Squat

Starting Position
Begin the exercise with the weight on the shoulders, as in a back squat. You may vary the grip for balance.

Action of the Movement
Stride forward with one leg until the foot is in a good split position. Stay in control. With the forward knee in line with the ankle, flex the forward hip so that it lowers while the rear leg is nearly fully extended. Note that the trunk remains upright. Recover from the position by tilting the barbell slightly backward, pushing off the rear leg, and pushing vigorously with the front leg. This is not a lunge exercise. Count the repetitions on the left leg and right leg together for a set.

Speed-Strength Coaching Tips
Before beginning, make certain the athletes are balanced in the starting position. All sports that use lunging movements followed by very rapid and dynamic recovery may benefit from the employment of this exercise. This exercise can also be performed with dumbbells held in each hand and repeated in the same form and method. This super movement improves flexibility of the hips and the ankles. There is tremendous pressure on the rear leg and knee during this movement. If

athletes feel knee soreness or quadriceps tendon pain, have them stop performing this movement.

One-Legged Squat

Starting Position

Stand on top of a box or scoop on a power rack and assume the starting position by standing on one leg.

Action of the Movement

Hold the rack for support as the body is lowered. Bend the support leg in the squat style, to a point where the calf muscle and hamstring are touching each other. Upon making the finishing movement, explode upward, back to the starting position.

Speed-Strength Coaching Tips

This is an excellent warm-up exercise. Not only is the flexibility increased but the full range of movement is increased as well. This exercise can be used with dumbbells and as an in-season competitive-period exercise. It can also be modified and used as an excellent knee-injury-rehabilitation exercise at the appropriate advanced stage of rehabilitation. Many athletes have an incomplete rehabilitation. This exercise can help teach the athlete to recruit the thigh and hip muscles again. The depth can be gradually increased.

Lunge

Starting Position

Start in the same position as in the back squat. Stride forward with one leg until the foot is in a good split position. Your thigh should be parallel with the ground and your knee should be at a 90-degree angle. You may vary the stance to achieve balance.

Action of the Movement

The action is the same as in the split squat. The difference between the two exercises is

Lunge walk A. Start the lunge walk with a dumbbell in each hand.

that each repetition in the lunge is alternated from one leg to the other. A single repetition consists of a left-leg lunge, then back to a starting position, followed by a right-leg lunge, and return to a starting position.

Speed-Strength Coaching Tips

This exercise is really good for athletes who need to improve their balance, athletic coordination, and footwork. The use of a plate may be of great help in strength development. By standing with the back leg on a plate, balance is thrust forward, and this places greater force on the lead leg. If athletes have developed patellofemoral pain (pain in the front of the knee), do not allow them to do this exercise.

Lunge Walk (Squat Walk)

Lunge, or squat, walking may be an important contribution to balance in the leg strength of hockey players (Morrow). The lunge walk should not be confused with the duck walk, a movement in which the athlete

Lunge walk B. Step forward into a lunge. The front knee should be at a 90-degree angle, with the thigh parallel to the floor.

drops down into a full squat position and remains there while attempting to "walk" or waddle. Although the duck walk was popular 25 years ago, it is not commonly seen today.

Starting Position

Start in the same position as in the lunge or split squat.

Action of the Movement

Stride forward with one leg until the foot is in a good split position, thigh parallel with the ground and knee at a 90-degree angle. Instead of pushing back and coming to an erect position, allow the pushoff to propel you forward so that you walk from this low position to the same position but with the opposite leg forward. The athlete can strive for distance, up to 25 or 30 meters.

Speed-Strength Coaching Tips

Dumbbells may be used for additional resistance when needed. The advantage of this exercise is that it helps build individual leg strength.

Step-Ups/Dumbbells

Starting Position

Grip a dumbbell in each hand. Face a box or power rack scoop to be used in the step-up exercise. Make sure the weight is equally distributed throughout the body.

Action of the Movement

Place one foot on the surface of the platform. As you make contact, drive the other leg and knee into a 90-degree angle at the waist. Then bring this leg back down to the floor. Repeat the movement with the same leg for the desired number of repetitions, then switch legs.

Speed-Strength Coaching Tips

This movement works really well with more than one step. For years the one step has been used, but the three-step approach gives the athlete greater follow-through and quicker reaction-strength development; it helps develop greater speed-strength because of the continued movement from step to step. Again, this is an excellent movement for balance, coordination, and body control. For players who do not have well-developed leg drives, this is a super addition to the back- and front-squat exercises. This exercise can be performed with a barbell as well.

Back and Hamstring Exercises

There are several exercises to choose from for effective strengthening of the leg, hip, and low-back muscles. All of the core exercises are performed in a weight-bearing or standing position. This is important for what is known as the "kinetic chain." These are the connecting anatomical and biomechanical structures (chain) that work or move together (kinetic). Some popular gym exercises are deliberately left out of this section because of their failure to address all of the key muscles that both condition and facilitate coordination. The following exercises have been established and have worked for all sports for decades.

The lumbar paraspinal muscles are unique in several areas. First of all, the erector spinae muscles consist of many sets of muscles that attach themselves along the length of the spine from the pelvis up to the base of the skull; although it may feel that way, there isn't just a single muscle that covers that entire distance.

Although most muscles respond well if exercises cover the full range of motion (for example, if you are performing a biceps curl, you would want the elbow to straighten completely and bend all the way up), the erector spinae does not work that way. In fact, exercise over a full range of motion in the lumbar spine may cause injury and will likely produce a great deal of low-back pain on a daily basis. Several studies (Kippers and Parker; Triano and Shultz) have investigated and confirmed the function of the erector spinae muscles in untrained individuals. EMG (electromyogram) studies of these muscles reveal that if a normal subject is in a standing position, the erector spinae muscles are very active. As the subject begins to perform a toe-touching movement with the hip bending and the back rounding, the muscle activity remains but begins to diminish. The farther that the subject bends forward, the less the erector spinae muscles work. When the subject reaches about 80 degrees of forward bending (almost two-thirds of an average toe-touch effort), the erector spinae muscles cease to work (myoelectric silence). This can be similar to the

position assumed during a faceoff. At the moment of reaching the two-thirds mark, the weight of the upper body is supported entirely by the ligaments and discs of the spine. This is a very vulnerable position. This is why a great deal of back rounding during back-strengthening exercises is undesirable. It is of interest to note that Olympic weight lifters rarely, if ever, round their backs during any exercise, and yet they have the most heavily developed erector spinae of any athlete.

Hyperextension Exercise

The hyperextension exercise, or "hypers," is a common low-back, glute, and hamstring exercise. The most common performance of this exercise is far more conservative than the name implies. The word *hyperextension* in this case refers to the motion in the spine. A rounding of the back is called flexion. Straightening of the back is called extension. Arching of the back is called hyperextension. Although the exercise is called "hyperextension" because of the way that it was originally performed, the "hyper" of today is best performed by having the athlete raise only to a parallel position. This prevents pain from occurring from small joints in the back (facet joints).

Starting Position

Position yourself facedown on a hyper bench or across a vaulting horse. Your feet should be stabilized and held securely, or they should be placed against a wall and the hips supported solidly so the upper body can hang over the bench or horse. Only the thighs are on the bench. The upper body and hips are off the bench. Lock the arms around the back of the head.

Action of the Movement

From the hanging position, lift the head and extend the upper body so the shoulders and

Hyperextension A. Begin the hyperextension exercise with the weight behind your head.

Hyperextension B. To complete the exercise, raise the back to the neutral position. The back should remain flat and the movement should be in the hips.

head come as close as possible to being at hip level. Hold for a two-second count at parallel, and then lower back to the hang position.

Speed-Strength Coaching Tips

Start with this exercise using no weight resistance, but as the player becomes more accustomed to the exercise, weight resistance should be added, as in the photos above. Different weighted medicine balls are excellent to use. Also, make sure the athletes do not start the movement by arching the low back first. Instead, they should try to make the hamstrings and glutes pull the upper body upward. This will assist in teaching athletes the difference between their hips and back.

This exercise is actually hip extension while the spine remains in extension or neutral position the entire movement, and this is as far as the body should be raised. If the body is raised further, then the athlete has ventured into a true hyperextension movement. This hyperextension motion is really not necessary, and if the athlete has degenerative changes in the small joints (facets) of the back, this exercise may produce pain. It is

necessary only to reach a parallel level. The athlete should allow the motion to happen in the hip joint.

Glute-Ham-Gastroc Raise

An exercise known as the glute-ham-gastroc raise was developed in the Soviet Union. The exercise targets the lumbar spine (erector spinae), gluteal, and hamstring muscles. It originated using a vaulting horse, and today there is equipment especially for this exercise. It was designed for the Olympic weight lifters but has carried over very well to football, especially for power coming out of the three-point stance prior to foot movement. It is also very applicable to hockey.

Athletes will most likely need to progress to this exercise because they may not be able to achieve a full range of motion raise at first. This is an advanced exercise, and athletes should become proficient at the hyperextension exercise first. Once they reach the position of a completed hyper movement, it is important that they keep an isometric contraction of the lumbar paraspinal and gluteal muscles while maximally contracting the

Glute-ham-gastroc raise A. The starting position for the glute-ham-gastroc raise is similar to the hypers start. The back is held flat.

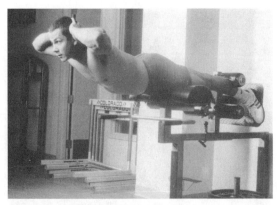

Glute-ham-gastroc raise B. Raise the back to the neutral position.

hamstring muscles, which will assist in stabilizing the knee. Some athletes with existing, significant knee injuries may not be able to perform the glute-ham-gastroc raise at all. For all the other athletes, weight can be added for resistance as strength increases in the glute-ham-gastroc raise. Famed Olympic weight-lifting record holder Vasily Alexeev used 60 kilograms (132 pounds) for three to five sets of four to six reps and 200 pounds for a single repetition. However, this exercise may be done without weight as a supplemental exercise.

Starting Position
Repeat the position used in the hyperextension. The incorporation of the glute-ham bench has advanced the glute-ham-gastroc raise.

Action of the Movement
The movement is identical to the hyperextension exercise, except in the hyperextension you stop at a position parallel to the floor. In the glute-ham-gastroc raise, you keep going until the thighs and legs are at a 90-degree position. This action incorporates the hamstring muscles into a maximum muscle contraction of a speed-strength movement.

Glute-ham-gastroc raise C. Finish the exercise by maintaining a flat back and bending the knees to raise the thighs, hips, and upper body.

Speed-Strength Coaching Tips
The movement from parallel to 90 degrees will help in the hamstring development. This exercise is often overlooked in speed-strength development programs.

Good Morning Exercise
The good morning exercise is a fine back-strengthening exercise. It is a full-range movement and will be a very important remedial exercise. In the beginning, it is wise to move smoothly and with control in both the

Good morning A. In the starting position of the standing good morning, the knees are bent slightly.

Good morning B. Hold the knees in the bent position and keep the back flat. Then bend forward at the hips.

flexing and extending movements, but as strength is developed, the extension part of the movement should become more dynamic.

Starting Position

Repeat the standing squat position, with feet a little over medium-width apart and the barbell resting on the shoulders behind the neck. The medium-grip position is the best for controlling and balancing the bar.

Action of the Movement

From a standing position, squat about a quarter of the way down, then curl forward so that the spine is mildly rounded. The legs are not really in a locked-out position but are slightly bent to relieve tension on the hamstring muscles. From this parallel position, uncurl the body back to the starting position. Keep the back tight and the neck "bulled" against the bar.

Speed-Strength Coaching Tips

The increase of lower-back strength will produce greater development and improvement in the hockey player. Having great strength in what otherwise is a vulnerable area affords the athlete a measure of protection from injury. Both small and large muscles surrounding the spine are strengthened by the good morning exercise.

Stiff-Legged Dead Lift

The stiff-legged dead lift is one of the best exercises for developing hamstring strength. This exercise allows the muscles to be stretched at both the knee and hip joints. Of course, this exercise carries with it an increased risk of injury, so we have a qualifying statement: if you have already incurred a significant back injury or have chronic low-back pain, do not perform this exercise.

Starting Position

The barbell starts on the floor. When you begin this exercise, stand on the floor. As your flexibility and strength improve, you may stand on a very low box or weights to give a greater range of motion. Do not begin this exercise by standing on a box. The medium-width grip is fine. You may use a clean posi-

Stiff-legged dead lift A. Start the stiff-legged dead lift with the barbell at midthigh. Very flexible athletes can stand on blocks of weights to deepen the bend.

Stiff-legged dead lift B. Bend forward with legs straight, as though doing a hamstring stretch.

tion to initiate the movement and stand upright with the bar at a full hanging position.

Action of the Movement

Bend forward, allowing the barbell to slide against the body at all times. Touch the weight to the floor, and return to a standing position. Keep the knees nearly completely locked (a very slight bend is OK). Do not round the back too much.

Speed-Strength Coaching Tips

This exercise does not allow for great speed of movement. However, it is excellent for developing hamstring strength. The hamstring is a two-joint muscle, and it must be stretched to be facilitated. A standard leg-curl machine does not accomplish this goal. For many years, I (JMH) have advised track athletes and hockey players to drop the leg curls from their training and substitute this movement, and this has been met with much success in reducing hamstring injuries. However, I now usu-

ally advise the athletes to use the Romanian dead lift (see next exercise). If you have had prior significant back injuries or if you have one now, do not choose this exercise.

Romanian Dead Lift

A special type of dead lift is utilized by Olympic weight lifters today. This exercise was brought to this country by Dragomir Ciroslan, the head men's coach for USA Weightlifting. Mike Reed, D.C., chair of sports medicine for USA Weightlifting, informed me (JMH) of the success that Olympic weight lifters were having with this exercise. I incorporated this movement immediately, and the athletes saw the benefit right away. This movement has become a mainstay in sports training today.

The Romanian dead lift is a modification of an exercise known as the stiff-legged dead lift. The difference in the Romanian dead lift is that the back is kept completely flat during the lift, and the knees are slightly bent. The

Romanian dead lift A. From this position, bend the knees slightly and hold.

Romanian dead lift B. With the knees bent and the back flat, bend forward at the hips.

bar travels close to the body, if not against it completely. Most people do not have sufficient flexibility to perform the lift all the way from an upright position to the floor. You must use the range of motion that you have available to you. To test your range of motion, attempt to touch your toes while keeping your back completely flat. If you can reach only slightly past your knees, that is OK. If you attempt to reach past your range of motion while holding a barbell, you will alter the technique, and this may cause an injury. The purpose of this exercise is to strengthen the hamstring muscles in the back of the thigh, the gluteal muscles of the hip, and the erector spinae muscles of the back. This exercise will help the pulls (clean pull, power clean, snatch pull). It will be difficult to ever attain heavy weights with this exercise, so don't worry about the poundage at first. Keep proper form, and progress reasonably.

The increased hamstring strength will serve you several ways:

1. The hamstring-to-quadricep strength ratio will be improved. A ratio of 0.6:1.0 is generally considered to be the minimally acceptable ratio. A ratio less than this is generally considered a predictor of hamstring injury.
2. A strong hamstring will reinforce the ACL of the knee. Many hockey players are ACL deficient (either torn or overstretched). Many athletes are functional without their ACL if the hamstring group is strong enough to compensate. Several years ago, a top college running back prospect was discovered to have previously ruptured his ACL. This deficiency was found at the physical examination at the NFL combine. Ironically, the running back had led his team to several winning seasons without an ACL.
3. Both hamstring strength and hamstring flexibility are important factors in maintaining low-back health.

There is a warning for both the Romanian dead lift and the stiff-legged dead lift: if you already have a serious low-back injury, then you probably need to avoid these two exercises. If you have only mild, occasional low-back pain, you may need to improve flexibility in your hips, and you may need to increase the strength of your hamstring, abdominal, erector spinae, and gluteal muscles. This exercise could be beneficial for athletes in this category.

Starting Position

Stand over the bar and then grip the bar with the hands slightly wider than shoulder-width. You may simply stand up with the bar in a dead-lift manner and then begin the Romanian dead lift.

Action of the Movement

As you begin to bend forward, you may bend the knees a little, but keep the back flat so the bend is happening entirely in the hip joints. Keep the bar against the body. The range limit will be determined by your hamstring tightness. As you return to a standing position, straighten the knees.

Speed-Strength Coaching Tips

Keep the reps low (five or fewer) on these types of movements. Training to failure or for high reps is not desirable for the back muscles. Dr. Mike Reed advises those athletes who have never performed a movement like the Romanian dead lift to start with an empty Olympic bar (45 pounds).

Dead Lift

The dead lift recruits the major muscles of the back, hips, and legs. This movement is performed slower than the power clean because of the significant weight that can be utilized. The dead lift is not a speed-strength lift.

Dead lift A. This is the starting point for the dead lift.

Starting Position

Begin with the bar on the floor. Get into a position similar to the power clean so that the feet are under the bar. Use a comfortable shoulder-width stance and a slightly wider grip.

Action of the Movement

Maintain a relatively flat back, and perform the lift with your legs and hips so that you end the lift by standing straight with the bar at full arm's length by your sides.

Speed-Strength Coaching Tips

If a player needs to perform this lift to overcome significant low-back weakness or an injury, then this style of lifting will later carry over very well to cleans or snatch pulls. This movement can build a tremendous amount of low-back strength. The key is to learn proper form and begin with a weight that the athletes can actually use instead of starting with a weight that they think they should be using. We want a training effect, not a straining

Dead lift B. Bring the bar up to midthigh.

effect. Remember, it doesn't matter where the athletes start in training. What does matter is where they end up and what they can do in their sport at a given time. Many low-back injuries could be prevented with adequate strength of the erector spinae, abdominal, hip, and thigh muscles.

This can be a substitute for the power clean if the quick pull of the clean causes low-back pain. However, before abandoning the power clean make sure that the athlete is using proper form and not using too much weight.

Another dead-lift technique flaw to avoid is the forward thrust of the hips at the top of the lift (near completion). This technique flaw developed because in powerlifting competition, the rules indicate that the shoulders must be pulled back at the top of the lift. The heavy weight that is usually pulled in the dead lift would prevent some lifters from being able to pull their shoulders back, so they thrust their hips forward to make it appear as though their shoulders are back. This places

an unnecessary strain on the low back. Make sure that athletes do not arch their back at the top of the dead lift.

Rotational Strengthening Exercise
Some rotational strengthening can be incorporated for sport specificity, but it should be kept to a minimum. Rotation that occurs during a slap shot takes place in many joints. It happens between the shoulder blade and the rib cage (scapulothoracic), the shoulder joint itself (glenohumeral), the thoracic and lumbar spine, and the hips.

Starting Position
Start in a standing or seated position. Using the low cable pulley, grab one handle of the weight stack.

Action of the Movement
Start to pull the handle as if you are performing a rowing motion. As the handle is reaching the halfway point, make sure to pull your shoulder blade back and slightly rotate the same shoulder back (thoracic rotation). This movement will not lend itself to a great deal of weight without losing technique, but it is worth performing for just a few sets.

Speed-Strength Coaching Tips
Rotational strengthening can be improved with the use of the medicine ball in the side pass and slap-shot pass movements (see the medicine-ball exercises later in this chapter).

"Do Not Do" Exercise for the Low Back

The various types of seated rotary torso machines should not be used in training. The reason for this opinion is that the machines do not allow the pelvis to be incorporated in the normal rotation motion. Rotation in sport does not come just from the spine. The rotation involves the pelvis moving with the rotation of the torso. Additionally, other muscles contribute in the rotation of the shoulder girdle. Furthermore, there are the large muscles of the hip and thigh, which have the capacity to generate enough power to rotate the pelvis along with the rotation of the spine.

Watch a professional golfer during a swing the next time that a tournament is on television. It is much easier to observe a golfer than a hockey player because the camera can line up better with a golfer, there is less distracting action occurring simultaneously, and sometimes a slow-motion replay is shown after a good drive. Notice how the entire pelvis rotates with the golf swing. The swing does not occur in a manner as in a seated rotary torso machine. This applies to hockey as well. The rotation is not entirely in the spine.

The rotation that occurs in a generic seated rotary torso machine is not duplicated in any sport. Rotation occurring primarily in the spine could lead to a disastrous and short-lived career. The rotation is very important to the shooting of a puck, so we want to make sure that the proper muscles are strengthened and that overrotation of the spine does not occur. There is no question that some rotation occurs in the spine. However, when one uses a seated rotary torso machine, the weight is being supported by the ischial tuberosities (portion of the pelvis that you sit on) and L5 (lowest lumbar vertebra) is rotating excessively on S1 (highest part of your pelvis). There is little rotation physically available at L5-S1, so there is a shearing effect on the L5-S1 disc. This can lead to disc pathology such as a disc protrusion. Simply put, do not use the seated rotary torso machine as it can lead to significant low-back injury. Also, do not perform leg raises as this can cause low-back pain.

Experience has demonstrated that players who are in their thirties and have not had supplemental training (weight training, various agility and conditioning drills, power-skating) throughout their career usually respond to minimal changes in training. This is not so much a factor of age as it is an issue of many more years of specific adaptation to a given movement. Also, hockey veterans have usually incurred many injuries. Dramatic changes in the way their body moves may not be helpful or painless. The bottom line for these few players is to make a few beneficial training changes. Keep it simple and slowly progressive.

Gymnastic Exercises

Gymnastics was the birthplace of weight-resistance exercises, and these exercises are still valuable to the trainer or coach in the development of hockey players. The importance of the gymnastic exercises is that they teach the athlete to control his or her body. These simple but difficult exercises have been the base for athletic progress. Programs of speed-strength training must teach and train athletes to master their body's weight. The only way to be able to achieve these movements is to practice. They are definite strength builders.

Pull-Up

Starting Position
Assume a hanging position on the chin-up bar. Place the palms forward, and use a medium grip. Then allow the body to drop into a hanging position.

Action of the Movement
Make a good even pull with the shoulders and arms, bringing the chest up to the bar before lowering the body back to the starting position. Try to keep the body as naturally loose and straight as possible.

Speed-Strength Coaching Tips

Many variations of pull-up exercises may be implemented by changing the grip position. Increasing the resistance of both the pull and the return to starting positions offers other variations.

Parallel Bar Dip

Starting Position

Start with the arms locked out, with one hand on each bar and the body hanging between the bars.

Action of the Movement

Lower the body by bending the arms and chest down until the elbows are almost at a 90-degree angle to the shoulders. Upon completion, return to the starting position by pressing with the arm and shoulder muscles back and up to arm's length.

Speed-Strength Coaching Tips

If the athlete maintains an upright position while executing the dips, then more stress will be placed on the triceps. When the athlete leans forward, there will be more movement of the deltoids and pectorals. As in the case of any gymnastic strength movement, greater resistance can be added by using dumbbells and weight plates. Hockey players commonly have problems with their AC (acromioclavicular) joint, therefore this may not be an exercise for some to include as the dip places enormous stress on the AC joint. If the athlete has shoulder pain while performing a dip exercise, stop the exercise.

Ballistics: Upper-Body Explosiveness

The medicine ball can be used in both training and evaluation. It is nothing new in training, although some "experts" are trying to make it appear so. The medicine ball dates back to at least the 1930s and perhaps a few decades earlier. However, methods of training with the medicine ball have certainly advanced. The training is more sport specific today. One distinct advantage that the medicine ball has is that it can be used ballistically (with momentum as in a throw) with relative safety. Many muscles are utilized at one time in a coordinated manner.

If the hockey player has wrist injuries, he or she is probably better off throwing the ball rather than catching it. The player can throw the ball against a concrete wall or across a grass field.

The use of the medicine-ball throw has already been found effective as it simulates the skills needed by an offensive lineman pass blocking, a wide receiver catching a football, a running back being hit by a tackler, or a defensive end pushing off a would-be blocker. Hockey players can use the medicine balls to learn to develop power quickly as in a check or slap shot.

Medicine balls come in various sizes, weights, and makes. Which ball will work best for the individual hockey player is determined by his or her level of strength. For standardized testing, the nine-pound (or four-kilogram) medicine ball would be ideal for the hockey player.

In his book *Bounding to the Top*, coach Frank Costello recommends six to eight minutes of medicine-ball training after every workout. The athlete should spend six to eight minutes in total. The number of drills incorporated on a training day should not be more than five or fewer than two. Any more drills or longer training sessions would decrease the overall explosive-strength development.

Briefly, the idea of using the medicine-ball throws and catches is important to teaching methods, form, and techniques involved with

Leg and hip strength are needed to stop or change directions quickly.

playing hockey. These drills allow the athlete to develop a feel for the ball and the ability to relax and concentrate upon impact with the thrown medicine ball.

Standing Overhead Throw

Starting Position

Start by placing the feet shoulder-width apart. Grip the ball with both hands, and bring the ball back as far as possible over the head.

Action of the Movement

Keep the arms bent at a 90-degree angle at the elbows. Use the stretch occurring in the shoulder, chest, latissimus dorsi, and leg muscles to help you know when to step forward with either leg and at the same time pull the elbows forward and throw the ball.

Speed-Strength Coaching Tips

Remind the athlete to grip the ball firmly and follow through with each throw. Distance

Standing overhead throw A. The ball is lowered behind the head and the abs are slightly stretched.

Standing overhead throw B. Follow through on the throw using the arms and legs.

should vary according to the strength level of each player and weight of the medicine balls.

Kneeling Overhead Throw

Starting Position
Start on your knees with the knees shoulder-width apart. Grip the ball with both hands, and bring the ball back as far as possible over the head.

Action of the Movement
Keep the arms bent at a 90-degree angle at the elbows. Use the stretch occurring in the shoulder, chest, and latissimus dorsi. At the same time pull the elbows forward and throw the ball.

Speed-Strength Coaching Tips
This throwing exercise requires strength in the upper and lower back. Be sure that the

athlete follows through after releasing the ball.

Standing Side Throw

Starting Position
Stand and hold the ball with an overhand grasp. The arm closest to the direction the ball will be thrown should be on top of the ball.

Action of the Movement
As you bring the ball back to one side, keep it away from the body. As you throw the ball back, rotate the hips forward to get a good stretch in the entire side of the body. The movement is similar to swinging a bat.

Speed-Strength Coaching Tips
Muscles in the rectus abdominis, external oblique, shoulders, hips and legs (to generate

---

Standing side throw A. Start the standing side throw by gripping the ball with both hands. The hand on top of the ball determines which side the ball will be thrown to.

Standing side throw B. The athlete has wound up and is ready to throw.

force), and paraspinal muscles are being worked. If the athletes have never performed this movement, start them out with slower tosses and increase the force and speed over a period of weeks.

Two-Hand Chest Throw

Starting Position
The starting position is the same as in the overhead throw, except the throw is from the chest.

Action of the Movement
As the ball is being brought to the chest, keep the elbows even at shoulder level. Step forward with either leg, push the throw through to full release, and follow through.

Speed-Strength Coaching Tips
Muscles being worked are those of the chest, shoulders, back, hips, legs, and arms. This is

Standing side throw C. Always follow through completely.

Two-hand chest throw A. Dip down into a shallow squat position to begin the two-hand chest throw.

Two-hand chest throw B. Explode out of the squat; use your whole body and both hands to push the ball forward.

an excellent drill for teaching shoulder, arm, and chest explosion. This will help the hockey player by giving him or her a ballistic training motion that resembles a check or even the normal protection while taking a fall to the ice.

Sit-Up Long Throw

Starting Position
Assume the bent-knee sit-up position while holding the ball.

Action of the Movement
Throw the ball as you are raising upward and forward. The bent position of the legs is for balance so that the throwing motion can occur. The position of the ball is similar to that used in the overhead throw. Rock back and accelerate by throwing the legs down, sitting up, and throwing the ball. Remember to follow through upon release.

Speed-Strength Coaching Tips
This is an excellent exercise for the midsection. It is also a good drill to use with a teammate or training partner for a combination exercise for throwing and stomach work. This drill is excellent for hip flexion development and coordination.

Underhand/Back Overhead Throw

Starting Position
Assume a standing position with feet shoulder-width apart. Reverse the movement of action in the overhead throw; this time the movement is from front to back.

Bench-press throw. In the bench-press throw, an exercise partner (not shown) will drop the ball to you. Lie on the ground with knees bent and the hands at the chest ready to catch the ball and throw it back up to the partner.

Action of the Movement

Keep the ball out front and away from the body. Squat to about three-fourths of the way to the ground. The action will be a sweeping movement up and over the head.

Speed-Strength Coaching Tips

Release of the ball will occur at the point of optimal stretching of the shoulders, back, arms, and legs. This is an excellent drill because hockey calls for the force of driving the arms and hands upward during checks.

Bench-Press Throw

This exercise should help improve the punching or striking speed-strength movement.

Starting Position

Lie down on your back with the arms extended upward and ready to catch the ball. Your workout parner will stand above you.

Action of the Movement

Your workout partner will stand above you and drop the ball to the center position on your chest. Catch the ball and immediately throw the ball back to your partner.

Speed-Strength Coaching Tips

This action will allow the player to use short, explosive arm and chest movements with no loading (pulling back) for the release. The nature of checking could easily require the use of this drill—one that should be employed time and time again. Because the athlete is lying on the floor, the elbows cannot extend past the sides. The players make use of the quick, explosive force that is generated.

Press Throw

Starting Position

Assume a shoulder-width standing position. Keep the head and shoulders tilted slightly backward.

Action of the Movement

Grip the ball with both hands. Stand with the head tilted upward. This will allow the back and hip position to prepare for the throwing motion. Use a push press–type motion by dipping the legs and driving the ball upward. Throw the ball as you drive back up from the dipping position, like a push press. Send the ball in an upward direction, and then prepare to make the catch, or step aside and let it fall.

Ballistic push-up A. To perform the ballistic push-up, place each hand on a low plyo box.

Ballistic push-up B. Drop your upper body to the floor, then do a push-up with enough force to bring your hands back onto the boxes.

Speed-Strength Coaching Tips

This exercise is excellent for all positions and is outstanding for eye-hand coordination and also for developing the ability to keep the opponent at arms' length from the body. Athletes tend to like this drill because they don't need a partner and they never have to retrieve the ball.

Ballistic Push-Up

The ballistic push-up incorporates speed-strength-training components and principles of upper-body explosion in a training movement. Exercises and strength movements using the hands (arm and shoulder explosion) can improve speed and strength, which can help hockey players when they are pushing for position in front of the net.

Starting Position

Place a box, 12–18 inches tall, under the feet and each arm. Separate the arms on each of the front two platforms and plant the feet together on top of the third platform. You should be in a prone position with the weight of the body separated equally at each point.

Action of the Movement

Lower the body by bending the arms and dropping down between the two front platforms. To start the push-up, repeat the downward push and explode upward by pushing off the floor with both arms and shoulders.

Speed-Strength Coaching Tips

This exercise begins with the regular push-up drill. After the regular push-ups are completed, have the hockey player start off with a minimum platform and gradually work up to a maximum height of no more than 18 inches. Remind the players to concentrate on exploding off the floor. Players with shoulder instability or rotator cuff tears will not be able to perform this exercise. Players who have had their shoulder capsules/ligaments reconstructed should not perform this movement.

Abdominal Exercises

The abdominal muscle region is the most highly visible area of the athletic body, yet it may be the most overlooked and underworked region in strength-development programs for athletes. This is particularly true for hockey players.

The development of abdominal strength is important to the athlete. The abdominal region is only as strong as the weakest link. Using speed-strength on the waist and abdominal areas coordinates all parts of the body. These areas contain about one-third of the body's weight. Failure to develop strength and flexibility in the stabilizing muscles of the lower back is one of the major causes of low-back strains and pains among athletes in hockey. The exercises described here are some of the best that can be incorporated into a speed-strength program.

Coach Francis discussed "specific core fitness" that has to be developed before it is possible to develop speed. He was specifically referring to the shoulders and abdomen. Fatigue in these areas would result in the degradation of sprinting technique. This is a function of abdominal strength that few consider. In fact, the stability and power that strong abdominal muscles provide during checking are rarely considered.

Definition and development of strength of the abdominal muscles is rarely understood. The reason for this is that most people unknowingly discuss muscular endurance as opposed to strength of the abdominal muscles. For example, if a player is told that he or she needs to increase abdominal strength, he or she usually responds with a comment like "OK. I usually do 50 sit-ups at a time, so now I will do a couple sets of 75 reps." Performing more repetitions does not create greater strength. If you needed to be faster, would you simply run farther? Of course not. So why would you simply perform more sit-ups to have stronger abdominal muscles?

Strength gain implies the need for progressive resistance training. The key word there is *progressive*. The abdominal muscles

need to be exposed to progressively more difficult training loads. This can be done several ways in training. The first is using the old standby of a weighted sit-up. You do not need to come up all the way during the sit-up, as the top portion of the sit-up is performed by the hip flexors as opposed to the spinal flexors (true abdominal muscles). Doing standard sit-ups all the way up may cause low-back pain in some people. Do not perform leg raises, knee-ups, hanging leg raises, Roman chair sit-ups, or full sit-ups because they cause you to strongly recruit your hip flexor muscles and alter weight distribution in your lumbar spine. As a hockey player, your hip flexors are overworked from all of the skating and forward skating position. The bottom line is don't perform pure hip flexion movements.

Abdominal strength is greatly needed in hockey in light of the near epidemic occurrence of abdominal tears, sometimes called "sports hernias." I (JMH) don't care for this term because it is a rather vague way to define an injury. The injury is an abdominal muscle tear or severe overstretch, which functionally behaves like a tear. Needless to say, all players should begin a true strengthening program in late high school ages.

Sit-Up with Resistance and Sit-Up Without Resistance

The weighted sit-up (with resistance) can be used on a progressive level. A beginning weight trainer can start with a five- or ten-pound weight held in back or in front. A progression of five pounds per two weeks during a training cycle is a very reasonable strength-gain rate.

Standards of strength exist for the abdominal muscles. Kreis has an abdominal-strength guideline for his University of Colorado football team, in which a lineman should be able to perform at least three sets of 10 reps with

55 pounds. Kreis would like to see the linemen perform 75 pounds for three sets of 10 reps. The strength of the abdominal muscles is critical for checking and stabilizing in hockey. Weakness can predispose someone toward injuries.

If an athlete as heavy as a lineman can be expected to perform a minimum of three sets of 10 reps with 55 pounds, then we should expect the larger hockey players to use at least 40 pounds for three sets of 10 reps as a strength guideline. The following is our suggested minimum guideline for hockey players.

American 77-kilogram-class weightlifter Greg Schouten performing sit-ups with 70 kilos!

Player's Body Weight in pounds	Minimum Recommended Sit-Up Weight
175–200	three sets of 10 reps with 35 pounds
200–220	three sets of 10 reps with 40 pounds
220–245	three sets of 10 reps with 45 pounds
245 and up	three sets of 10 reps with 55 pounds

These weights are, of course, built up over time. A player who has never performed weighted sit-ups should begin with a 10-pound weight or plate. It will probably take months to build up to 40 pounds. Athletes may hold the weight behind the head or in front of the upper chest. They may also progress to heavier weights. A heavy dumbbell can be used instead of plates.

There are a few key examples of the use and benefit of sit-ups with resistance. One of the Long Beach Ice Dogs wings, Barry Neickar, worked up to sit-ups with a 70-pound dumbbell during his 1996–97 season with this type of training, and he weighed 218 pounds. Neickar worked up to 100 pounds in the sit-up during the 1997 off-season. Wing Patrik Augusta worked up to 55 pounds during his first off-season program, and he weighed 188 pounds. Luc Robitaille had surgery for an abdominal muscle tear in the spring of 1998. By June 1998, he started his sit-ups with a 10-pound plate. December 1998 found him performing three sets of 10 reps with a 75-pound dumbbell. Robitaille wound up performing 90 pounds for three sets of 10 reps. Kings' captain Mattias Norstrom performed three sets of 10 reps with 100 pounds.

Abdominal strength is significant in other sports as well. This is demonstrated by athletes such as Sherri Howard and Greg Schouten. Howard is an Olympic gold and silver medalist in the 400-meter run. She performs sit-ups while holding two 25-pound plates, and she weighs only 124 pounds. Schouten is a 77-kilogram-class American weight lifter and was having episodes of low-back pain. He began performing sit-ups with a 5-kilogram plate and has worked up to 70 kilograms for three sets of eight reps in the sit-up. Schouten has not had back pain since starting the weighted sit-ups.

Sit-up with resistance A. Start the sit-up with resistance with the weight at your chest or in front of your face, as shown here.

Sit-up with resistance B. Perform the sit-up with abs and the low back on the floor.

Starting Position

Assume the supine position on the floor, with legs bent. If someone cannot hold your feet down, hook them under a bench or barbell to keep them still. When you use weight resistance, place it behind the head or on the chest. Weight plates, dumbbells, and medicine balls are excellent resistance implements.

Action of the Movement

Sit up by reaching forward with the head. The knees will be bent during the movement as the athlete drives forward and upward. Keep the abdominal muscles tight at all times.

Speed-Strength Coaching Tips

Use some form of weight resistance after the initial sit-up has been mastered. This exercise is excellent for the development of the abdominal muscles (spinal flexors). Unfortunately, there will be some recruitment of the hip flexors during this movement, but that is unavoidable. The increased strength of the abdominal muscles is critical for hockey players, especially considering the substantial increased incidence of abdominal muscle tears.

Crunch

The crunch sit-up has gained popularity over the past 20 years, and rightfully so. The crunch is an exercise that attempts to isolate the abdominal muscles as much as possible, although true isolation is nearly impossible. The crunch is performed with the athlete on his or her back and the lower legs up on a chair, couch, or bench. This places the upper thighs in a vertical position. The purpose of this position is to flatten the lumbar spine (low back) and attempt to limit the use of the hip flexor muscles. The first one-third to one-half of a sit-up is performed. This is the only amount of true spinal flexion available. This is biomechanically correct, and it is a good exercise. The only drawback with this exercise is that the leverage is so poor that a true strengthening effect is not possible. So this exercise can be used as a supplement to the abdominal training. For example, if the athlete performed a weighted sit-up earlier in the week and the team is now on the road, the crunch could be used as an alternative, and in reality, it would serve as a "light day" of training for the abdominal muscles. This is an excellent exercise of choice during the recovery/rehabilitation phase after a back injury.

Starting Position

Lie on the ground with your feet over a bench; let the legs relax.

Action of the Movement
Perform the first one-third of a sit-up by rounding the shoulders off the ground. There is a limited amount of spinal flexion (bend), so you will not be able to raise the upper body very far.

Speed-Strength Coaching Tips
This is an excellent rehabilitation exercise, and it is one of choice for a deconditioned player. This is a superior exercise from a biomechanical viewpoint, but it does not allow for significant increase in strength.

Pulley Crunch
The pulley crunch requires the use of a weight stack and pulley in a gym or a lat pull-down machine.

Starting Position
The pulley crunch requires you to kneel in front of a cable apparatus while holding onto rope handles or straps.

Action of the Movement
Begin with the torso in a relatively straight position and then crunch (flex) the torso, bringing the elbows toward the knees. While holding onto the rope handles, keep the shoulders in a fixed position and round the back only as you pull your elbows toward your knees. Return to the starting position.

Speed-Strength Coaching Tips
This exercise offers two distinct advantages. First of all, it allows for progressive strength training—the weights on this machine can be increased in 10-pound increments, or you can place smaller plates on top of the weight stack. Second, the body is allowed more free motion than lying on the floor permits. Sit-ups can sometimes bother the pelvis and tailbone (coccyx) region; this position is a good way to avoid that compression.

Janda Sit-Up
A Czechoslovakian physiatrist (doctor specializing in physical medicine), Vladimir Janda (pronounced yawn-da), developed a sit-up to eliminate or at least substantially reduce the use of the hip flexor muscles. Dr. John Scaringe of Whittier, California, has been instrumental in getting Dr. Janda's work out to the sports medicine field. A training partner or coach is best used during the learning process of this sit-up.

Starting Position
Lie on a high table, bench, or floor in a standard sit-up position. The amount of knee bend is unimportant. The coach should stand at the foot of the table or kneel by your feet. The balls of your feet should be against the thigh of the coach. The coach then places both hands under your lower legs, near your Achilles tendon.

Action of the Movement
Follow these instructions from the coach:

1. "Press the balls of your feet into my leg (or knee)."
2. "Dig your heels down into the table or floor." (The coach must be aware of these two pressures exerted by the athlete. These pressures must be maintained at all times.)
3. "Perform a crunch sit-up while still digging your heels down and pushing the balls of your feet into my legs." (The coach pulls slightly upward against the lower leg of the athlete. If the legs lift easily, then the athlete has already recruited the hip flexor muscles. It is difficult for even world-class athletes to perform this at first.)

Speed-Strength Coaching Tips
The key component is that when the athlete digs the heels into the table or floor, he or she

has performed hip extension. There are neurological functions that make one muscle relax if the opposing muscle contracts. For example, if you perform a biceps curl, the biceps has been recruited and at the same time the opposing muscle, the triceps, has been inhibited or relaxed so that it does not interfere with the biceps muscle. That is exactly what is happening during the Janda sit-up. The action of isometric hip extension (digging your heels into the floor) inhibits the hip flexors. Once athletes can consistently perform this exercise, then they do not require assistance. All they have to do is lie on the floor and press the balls of their feet against a wall and dig their heels into the floor.

Again, this should be used as a supplemental abdominal training exercise. It is very difficult to add resistance to this exercise.

The Janda sit-up reduces the use of the hip flexor muscles during the sit-up. These muscles are a common culprit in low-back pain because they are too strong, too tight, or recruited incorrectly. This is an excellent exercise during rehabilitation and for a supplement to the abdominal-strength exercises.

Dumbbell Side Bend

Starting Position
Hold the dumbbell in one hand; place the feet about one foot farther apart than hip-width, and keep the knees braced. You may instead hold a plate behind your head.

Action of the Movement
Bend the body mildly over to the opposite side by lateral flexion of the trunk. With the hips positioned slightly forward, lean laterally to the side of the dumbbell. Place the opposite hand behind the head.

Speed-Strength Coaching Tips
Have athletes try to perform this exercise while maintaining the proper stance. Setting the hips slightly forward in the starting position prevents athletes from bending forward. They must keep the feet flat and knees braced. Make sure that the exercise involves both sides of the trunk. The athletes should not attempt to bend excessively.

"Do Not Do" Exercise for the Abdomen

There are a number of exercises that can pose a problem for those who already have low-back pain and for those who are underconditioned. There are some elite athletes in superior condition who are able to perform leg raises. However, if low-back pain develops while performing this exercise, it would be wise to drop the exercise from your training.

Leg raises were previously mentioned, but because of their popularity, we wanted to make sure that they were addressed sufficiently. The leg raise is an exercise that needs to be reevaluated for its use in a training program. I (JMH) always take athletes away from the leg raise due to the excessive recruitment of the hip flexor muscles, which, as we noted previously, can cause low-back pain. Skating and sprinting on the ice, especially in the skaters' position, recruits and develops the hip flexors more than adequately, and additional hip flexor training is not advantageous and may cause sufficient low-back pain to interfere with playing time or training. Also, many athletes have very thick legs, which serve as a significant weight to raise up and down. Many NFL teams dropped the leg raise because of the pain the players were having from it.

Neck Exercises

It has been well established for decades that the high impact of football necessitates the resistance training of the neck muscles. The results are certainly most visible during the television pregame introduction of both collegiate and professional football players (especially linemen and linebackers) as they are presented to the audience and cameras. Athletes with larger neck circumferences have always been associated with football and wrestling. There is a reason for this. Wrestlers use their neck to form a bridge to avoid being pinned. Football players require the neck development for their own protection and safety in their sport. Hockey players require the same protection as football players.

Hockey certainly must rank no less than second to football as a contact sport, yet very few professional hockey players, perhaps only a very small percentage, actually perform any type of neck training. We believe that neck training should be a significant component of training in a contact sport and especially in a sport that is gaining in its physical performance. As the speed and impact of the game increase, hockey is beginning to display the serious and catastrophic neck injuries that have been known in football for quite some time. The impacts from falling to the ice, from falling against the boards, and from the various pushing and shoving that takes place in the corners, against the boards, in front of the net, and during fights are major risks to the neck. The neck is simply another portion of the spine; it is very important that the muscles surrounding it become strong and stay strong to help maintain spinal stability. Many athletes who have had low-back injuries are afraid to train their back or their neck because they fear reinjury. Although this is an understandable fear, the problem is made worse when the muscles surrounding the spine weaken, increasing the likelihood of injury. The spine is designed to have a balance of muscle strength surrounding it. This includes back muscle strength.

Neck training can be easily incorporated throughout preseason training, during summer camp, and throughout the season. The neck can be trained with a variety of methods including using a neck harness, using a weighted helmet, using manual resistance with a towel, or pushing against the head. A training partner or a teammate can easily provide this form of help. Neck training does not have such an exhaustive effect as training the larger muscles of the body. Neck training can be performed in a short period of time and is a vital component to the overall safety of the player. It can also easily be performed on a road trip because equipment isn't necessary.

A neck warm-up takes only a few minutes, and it can consist of rotation, flexion and extension, and lateral flexion. The neck should not be exercised with jerking or uncontrolled movement. The fullest possible range of motion should be achieved without undue forcing of the movement.

Crouch feels that neck exercises should be in flexion and extension only. We feel that resisted rotation may be performed carefully and most likely with manual resistance. Lateral flexion (side bending) should be avoided because of the stress it places on the cervical discs. By avoiding this motion, you also avoid any potential of compression of a nerve root by narrowing of the area of exit for the nerve (neural foramen). Isometric training for the side motion (lateral flexion) strength is acceptable and advisable.

One point to keep in mind is that neck training after an injury can begin with isometric training. Isometric training refers to resistance without moving. A strength coach, athletic trainer, or teammate can provide gentle resistance or pressure, while you keep your head still and do not let your neck move. For example, if you are sitting on a chair or bench, your teammate can place his or her hands on your forehead and apply pressure that would push your head backward. You resist that pressure and hold this position for approximately six seconds. Do not use maximum pressure after an injury (or if you are a beginner).

Strength gains in isometric training are very specific to the position that you train, plus or minus a few degrees. Therefore, you must use multiple positions in each motion. If you start with pressure being applied to the forehead with the athlete in a normal, upright position, you can follow with the athlete dropping the chin a little bit and again using pressure against the forehead for six seconds. Then have the athlete drop the chin a little further and repeat. The same process happens for other movements. The whole isometric neck training program is divided into four groups with approximately five positions for each movement:

1. flexion (bending forward)
2. extension (bending or arching backward)
3. rotation right (turning right)
4. rotation left (turning left)

Another important factor in maintaining neck strength is upper-back strengthening. The major upper-back muscle is called the trapezius ("traps"). The trapezius also attaches to the base of the skull and to the neck. The stronger the trapezius becomes, the more support your neck will have. The trapezius will become developed by the power cleans, clean pulls, snatches, or dead lifts. If you have injuries that prevent you from performing these exercises, then you should perform the shrug exercise (see page 126).

The following are additional special exercises for the neck.

Wrestler's Bridge

Starting Position

You can perform this exercise while lying on the back or on the front. Lying on the back, slowly arch upward, keeping the weight on the heels and the back of the head. Lying on the front, round upward, keeping the weight on the forehead and toes.

Action of the Movement

Place your body's weight on the heels and the back of the head (if starting on your back). This helps you generate the amount of weight and pressure the neck can absorb. Under control, rock back and forth. Then straighten the body out again. The front bridge is performed in similar form, except that the pressure is on the forehead and toes. Placing your hands against your thighs helps provide balance and support.

Speed-Strength Coaching Tips

Both versions of the wrestler's bridge are tough exercises and should not be completed without some form of slow warm-up at the beginning. If the athlete has degenerative changes (arthritic changes) in the neck, particularly involving the small joints that guide the movement (facet joints), then this is not an exercise of choice. The same would apply if the athlete has had disc injuries or disc protrusions, and the exercise should probably be avoided in athletes who have symptomatic central stenosis (narrowing of the spinal canal) in the cervical spine. Also, if pain occurs during this exercise, the exercise must be eliminated.

Neck Harness

Starting Position

Place the neck harness apparatus over the head so it hangs down over the head. Once the weight implements are loaded, the neck is free to support the weight in a free-hanging position with the neck flexed slightly forward.

Action of the Movement

The action of the neck movement is usually completed by lowering and raising the neck.

Neck harness A. The neck harness is used to strengthen the extensors of the neck.

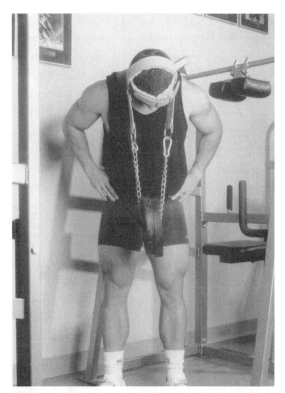

Neck harness B. Lower your head forward and then raise it to the starting position.

Avoid using too much range of motion while bending the neck backward (extending).

Speed-Strength Coaching Tips

Forward and backward movement of the neck occurs more at certain points in the neck than others. Too much motion with weight will place too much stress on the discs at these levels.

The use of neck harnesses, helmets with weights attached to them, and resistance of manual pressure are all excellent little extras that help develop the muscles of the neck. Remember that the incorporation of the snatch movements, cleans, and presses have already started the neck strength development in the speed-strength-training program. Start this exercise with light weight. Some athletes are capable of handling fairly heavy weight over time.

Manual Neck Training

Manual neck training is perhaps the original and most versatile form of neck training. All one needs is a teammate or training partner to provide resistance. Resistance can be safely applied to flexion, extension, and rotation.

Lateral flexion or side bending of the neck is not advisable. Isometric (no motion) neck training can be a good place to start for many athletes who have never trained their neck before or who have had neck injuries.

Starting Position

You can either be seated or on your hands and knees.

Action of the Movement

Your teammate will provide resistance (light resistance at first) against the back of the head and allow you to push back. Then the teammate must gently push forward while you resist the motion and lower your chin to your chest. You want to feel resistance at both stages of the exercise. The teammate can then provide resistance against the forehead while you allow the head to tilt backward a little. Do not allow your head to go all the way back. That can be hard on the discs in the middle of your neck. Then the teammate can resist and allow you to push your head forward so that your chin goes toward your chest. Next, the teammate can provide resistance to one side of your head, and you can then turn to that same side against resistance.

For isometric training, start with the neck in a neutral position. The training partner places his or her hands on your head and gently attempts to move the head in the directions just described. This resistance should be applied for approximately six seconds. The partner should begin with very little pressure and never push explosively against the head. Most people (athletes included) do not have much neck strength. Pushing too hard and too quickly can result in injury to the neck muscles.

Shoulder and Rotator Cuff Exercises

Shrug

A major muscle of the upper back and shoulder girdle is known as the trapezius (or, more commonly, the "traps"). The trapezius is important because it is a main stabilizer of the shoulder blades (scapulae), and it is involved in rotation of the shoulder as well as movement of the neck. The trapezius is developed by performing power cleans, clean pulls, and dead lifts. If various back injuries prevent those movements from being performed, then the shrug should be used as an alternative for building upper-back strength. The shrug would not be considered a speed-strength movement, but this may be the only alternative for an injured player.

Starting Position

Place the bar in the power rack, and set the pins just a few inches below the beginning height of the lift so that the stress on the low back can be minimized.

Action of the Movement

The movement begins with the bar at arms' length by your side. Complete the exercise by shrugging straight up. Then lower back to the beginning point and repeat. Do not relax at any time during this lift.

Speed-Strength Coaching Tips

The athlete does not need that "extra stretch" at the end of the movement. If he or she has achieved a full range of motion, then that is all of the stretch that is necessary. Additional stretch is usually gained by relaxing certain muscles. If the athlete relaxes during the bottom position of the shrug, he or she will suddenly place a traction force on the ligaments of the shoulder and also upon the rotator cuff and will most likely incur an injury. We have seen this very injury in several world-class bodybuilders (professional and amateur). The trapezius is a powerful muscle, and it will not be difficult to achieve significant poundages in this exercise.

This exercise is also very important for stabilizing the acromioclavicular joint, more commonly known as the AC joint. The trapezius surrounds the AC joint, and the increased strength of the trapezius will help to hold the AC joint stable. Two studies of professional hockey revealed that 45 percent of the players had abnormalities in their clavicle (collar bone) and AC joint. So the strength of the trapezius is a critical component.

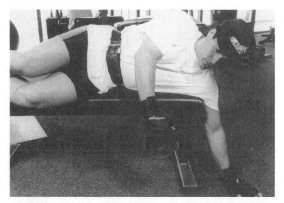
Lying fly A. Keep the elbow slightly bent.

Lying fly B. Raise the arm toward the ceiling, then return it to the starting position.

Rotator Cuff Exercises

There are four muscles in the shoulder that make up what are known as the rotator cuff muscles. These muscles are the supraspinatus, infraspinatus, teres minor, and subscapularis. The main function of these muscles is to stabilize the head of the humerus (ball) into the glenoid fossa (socket). These muscles also provide external rotation for the shoulder and assist in internal rotation. They are frequently weak because they are overlooked in training or they are compromised as a result of muscle imbalances from training.

A few simple exercises can be used to strengthen the rotator cuff. A few sets should be more than adequate for these small but vital muscles. Four exercises should suffice unless you have dislocated your shoulder. The number and choices of exercises, in that case, would depend upon how long ago the dislocation occurred.

Lying Fly

Starting Position
Lie on your side on a bench. If you are lying on your right side, then your right hand should be on the floor to stabilize yourself. Your upper hand should be holding a light

dumbbell, and your arm should be positioned across your chest. Your palm should be facing toward the bench.

Action of the Movement
Keep your elbow slightly bent, and raise the weight toward the ceiling. Do not let your arm extend past the vertical position.

Speed-Strength Coaching Tips
The athletes should not let momentum do the work for the muscles. This exercise works the posterior aspect of the deltoid ("rear delts") and the trapezius, rhomboid, and rotator cuff muscles.

Lying "L" Fly

The purpose of this exercise is to strengthen the muscles that perform external or lateral rotation of the shoulder. These rotator cuff muscles are very important in the role of stabilizing your shoulder.

Starting Position
Lie on your side on a bench. If you are lying on your right side, then your right hand should be on the floor to stabilize yourself. Bend your upper arm 90 degrees at the elbow,

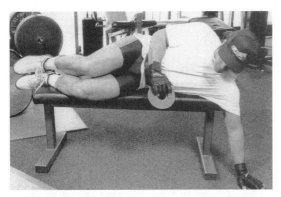

Lying "L" fly A. To begin the lying "L" fly, the elbow should be bent 90 degrees, with the forearm across the abdomen and the wrist straight.

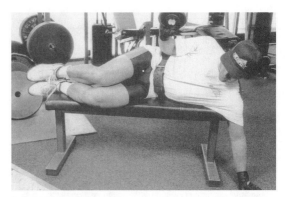

Lying "L" fly B. Raise the forearm, keeping the wrist straight.

and keep your elbow and upper arm against your side.

Action of the Movement

While holding a very light dumbbell, allow the hand that is holding the dumbbell to cross your chest/abdomen. Then return the dumbbell to a more upward position.

Speed-Strength Coaching Tips

The arm does not usually have enough range of motion for the forearm to reach a vertical position, so don't worry about it if it doesn't.

If you have the athlete try to push for more range of motion at the top position, you will probably cause shoulder pain and strain. This exercise does not allow for heavy weight.

Begin with either a 1-pound dumbbell or with a 1¼-pound weight. This latter choice is a very easy and inexpensive way of gradually increasing the weight. If you begin with a 1¼-pound weight, you can increase by a conservative and effective 1¼ pounds per week. Below is a sample resistance increase using a 1¼-pound weight, a 2½-pound weight, and a 5-pound weight.

Ideal Rotator Cuff Strength Progression for an Athlete

Week	Weight (Resistance)	Frequency
One	1¼ pounds	daily
Two	2½ pounds	daily
Three	3¾ pounds	three times per week
Four	5 pounds	two times per week
Five	6¼ pounds	two times per week
Six	7½ pounds	two times per week
Seven	8¾ pounds	two times per week
Eight	10 pounds	two times per week

Side raise A. At the start of the side raise the arm should be straight and flat against the side.

Side raise B. Keep the elbow straight and raise the arm 45 degrees. Do not raise the arm all the way up.

First hold the 1¼-pound weight in your hand. Next week, hold the 2½-pound weight. The following week, hold the 1¼-pound and the 2½-pound weight (totaling 3¾ pounds). The fourth week you will hold the 5-pound weight. The fifth week you will hold the 1¼-pound and 5-pound weight (totaling 6¼ pounds), and so on. These three plates will cost approximately five or six dollars to purchase, and they can provide seven weeks of rotator cuff rehabilitation exercise. The light weights are necessary for several reasons. First, the rotator cuff muscles are small. Second, if there has been an injury or strain, the rotator cuff muscles will not respond the same as a noninjured muscle, and they may be somewhat deconditioned because of decreased use. We must coax these muscles along and not force them to gain strength. Forcing these muscles may result in injury, which will set the athlete back even further.

Side Raises (Side-Lying Abduction)
The side raise or (side-lying abduction) is an important exercise for strengthening the rotator cuff, especially the supraspinatus muscle. However, the subscapularis, infraspinatus, and deltoid are exercised as well. A recent research project by one of the authors (JMH) revealed that when the side raise was compared with the military press and a more common exercise—known as the "supraspinatus fly," "empty the can," or "Jobe's exercise"—the side raise was most effective.

Starting Position
Lie on your side on a bench. Your top arm should be down against your side with your palm facing your thigh.

Action of the Movement
Hold a light weight in the top hand and raise it to a 45-dgree angle. Do not rotate your hand or arm.

Speed-Strength Coaching Tips
Do not allow the athlete to use high speed or momentum to perform this movement.

"Hitchhiker" (Blackburn's Exercise)
Another exercise for the rotator cuff muscles, particularly the supraspinatus, infraspinatus, and teres minor, was devised by Blackburn, a noted physical therapist. This exercise also

Hitchhiker A. This is the proper starting position for the "hitchhiker" exercise.

Hitchhiker B. Finish the "hitchhiker" with the arm parallel to the floor. If the shoulder is stable, you may be able to raise your arm higher.

targets some of the muscles that stabilize the shoulder blade muscles (scapular stabilizers) such as the middle and lower trapezius and the rhomboid muscles. This makes this a valuable exercise. For simplicity's sake we will call this exercise the "hitchhiker" for obvious reasons.

Starting Position

Begin by supporting yourself on one knee with your back parallel to the floor. Your hand should be all the way to the edge of the bench, and your arm should be hanging down toward the floor. If a bench isn't available, you may lean forward while supporting yourself on the floor making sure to keep your back flat and stable. You will hold a very small weight with this exercise.

Action of the Movement

Turn your hand so that it is facing forward and point your thumb outward (as if you were hitchhiking); this amount of rotation should remain throughout the exercise. Raise your arm up and out to the side. Do not raise

your arm above parallel with the ground if you have been told that you have shoulder instability. Let your arm return to the bottom position and repeat.

Speed-Strength Coaching Tips

Make sure that those who experience pain and have shoulder (anterior glenohumeral) instability do not raise the arm above parallel. If this exercise causes pain, have the athlete stop performing it. Consider trying the exercise again in a few weeks once the shoulder is further rehabilitated.

Internal Rotation

Internal rotation of the shoulder is provided by many muscles: the pectoralis major ("pecs"), latissimus dorsi ("lats"), teres major ("upper lats"), as well as one of the rotator cuff muscles—subscapularis. One rarely finds weakness in the subscapularis when the muscle is tested. This is the reason that I (JMH) rarely advise the use of internal rotation strengthening. However, there is a group of patients/athletes that does require internal

Internal rotation A. Note the starting position when using a low pulley.

Internal rotation B. Keeping the upper arm steady, rotate the forearm across the abdomen to complete the movement.

rotation strengthening. Anyone who has dislocated or nearly dislocated his or her shoulder, or anyone who has an unstable shoulder in the forward direction (anterior glenohumeral instability) should include internal rotation exercises. This will help keep the shoulder stable when the arm is close to the body.

Starting Position

There are three ways to do this exercise. If you are using a free weight, you can lie on your back or on your side. When lying on your back, your arm should be 30 degrees away from your side, with the forearm pointing straight up. When lying on your side, lie with the bottom elbow bent at 90 degrees

and a weight in that hand. (The arm you are working is underneath you.)

A third method is to sit on a stool and grab a low-pulley handle.

Action of the Movement

If you are lying on your back, let the dumbbell move toward the floor about 60 degrees. Do not let the dumbbell reach the floor. Return the arm to the original position.

If you are lying on your side, rotate the dumbbell across to the abdomen. Most of the movement will be in your forearm, but the rotation will be in your shoulder. Return the arm to the starting position.

If you are seated, position yourself slightly behind a pulley. Your arm should be bent at a

90-degree angle with your elbow by your side. Pull the weight across to the abdomen. By sitting behind the pulley, you ensure that your arm will rotate only 60 degrees. Your forearm should never be pulled straight out to the side.

Speed-Strength Coaching Tips

Internal rotation is a good exercise for athletes who have shoulder instability.

"Do Not Do" Exercises for the Shoulders

The following common exercises should not be performed because of the risk of shoulder injury and pain:

Upright Row

The upright row is a popular gym exercise that can wreak havoc on your shoulder. The exercise targets the deltoid and trapezius muscles as well as the biceps, brachialis, and brachioradialis muscles. However, the upright row is an unnatural movement for the shoulder in that the shoulder is internally rotated during the movement and this causes the rotator cuff and biceps tendon to become trapped or impinged against the roof of the shoulder (acromion and coracoclavicular ligament). This can cause chronic pain and a wearing-away effect on the tendons. The bottom line is that you have little to gain from this movement.

Front Delt Raise

This is another popular gym exercise. This movement also causes the rotator cuff and biceps tendons to be impinged against the roof of the shoulder. A fluid-filled structure, known as a bursa, is also impinged and becomes inflamed during impingement motions. Again, do not perform this movement. It can cause long-term shoulder pain.

Supraspinatus Flyes

This movement is similar to a front deltoid raise except that it is performed more to the side and with internal rotation. There is risk of impingement around 90 degrees of elevation. The side raise targets the supraspinatus more effectively and without risk of shoulder impingement.

Wrist Exercises

The wrist exercises are simple to perform and are usually included in a wrist rehabilitation program. There are numerous wrist injuries that occur in hockey. These are primarily the result of falling on the ice, but they can also occur from slashing. The following exercises may be useful for those with wrist injuries.

Wrist Curl

Starting Position

Sit on a bench and place the forearms against the thighs. Lean slightly forward so that the wrists are past the knees. Hold the bar with the palms facing up.

Action of the Movement

While holding the bar, let the wrist bend down and then up.

Speed-Strength Coaching Tips

This exercise will strengthen the muscles of the underside of the forearm (wrist flexors). I (JMH) do not advise allowing the bar to roll down the fingers as this can place a great deal of stress on the flexor tendons. This exercise is needed only if a wrist injury has occurred

Wrist curl A. Start the wrist curl with the barbell resting on the palms.

Wrist curl B. Curl the wrists toward you to finish the exercise.

and the area needs to be specifically rehabilitated or strengthened.

Reverse Wrist Curl
Just as the name implies, this movement is the opposite of the wrist curl.

Starting Position
Place your forearms on your thighs with your palms facing down as you hold a bar.

Action of the Movement
Allow your wrist to drop downward and then back up again.

Speed-Strength Coaching Tips
This exercise targets the muscles on the top of the forearm (extensors). These muscles do not have the same mass and leverage as the flexors, so the athlete will not be able to use

as much weight. Again, this exercise is best used for rehabilitative purposes.

Pronation/Supination
There are muscles that turn your palm up (supination) and down (pronation). These same muscles help to stabilize the wrist. The best way to train these muscles is to obtain an old-style dumbbell handle with collars and a sleeve that can be completely removed. Place one collar on one end of the dumbbell handle and fasten it. Place a small weight (1¼ pounds) on the dumbbell next to the collar. Place the second collar on next to the weight and fasten it. It should have all of the weight on one end and look like a hammer. The dumbbell handle is now ready to use.

Starting Position
Place your forearm against your thigh with your hand and wrist off your thigh. Hold the

dumbbell on the end without the weight. Begin with the dumbbell pointing straight up.

Action of the Movement
Allow the dumbbell to rotate first to one side and then the other.

Speed-Strength Coaching Tips
This exercise will allow only light weight. As with any exercise, if this causes undue pain, have the athlete stop performing the exercise.

Swiss-Ball Lumbar Stabilization

The large Swiss-ball exercises are common in rehabilitation today. Their primary function is to improve the athlete's awareness (proprioception) of his or her low back and abdomen. This is accomplished through a variety of movements performed lying face up or down on the ball. These movements can help teach patients to utilize muscles that they may not normally have recruited.

These exercises can be used after an injury, after surgery, or as a warm-up to the athlete's speed-strength program. However, it is important to remember that a trainer cannot rely on these exercises exclusively to return an athlete to play. The injured athlete needs to be placed in a more functional, closed-chain, and explosive training pattern before he or she can safely be exposed to and experience the speed, explosive power, and physical impact that is an integral part of hockey game situations.

Also, we strongly advise against the growing trend of performing squats while standing on a Swiss ball. There is great risk of injury by performing such a movement. Strength training requires a stable environment or surface for it to be performed safely and effectively, and the Swiss ball is not a stable surface. We also do not support the idea of performing squats while standing on a balance board. Again, an unstable surface may cause the muscle-firing pattern to change and expose the athlete to injury. Additionally, a loss of balance while the spine and body are under load may cause significant injury.

5

MODIFYING TRAINING BECAUSE OF INJURY OR INEXPERIENCE

One area of training that must be (but rarely is) addressed concerns training with, or around, an injury. Obviously, there are acute injuries that must receive appropriate diagnosis, treatment, and rehabilitation. However, some injuries have long-term effects, limitations, and pain, and the athlete will play for a number of years with the effects of the injury. In a case such as that, it is completely unacceptable and absurd to tell a player to avoid training. How sensible is it to allow a player to generate enormous forces skating, withstand the forces of delivering or receiving a check, hit the boards, struggle for the puck in the corners, battle for position in front of the net, deliver maximum-velocity slap shots, and possibly fight, but not let the player perform strength and conditioning exercises?

Conversely, the player must find a way to train around the injury. This is where the training knowledge of the doctor and strength coach comes into play. Their communication is vital and indispensable. A doctor whose only knowledge about training is limited to his or her own spa workout is of little applicable value in this scenario and does not know how to improve the performance of an athlete. However, the doctor's input is vital because the strength coach may not have enough clinical understanding to structure a training program around the athlete's injury.

The techniques for the exercises that are identified as potential problems and their replacements can be found in Chapter 4. The athlete with long-term injuries requires modifications in training. A few examples of modification are listed here.

Wrist Injuries

The position that the wrist is placed in during the catch phase of a power clean may be too difficult or painful for players with wrist injuries. A simple substitute for the power clean is the clean pull. The pull can be performed with a variety of grip widths, poundages, and heights pulled (snatch pull, hang pull, high pull). The clean pull movement is just like the power clean, except at the top of the pull, do not catch or rack the weight at your shoulders. Instead, allow the weight to drop back down to the floor under slight control. This is why rubber bumper plates and lifting platforms are used. These pieces of equipment are designed for just that. If you are training at a gym without lifting platforms and rubber bumper plates, place several rubber mats under the plates to cushion the force (and noise), and use more effort to slow the descent of the bar. If you are training at home, you must also be careful. You certainly do not need to drop a heavy weight and crack your house foundation.

If the push press movement is too stressful on your wrist, first try the slower military press. If you already tried to substitute the military press and they both caused too much wrist pain, then you will have to settle for lesser exercises for the shoulder girdle power. You can substitute the lateral raise for the deltoid strength. This is less effective because of a lesser range of motion; it is also more isolated in nature, and the shoulder girdle is exposed to less weight. However, this exercise is certainly better than no shoulder exercise at all. A word of warning: use this movement only if you have an injury to work around. If you are healthy, this exercise is not enough for the demands on the shoulder from ice hockey.

The wrist position during a barbell bench press may also cause too much pain. If that is

the case, substitute dumbbells for the barbell. The use of the dumbbells may allow you to find a more comfortable position than the bar permitted. The dumbbells must be lighter because of the difficulty in balancing them. Additionally, the weight that you used during a barbell bench press cannot simply be divided into two dumbbells. For example, if you were performing repetition bench presses with 225 pounds, do not attempt to use 110-pound dumbbells. The mathematics of the transition for barbells to dumbbells does not work that simply. Try no more than 75-pound dumbbells in this case and see how your wrist feels. You may (and more wisely) have to begin with 40- or 50-pound dumbbells until you develop the balance needed for the exercise and increase from that point. This will allow you to adapt to the increased need for balance and also to a slightly different range of motion. If you lose control of a dumbbell during the lift, *do not attempt to regain control*. Dump the dumbbell and roll off the bench in the direction of the dumbbell you are still holding. If you continue to hold onto a dumbbell when you have lost control, you may suffer a major injury such as a rotator cuff, capsular, or labrum tear, and your shoulder may never be the same. The dumbbell bench press requires your full attention. If you already have shoulder instability, then the dumbbell bench press is a bad idea because the bench-press movement can cause the instability to be worse during the movement. If the shoulder has been reconstructed already, you do not want to overstretch the repaired ligaments with the dumbbell-bench-press movement.

There can be no fooling around in the gym either. We are in favor of providing a positive environment for the athletes to train, be coached, and receive proper medical assistance. However, clowning around in the weight room can cause a permanent (and possibly career-ending) injury; it cannot be tolerated and should incur a fine on the professional level and parallel consequences in the amateur ranks. Give the weight room and weight training the respect they require, and you will perform better and remain in better health.

The weight-training portion of wrist rehabilitation can include three or four exercises. If you've had an injury to the wrist, make sure that you have sought professional advice from a health care provider before embarking on a weight-training rehab program. If a physician has told you to not lift weights, demand to know the reasons he or she reached this conclusion. You need to be given sound, rational reasons to not train. If limitations are advised, ask how long the limitations will be in effect. The wrist exercises as described in Chapter 4 should be used. These exercises include the wrist curl, reverse wrist curl, and pronation/supination.

Elbow Injuries

The elbow is another area of injury concern. If the bench press produces too much pain, then perhaps a slightly wider grip may reduce the strain on the elbow. The next step would be to try dumbbell bench presses with all the cautions that have already been described in this book.

The push press can also produce stress on the elbow. The speed factor may be more than an injured elbow can tolerate. The substitute for this is the military press. The slower speed of the military press may be much more tolerable. If you are unable to perform either of these exercises because of elbow pain, then a less effective and perhaps less painful substitute can be a last resort. An exercise that is known as a push-down may be that last resort; however, it has little appli-

cability to hockey. To perform the push-down, use a standard "V" bar. Stand straight and place the hands on the bar, elbows at your side. Keeping the wrists straight and the elbows close to your side, straighten your elbows by pushing the bar down to the thighs. We would advise against performing the push-down with a rope unless you have performed it many times before (and we hope you haven't). Don't use the push-down unless all other pushing movements cause pain. If all the other exercises produce elbow pain, make sure that you have had your elbow examined by a health care practitioner.

Shoulder Injuries

The shoulder can be injured a number of different ways, and, fortunately, there are a number of substitutes for training in the shoulder. The bench press is seen as a common villain when it comes to shoulder pain that is produced by weight training. However, it is not always the bench press that causes the problem; rather, the injury symptoms are produced or magnified by the bench press. If your doctor has told you that you have shoulder instability, you probably cannot perform the standard bench press. Painful limitations in the bench press may occur with rotator cuff strains or various types of bursitis in the shoulder.

One substitute that can allow many people to train around these injuries is the reverse-grip bench press. The grip is an underhand grip. The groove of the reverse-grip bench press is different when compared to the standard bench press. Please refer to the technique instructions in Chapter 4. This movement can provide an excellent substitution for the regular grip.

Another substitute is to perform a bench press in a power rack with the pins set at a height that allows the bar to travel only halfway to your chest. This point in the path of the bar should not produce shoulder pain related to instability, but it will still allow you to perform the movement with sufficient weight.

If the bench press produces too much pain, then perhaps a modified triceps extension can be used to train the triceps for upper-extremity power in checking and pushing off of the boards and other players. The modified triceps extension is used by many powerlifters to increase their arm power. The standard lying triceps extension has the athletes lying faceup on a bench with a bar in their hands, held straight-armed over their head. The athletes would then keep the elbows pointing up and bring the bar to the forehead or nose and then straighten their arms again. This can cause a great deal of elbow pain. A modified triceps extension has the athlete begin in the same position. However, the movement is like a blend of the close-grip bench press and the standard lying triceps extension. The elbows are allowed to lower a little and the bar is lowered toward the throat, but the bar stops six to eight inches above the throat. The elbows are bent (flexed), and this requires the triceps to straighten the elbows. The athlete then pushes the bar back to the starting position. This movement greatly reduces, or eliminates, elbow pain during the movement. An athlete could expect to handle 100 percent more weight than in the standard lying triceps extension. Use this type of movement only if injuries prevent you from training with the desired lifts.

If the push press causes shoulder pain, then the first substitute is the military press. The lower ballistic force may make the exercise more tolerable. We would not advise the use of the press behind the neck for two reasons: (1) many players have poor shoulder rotation and may not have sufficient range of motion for this movement to be performed safely, and (2) many players have had shoulder injuries that include instability, AC joint pathology, glenoid labrum tears, and rotator cuff tears, and their shoulder joint may be too loose and sloppy for the press behind the neck. If the military press does not work for you either, then substitute the lateral raise as previously described. Additionally, if overhead lifts continue to cause shoulder pain, you may need to have x-rays of your shoulder taken, specifically an x-ray that is called a scapular outlet view. The scapular outlet view allows the roof of the shoulder (acromion) to be seen and evaluated. Unfortunately, not all acromions are flat (type I). Some are downsloping (type II), and some actually are hook shaped (type III). If you are informed by your doctor that you have a type III or hooked acromion, then you may have to eliminate the push press or military press because the rotator cuff tendons, biceps tendon, and subacromial bursa are being impinged against the hooked acromion. The next viable substitute is the half press. Begin with the bar in the starting position on your chest, and press the bar to the same height as the top of your head. This will allow you to develop power and still stop the motion before the impingement can occur. If all of these alternatives fail, then and only then substitute the lateral raise as a last resort.

The high-pull exercise may cause a problem in your shoulder that is technically known as subacromial impingement syndrome. The internal rotation of the shoulder coupled with the amount of elevation of the arm that occurs in a high pull, or even an upright row, entraps, or impinges, tendons and a bursa in the shoulder, thus causing pain. So if the high pull is causing pain, try to not pull the bar as high. You will probably be able to use a little more weight because you will not be pulling as high. If the high pull is causing pain, you should have scapular outlet view x-rays taken.

Another substitute for the upper-back (trapezius) development is the shrug. Start with the bar at full arm's length. It is usually easiest to use a power rack for this. Shrug your shoulders upward and back down again. Do not roll the shoulders back, and do not relax while holding onto the bar.

Rotator cuff exercises should be included in the program on a preventative basis. Additionally, the strength of the scapular muscles is critical. A buzzword in rehab today is *scapular stabilization*. Scapular muscle exercises are commonly prescribed. However, if you are following a good program as suggested in this book, you will target those muscles. Here is a list of the exercises that accomplish this:

- trapezius—power clean, clean pull, snatch, snatch pull, high pull, shrug
- serratus anterior—push press, military press
- rhomboids—hitchhiker exercise, dumbbell row

Knee Injuries

If you have knee pain, you can also work around it. Many of the injuries in hockey are to either the anterior cruciate ligament (ACL) or the medial collateral ligament (MCL). If an ACL injury or ACL surgical reconstruction occurs, then it is vital for you to increase your hamstring strength as much as possible. The hamstring muscles balance the anterior cruciate ligament, and the quadriceps muscles balance the posterior cruciate ligament. Therefore, the stronger your hamstring muscles are, the more support you provide for the ACL. You can strengthen your hamstring

muscle by performing the stiff-legged dead lift, the Romanian dead lift, other pulls off the floor, the seated leg curl, hyperextensions, and the glute-ham-gastroc raise. These exercises are described in Chapter 4. The leg curl that is performed laying facedown is a mediocre hamstring exercise at best. The hamstring muscle is stretched at the knee only. The straight position of the hip reduces the stretch on the hamstring significantly and therefore reduces the recruitment of the muscle.

Conditioning after an ACL reconstruction is a major area of interest, where the needs of athletes and coaches are sometimes confusing. In question is the return to full function and return to play for a player who has had knee surgery, particularly ACL reconstruction. The early and middle stages of physical therapy and rehabilitation have been well established and published. The late stage of rehabilitation and particularly the transition from rehab to higher athletic function has not been well established. Too frequently, the orthopedic surgeon will tell a player, "Go strengthen your leg," and neither the player nor the doctor has any idea how this should be performed. If the athlete has access to a good athletic trainer, strength coach, physical therapist, or sports chiropractor, then the results may be excellent. If the player does not have this access or good fortune, then the results may be disappointing. A training program to address this need has been designed by a joint effort between the Soft Tissue Center and the West Coast Center for Orthopedic Surgery and Sports Medicine. The program is made for an athlete who has successfully completed the early and middle stages of rehabilitation and does not have complications (failed reconstruction, recurrent instability, infection, lasting patellar tendon pain, etc.). The advanced ACL rehabilitation protocol for an athlete is as follows.

ACL Rehabilitation Protocol

Level 1: 12–16 weeks post-op

Strength: low-velocity movement
1. Romanian dead lift (hams, glutes, paraspinals)
2. good morning exercise (hams, glutes, paraspinals)
3. power squat (glutes, hams, quads, paraspinals)
4. leg press (glutes, hams, adductors, quads)
5. calf raise (gastroc)

Proprioception
1. ball catch while standing on a trampoline
2. balance board

Level 2: 17–20 weeks post-op

Strength: high-velocity (speed-strength) movement
1. power clean (hams, glutes, quads, paraspinals, traps, gastroc)
2. snatch pull (hams, glutes, paraspinals, traps, quads, gastroc)

Strength: low-velocity movement
1. power squat (hams, quads, glutes, adductors)
2. Romanian dead lift (hams, glutes, paraspinals)
3. snatch squats (glutes, hams, quads, paraspinals, traps)

Proprioception
1. advanced balance board

Agility/recruitment drills
1. forward running (progressive)
2. backpedal running (progressive)

Level 3: 21–24 weeks post-op

Strength: high-velocity (speed-strength) movement
1. power cleans
2. snatch pulls

Strength: low-velocity movement
1. power squat
2. Romanian dead lift
3. snatch squats

Proprioception
1. advanced balance board
2. advanced trampoline

Agility/recruitment drills (alternate workouts A and B)

Workout A
1. cone sprint (narrow placement of cones, five yards apart), two to four for 40 yards
2. skate jumps, five for 20 yards
3. carioca, four for 10 yards
4. lateral shuffle and turn, four for 10 yards
5. side-lunge hops, three at 30 seconds
6. backpedal and turn, two for 20 yards

Workout B
1. run-shuffle-run, 20 yards—10 yards—20 yards, four times
2. carioca/carioca and turn, two for 20 yards
3. Heiden (slide) board, three for 30 seconds with 45-second rest between sets
4. double-leg hops, four for 15 yards
5. lateral shuffle, four for 10 yards

Level 4: 25 weeks and up post-op

Strength: high-velocity (speed-strength) movement
1. power clean
2. snatch pull

Strength: low-velocity movement
1. power squat
2. Romanian dead lift
3. snatch squat

Proprioception
1. advanced trampoline
2. advanced balance board

Agility/recruitment
1. run-backpedal-run, two for 40 yards
2. run-carioca-run, 20 yards—10 yards—20 yards
3. sprint with surgical tubing assistance (not resistance), four to five sprints
4. cone run (wide placement of cones, five-yard width with five-yard intervals), two to four for 60 yards
5. 300-yard shuttle run (20- or 50-yard distance between turns)

Often, players are returned to play once their symptoms cease. Some of these athletes are not fully prepared for the forces of starting and stopping, changing directions, checking, and being checked. Our goal is to assist the transition from a relatively pain-free state to an athletically functional state.

Overall strength of the knee can help to stabilize an MCL-deficient knee. The use of an "inner/outer thigh machine" can help. Find the machine that allows your leg to be relatively straight and not bent at 90 degrees at the knee. This type of machine should also have pads for the inner knee to push against. There is a muscle (gracilis) that overlies the MCL, and increasing the strength of the gracilis can help. Do not, under any circumstance, use a cable and strap around your ankle for inner-thigh exercises. This stress on the knee can further injure your MCL. There is too long of a lever involved, and the knee is unsupported. The RDLs (Romanian dead lifts) will also help support the MCL as one of the hamstring muscles overlays the MCL. As the athlete improves, all the key movements (clean pulls, snatches, snatch pulls, squats) recruit the hamstring muscles.

Pain can also develop around and behind the patella (kneecap). This collective pain is classified as patellofemoral pain syndrome. There are a variety of reasons for its occurrence; muscle imbalance in the quadriceps is one of the most common. Also, there can be excessive tightness of the connective tissue on the outside (lateral) aspect of the patella. Another cause of pain around the patella is overuse. Improper squatting technique can produce the pain as well.

There are standardized techniques of squatting, but they may not be suitable for those that have patellar pain. Frequently, there is an excessive amount of forward movement of the lower leg (tibia) during the squat. This places too much shearing force on the patella. A modified type of squat may work around this as well. This is the power squat, which was described in Chapter 4. You sit back into the power squat more than you do into a regular squat. The pivot point almost appears to be at the knee. The back remains flat but not vertical. The eyes look forward and slightly down, not upward. This assists in keeping you from arching your back excessively, which places undue stress on the small joints of your back (facet joints). You may also straddle a bench to perform this lift. This may assist in learning the technique of reaching back with your hips and butt while keeping a flat back and a forward lean of the body from the hips.

If you have been told that you have weakness in the vastus medialis oblique (VMO) and this is producing a patellar tracking problem, then you must strengthen the VMO. The VMO is the muscle on the lower, front, and inside area of your thigh. It is vital for the last range of motion when straightening the knee. Some research indicates that the last 30 degrees of knee extension is not possible without the vastus medialis. Other research indicates that VMO atrophy is really nothing more than a sign of overall quadriceps atrophy and associated weakness. Biomechanically, the oblique portion of the muscle pulls the patella inward (medially) and allows it to move up and down properly.

The best way to target the VMO is to perform what is known as terminal extension (last 30 degrees of knee extension). This can be done on a leg-extension machine (open chain), in a standing position (closed chain), or on a leg-press machine (closed chain). The closed chain is gaining more favor today from biomechanists, physical therapists, sports chiropractors, and athletic trainers. The top portion, or slight knee dip, of the squat is all that is needed. There is much debate about foot position during the leg extension. If the feet are turned in or out too much during a leg extension, then it may create a patellar tracking problem and make matters worse. We advise you to keep the foot in a neutral (straight) position during the leg-extension movement. You may be better off not performing the leg extension at all because of the compressive forces of the patella against the femur.

Low-Back Injuries

The low back, or lumbar spine, is always an area of concern with regard to injuries and training. One common problem in training by those with a lumbar injury is that the fear of reinjury causes them to avoid training the erector spinae. This can actually make the lumbar spine pain worse by creating imbalance. The abdominal muscles are certainly important. However, the paraspinal muscles must also be kept strong. Many neurosurgeons subscribe to the "three-column theory." Ian Armstrong, M.D., chief of neurosurgery at Century City Hospital, states, "The three-column theory is the spine is made of three columns. The first column is the abdominal muscles. The second column is the spine itself. The third column is the paraspinal muscles in the back. The first and third columns must be strong to protect the second column."

There are several things that need to be evaluated for low-back strengthening. The first and foremost is the diagnosis, condition of the athlete, and time frame of estimated return to play. Obviously, if the patient had surgery, then a true rehabilitative program is needed and the spine may not be significantly loaded (compressed with weight during an exercise like the squat) for 12 to 16 weeks.

The exercises of choice are the dead lift or the clean pull. The name "dead lift" conjures up images of massive weights being lifted

with the back straining. The dead lift can be performed with any amount of weight, even starting with a broomstick, dowel, or PVC pipe. I (JMH) frequently use a PVC pipe that weighs half a pound. It is critical for the patient to learn proper form; this is what will allow the development of strength and stability in the back. If the ballistic type of movement such as the power clean is painful, then substitute the more controlled dead lift. If the dead lift is not possible either, then try the hyperextension exercise. If all three of these fail, then try one other movement: the top-half dead lift. The top-half dead lift is performed in a power rack with the pins set just above knee height, and is simply the top half only of the movement of a standard dead lift. This exercise will allow the spine to remain in a good position. The paraspinal muscles will still be loaded, and you will be exposed to significant training loads. Remember to always begin with a poundage that is easy for you. You can use periodization training to increase the weight. Those who are unfamiliar with rehabilitation or training will be apprehensive about performing these types of movements, even with a half-pound PVC pipe. They fail to recognize that our daily activities of standing out of chairs and cars (squats) and picking up grocery bags and children (dead lifts and cleans) require strengthening and preparation.

It is a mistake to think that if you don't train your lower back you will therefore avoid injury. Not only might you create a muscle imbalance, but as soon as your back is challenged on the ice, you may have reinjury.

The abdominal muscles can be trained in a way to help avoid excessive stress on the low back. Sit-ups with weight can bother the low back for a few people. This is usually due to the recruitment of the hip flexors. A suitable alternative is the pulley crunch, which allows for progressive resistance training to occur and will make the abdominal muscles stronger. If neither the weighted sit-up nor the pulley crunch are possible, then you may have to substitute the exercises with the medicine ball and the standard crunch.

Neck Injuries

The cervical spine is an area that must be trained. The most significant concern is if there has been a previous neck injury. If there has been a previous injury, then you may have to use isometric resisted exercises rather than full-range-of-motion resisted-moving exercises. Using the isometric exercises is certainly better than not training the neck at all.

A stronger neck will protect the neck itself and may also contribute to decreased risk of concussion. All of the major published articles on neck trauma in hockey indicate that neck strengthening should be used. The stronger neck will also slow the movement of the head during an impact. This may allow for less acceleration/deceleration forces on the brain.

If you require other modifications due to an injury, then you should consult a strength coach and your doctor.

Varying Training Experience

There is another area that requires attention, and that is training experience. It is included in the section dealing with injuries due to the fact that a novice trainee needs to be approached with caution. There is a range of players: a few have proper training experience; many have dabbled in a gym setting (mostly without instruction or suitable exercises); some players do not have any experience. Those players with little or no experience are truly beginners; their programs need to be simple, and they also need instruction and supervision. The athletes that have dabbled in weight training may require the most supervision due to the fact that they may not fully comprehend that they do not know how to perform the new weight-training movements. Time can be set aside in camp, during preseason, and at key rest points during the season to review and teach proper technique.

The instruction in the Olympic lifts can begin with PVC pipe, a wooden dowel, or an empty bar. It is important for the novice to learn proper technique; this must take precedence over the amount of weight lifted.

6

PLYOMETRICS: LOWER-BODY EXPLOSIVENESS

"Depth jumps and compression jumps are events in themselves and to train these jumps requires specific progressive training. Athletes are undergoing a multidimensional program already, which doesn't leave much time or energy for heavy plyometric work without increasing the expectation of injuries. If one doesn't have the time to approach the jumps as an event in and of itself, then a moderate approach should be taken."

—CHUCK DEBUS

Plyometrics is a form of emphasis training that revolves around the jump movement. In the Soviet Union, there is no word like *plyometrics*; these jumps are simply called "hit" and "shock." U.S. trainers call these same movements "jump" and "depth jump." Plyometric jumping incorporates different forms such as: (1) jumps for height; (2) jumps for distance; (3) single-leg jumps; (4) double-leg jumps; (5) hops; (6) depth jumps with a single-, double-, or triple-rebound effect; (7) reaction speed-strength plyometrics; and (8) reaction speed-strength sprinting skills. Some actions are singular in nature, and some work in series, sets, or combinations. Although acceptance of plyometrics was relatively slow in the United States, the use of plyometrics gradually found its way into professional, col-

lege, and high school conditioning programs. With speed-strength training emphasizing starting, reaction, and explosive strength, the competitive edge is being gained by those who have utilized plyometrics as another way to vastly improve their athletes.

Plyometric movements help improve the quickness and explosiveness of the athlete. When an athlete improves his or her vertical, horizontal, and reaction strength, his or her starting and explosive strength also improve. Thus, the level of absolute strength is improved for the hockey player.

Today, speed is even more a measure of successful competition. To develop lower-body explosive strength, an excellent leg speed-strength program should complement weight training. Jumping, depth jumps, hop-

Former captain of the Long Beach Ice Dogs Darryl Williams.

ping, bounding, and squat jumps contribute to explosive leg strength. This approach helps develop faster movement in starting and reaction speed as well as greater speed-strength. The coach or trainer can review in this chapter different exercises involving plyometric movements and select from different drills used for the development of speed-strength. When planning speed-strength training during the main competitive period, coaches should allow two days off from heavy plyometric exercises before a game.

Jumping Drills

Incorporating jumps into a training program utilizes the simplest form of plyometrics. Jumping involves either one leg, both legs, or alternating between legs. Beginning hockey players should start with double-leg jumps until the legs are accustomed to the jumping movements. It is important that the trainer or coach remembers that the amount of force generated in a single-leg jump is about twice that of double-leg movement. If the young athlete's muscles are not prepared for this force, it could be injurious.

Jumping exercises, including jumping on and off various platforms, can be used to duplicate different heights and directions. Jumping over an object is more effective for a hockey player than simple jumping because it forces the athlete to jump a little higher, which in turn creates greater force upon the landing. Jumping over different heights and obstacles allows for a progressive development that in time will allow the athlete to jump even higher.

The nervous system is exposed to different amounts of force from different jumps, which provides for greater leg explosiveness and development. The following plyometric drills serve as examples of the types of jumps that

the coach/trainer may use in the speed-strength-training program.

Platform Jump (Box Jump)

Starting Position
Assume a solid standing position on the ground with the pressure on the balls of the feet and the knees slightly bent. Using the arms to balance, "psych up" for maximum explosion upward and onto the platform.

Action of the Movement
From the explosion upward and slightly forward, the amount of force will allow you to land on both feet on top of the platform. Upon landing, you may repeat the platform jump exercise or the depth jump followed by platform jumping to another platform.

Speed-Strength Coaching Tips
This is an outstanding exercise for beginning athletes who have a strength deficit in the lower body. The starting height should be 18 to 36 inches, depending on the level of the athlete. I (EJK) recommend the following workout program for a hockey player: three sets of six repetitions one time per week during the competitive period (in-season) and two to three times per week during the preparatory phase (off-season).

Over-the-Top Side Jump

Starting Position
Standing erect, place the feet a heel's distance apart, with the knees slightly bent.

Action of the Movement
Stand to the side of the blocking bag (approximately 12 to 18 inches high), and hop back and forth over the blocking bag, landing on both feet each time. Small hurdles or cones can be used too.

Box jump A. Start the box jump standing in front of the box ready to jump.

Box jump B. Explosively jump onto the box, then step down.

Over-the-top side jump A. Starting position for over-the-top side jump using low hurdles.

Over-the-top side jump B. Quickly hop over each hurdle.

Straddle bench jump A. To begin, keep the knees slightly bent.

Straddle bench jump B. Explode upward and land with both feet on the bench.

Speed-Strength Coaching Tips

Quickness is important here, so keep a record of how many jumps are achieved in a recommended time period.

Straddle Bench Jump

Starting Position

Stand erect with the knees slightly bent, similar to the front- or back-quat starting position. The only difference is that the flat bench is being straddled.

Action of the Movement

Jump downward until you barely make contact with the top of the bench. When contact is made, explode as quickly as possible in order to be able to have both feet land on top of the bench with full extension achieved; then return down into the starting position.

Repeat the process until the desired number of repetitions is completed.

Speed-Strength Coaching Tips

The straddle bench jump can be performed with or without the use of weight resistance. Remind the athletes to explode and try to land with control.

Depth-Jump Drills

Fred Hatfield and Michael Yessis say that the most effective height for the depth jump is between 30 and 40 inches. For beginning athletes, the coach should lower the height until the proper form and technique are mastered. Hatfield and Yessis also state that "as a general rule of thumb, your depth jump height should be no more than a foot above your vertical jumping ability." Depth jumping from too great a height should be avoided. Many beginners and second-year players usually function on the principle that "the more I do, the better I get," and because of these ideas, they increase the height to amounts that are beyond their capabilities.

When you jump from a box that is too high, there is too much flexion in the legs, which absorb most of the force of the landing, and thus there is very little force to propel you upward. You thus end up with a weaker lower jump. Jumping from boxes that are too high also involves different takeoff mechanisms. It is also important to keep in mind that it is most advantageous to execute depth jumps only after adequate strength preparation (preparatory period of training).

Some authors recommend that athletes be able to squat two and a half times their body weight before undertaking maximum depth jumps (Yessis and Hatfield). We think this varies with the age and weight of the athlete. Young, lightweight athletes may be able to get by with this very easily, but large athletes may need the strength.

An unpublished review of elite athletes with jumper's knee associated with depth jumps revealed that the average jump height was from a box of 36 inches. A height of no more than 20 inches is recommended. A limited number of weeks of depth-jump use each year is also advised. Additionally, I (JMH) examined an NHL player who weighed approximately 245 pounds who had ruptured a lumbar disc from jumping from too great a height. To make matters worse, this player had no experience with jumping. His team let the players choose between performing the plyometric jumps after a game or on the following morning. The players chose to perform the jumps after the game when, of course, the local muscle fatigue of the legs is

Depth jump A. Step off a box to start the depth jump.

great and the central nervous system fatigue is significant after sprinting, shooting, checking, fighting, and reacting quickly. Plyometric training is best used when the athlete is not fatigued. Very large athletes may also be advised to use only the box jumps.

Depth Jump

Starting Position
Stand on top of the platform.

Action of the Movement
When stepping off the platform, drop straight down, landing on both feet together at the same time. Keep the knee and hip bending to a minimum. As you make contact

Depth jump B. Land with a minimum amount of bend in the knees and hips.

Depth jump C. From the landing position, explode into a vertical jump.

with the surface, immediately jump straight upward and slightly forward, obtaining as much height as possible on each jump. Upon landing, try and be as vertical as possible so that the maximum load can be placed on the leg muscles. The landing should first be on the balls of both feet and then on the whole foot, followed by the ankle, knee, and joint flexion.

Speed-Strength Coaching Tips

Remember to use a good landing surface. The number of rebound jumps repeated should not be more than three repetitions.

A recommended workout for a hockey player includes two sets of five repetitions with a triple rebound one time a week during

the main competitive period (in-season) and two to three times a week during the preparatory phase (off-season). Allow two days off before a game.

Shock Jump

Starting Position

As in the depth jump, assume the starting position on top of the platform.

Action of the Movement

The movement is the same action used for the depth jump. As you step off and make contact with the surface, the action is completed. Land in an upright position with feet wide apart and knees slightly bent in a ready posi-

Front-hurdle hop A. To start the front-hurdle hops, stand in front of a row of hurdles or cones.

Front-hurdle hop B. Hop over each hurdle or cone.

tion so that the maximum load can be placed on the leg muscles. The landing should first be on the balls of the feet, transferring the weight to each foot, followed by ankle, knee, and hip joint flexion. Keep the knees in the bent position with a wider base.

Speed-Strength Coaching Tips

Remember to use a proper landing surface. Make sure that the athlete uses the prime movers of the legs and hips to absorb the major force and flexes on the landing. Have the athlete stop using this drill if pain occurs.

Hopping Drills

The hopping drills are excellent for developing overall coordination, balance, agility, and arm position.

Front-Hurdle Hops

Starting Position

Five low hurdles should be placed one and one-half yards apart. Stand on both feet in front of the first hurdle to be hopped.

Action of the Movement

Jump over the hurdle and land on both feet. Then quickly repeat the jump up and over the next four hurdles one by one until the last hurdle is cleared. Use the arms to help you balance and coordinate the movement. Drive the arms upward as the hop occurs. The action is to maximize height, not distance.

Speed-Strength Coaching Tips

The idea is to spend as little time as possible on the ground between hurdles. Athletes should not wear ankle weights or a weighted vest in this drill. Start with the hurdles at the lowest level and slowly move the hurdles up as the athlete makes improvements.

Double-Leg Hops

Starting Position

Assume the standing position used in the front-hurdle hops. In this exercise there are no hurdles.

Action of the Movement

Jump forward and land on both feet. Upon landing, quickly repeat the hopping motion for the required distance. Use the arms to help

Double-leg hop A. This athlete has already left the ground.

Double-leg hop B. Land after one hop and immediately jump again.

you balance and coordinate the movement. Drive the arms upward as the hop occurs. The idea is to maximize distance, not height.

Speed-Strength Coaching Tips

Again, the idea is to spend as little time as possible on the ground between double-leg hops. Require good form and technique. These hops are recommended for use in the warm-up plan. This is a very simple movement and is excellent for beginning athletes to use in warm-up drills before weight training as well as for cooldown after finishing drills.

Single-Leg Hop

Starting Position

Stand erect in a relaxed position. Cones or small hurdles can be used.

Action of the Movement

Thrust the right knee forward and upward, and at the same time hop forward on the left leg. Repeat the action several times for a given distance. Hold the left arm up in proper running form using a pumping movement

Single-leg hop. To perform the single-leg hop, spring over a series of cones or hurdles.

back and forth. The right arm serves as a balance of control to help in the hopping action. The landing should be flat-footed on the ground.

Speed-Strength Coaching Tips

The arms should help the athlete balance and coordinate the movement. Because it is difficult to hop on one leg while keeping the other leg up as high as possible in readiness for the next hop, the single-leg hops are an excellent exercise for the development of leg coordination and increased speed.

Reaction Speed-Strength Plyometric Drills

This series of reaction speed-strength plyometric drills is designed to increase the reaction speed of the leap. Track coach Dean Hayes best explains these drills: "These exercises help the legs learn to snap back off the ground more quickly, thus teaching you to automatically respond and increase faster improvement of reaction speed." Over the years, coach Hayes pioneered and formulated many concepts and ideas that have been implemented by world-class long and triple jumpers and sprinters alike. These drills have obvious benefits for hockey players and have become invaluable plyometric exercises. These are the reaction-strength plyometric drills:

1. Hayes double-leg top hop
2. Hayes double-leg-in-the-hole hop
3. Hayes single-leg top hop
4. Hayes single-leg-in-the-hole hop

These drills will make a difference in the improvement of speed development.

Hayes Double-Leg Top Hop

Starting Position
As in the platform jumps, assume the squat stance starting position.

Action of the Movement
The difference between the platform and the Hayes double-leg top hop is the series of platforms to be used. The number of jumps is determined per set by the number of platforms. Make every movement a forceful drive.

Speed-Strength Coaching Tips
A recommended workout program would be between four and ten platforms and two and five series. Try, as a rule of thumb, to start low, and as the athletes become more skillful, then add to the number of platforms and number of series. Another reminder is to keep the height of the platform between 12 and 18 inches. Start with a short distance between each platform. As the hops become easier, move each platform a little farther apart. This drill can also be performed using one leg.

Hayes Double-Leg-in-the-Hole Hop

Starting Position
Assume the same starting position as in the Hayes double-leg top hop.

Action of the Movement
Again, as in the Hayes double-leg top hop, you will be moving over multiple platforms. The difference is that this time instead of landing on the top of each platform, you will land on the ground space between each platform.

Speed-Strength Coaching Tips
The recommended number of platforms is between four and ten and two and five series. Remind the athlete that ground recovery time is to be kept at a minimum. Be aware of athletic form and technique. This drill can also be performed using one leg.

Reaction Speed-Strength Sprinting Drills

Integrating these three running drills—bounds, skips, and running As—into the overall speed-strength-training program will help in the development of sprint speed. They will help athletes to identify wasted motion and movements that hinder their ability to obtain

Bounds A. Switching from leg to leg, bound forward, landing on the balls of the feet. Bounds help train the body to propel forward with more force.

Bounds B. Use forward and upward drive when performing bounds.

maximum running speed. Each of these drills requires the use of knee-lift-to-arm action in teaching the athlete the correct and simplest technique in sprinting-speed improvement.

Bounds

Bounding is an excellent plyometric drill for developing speed, balance, coordination, and agility. Bounding incorporates the skill of jumping and the mechanics of running all in one. The athletes' improvements are in stride length and stride frequency, two factors that make up running speed.

Starting Position

Assume a good relaxed standing position at a defined starting line or point. You can have both feet together or in a split-leg position.

Action of the Movement

Bound as far as possible from one leg to the other, going up and forward on each leg. Land

lightly on the balls of the feet and on to the toes. The center of gravity must be behind on each step and then pulled forward. The action is repeated several times for a given distance.

Speed-Strength Coaching Tips

By varying the workouts, the athlete can bound for distance, which is excellent for speed-strength, or take short, fast bounds, which are good for speed explosion. This is a very simple drill, but the payoff is huge. Suggested distance, sets, and repetitions are 20 to 60 yards, two to four sets, and two to six repetitions per training day. Suggested number of days is two to three per week.

Skips

Starting Position

Assume a good relaxed standing position at a defined starting line or point. Have both feet together or in a split-leg position.

The need for strength, balance, coordination, and an awareness of one's own body, opposing players, the boards, and the puck are what make hockey the great game it is.

Action of the Movement

In mastering the skip drill movement, you should start with the walking position movement first. As the right leg touches the ground, the left arm should make a light touch to the right knee. As the left leg touches the ground, have the right arm lightly touch the left leg on the downward motion. Skipping incorporates rhythm, coordination, and balance. As you advance from walking to slow running to the actual speed skip, you will be up on the balls of your feet, exerting smooth arm action.

Speed-Strength Coaching Tips

For any athlete just starting, the skips allow for proper sprinting mechanism and proper balance awareness. Corrections of running form and techniques can be evaluated, and technique can be corrected. Distance, sets, and repetitions are 20 to 60 yards, two to four sets, and two to six repetitions per day. Suggested number of days is two to three per week.

Running A

Starting Position

Assume a good relaxed standing position at a defined starting line or point. You can have both feet together or in split-leg position.

Action of the Movement

The running A drill utilizes the maximum training movements for speed sprinting development. This drill is similar to the skip drill with the exception that the knee and arm action is at rapid movement speeds. Right-arm-to-left-leg action and left-arm-to-right-leg movement occur in rapid succession. The idea is to develop proper knee lift and arm action to promote faster reaction strength.

Speed-Strength Coaching Tips

Make sure the knee lift is brought right above the belt line. Also, make sure the athletes pump the arms slightly past the upper-torso side, a movement very similar to drawing a pistol from a holster. They should stay on the balls of their feet. Suggested distance, sets, and repetitions are 20 to 60 yards, two to four sets, and two to six repetitions per training day. Suggested number of days is two to three per week. This drill can also begin with marching As until the skills are improved and then progress to skipping As before graduating to running As.

7

RECOVERY

There are several theories of recovery from training that originated in what used to be the Eastern Bloc of Europe. One theory's main point is to monitor central nervous system (CNS) fatigue. The central nervous system is a critical component of performance and training. Strength is largely determined by the speed the nerve fires and the number of motor units that the nerve recruits. A motor unit is a bundle of muscle fibers. The nerve must also coordinate the various muscles at the right time and in the right sequence, as well as relax opposing muscles at the right time. Because strength is a neurological phenomenon, the fatigued nerve will contribute to decreased strength and performance. Fatigue reduces the effect of muscular force and interferes with movement patterns—especially high-power, technique-oriented activities. During high-volume training when fatigue levels are high, care should be taken to reduce the number of highly technique-oriented power exercises. Performing these exercises during a fatigued state may interfere with learning or maintaining proper technique, and this results in diminished adaptations for maximum strength and power.

Simply stated, the nerves fatigue as do the muscles. Once the nerves are fatigued, they cannot fire as quickly, or as often, as nonfatigued nerves.

Central fatigue was observed in 1903 and was described as the "Setchenov phenomenon." The basic principle of central nervous system fatigue is that there is a "neurotransmission fatigue taking place somewhere between the brain and the motor end plate," as one of my (JMH) former college professors put it. There are entire textbooks on the subject now.

One physiology researcher, E. Asmussen, defined fatigue as situations where a transient decrease of working capacity results from previous physical activity. It is believed by some physiologists that only one form of fatigue exists and that it originates in the nervous system. Others feel that it can occur in the muscle as well. Asmussen defined this more clearly as "central" fatigue and "peripheral" fatigue. "Central" is defined to be mainly in the brain. "Peripheral" is defined to be the motor neurons, peripheral nerves, site of motor nerve attachment (motor end plate), and muscle fibers themselves. These two forms have been separated and identified in laboratory settings. The fatigue at the peripheral aspect is occurring at one of two locations: the neuromuscular junction (transmission mechanism) or the contractile mechanism (muscle filaments). The peripheral fatigue may be either an accumulation of "fatigue substances" as a by-product of muscle work or a depletion of substances that produce the work.

Another neurophysiological theory about central fatigue is that impulses from the fatigued muscle back to the brain cause this part of the brain to inhibit (use less of) the muscle. This would then cause fewer impulses or signals from the brain to make the muscle work or contract. However, other types of signal input (from other locations) could cause the brain to improve impulses to the working muscle. In other words, changing the training can cause other areas or centers of the brain to send impulses, and this can improve, or remove, the inhibition to the area that was causing the original muscle to contract. This gives the appearance of improving the recuperation process.

It is quite interesting that this scientific research falls right in line with the observations on the track and in training halls by coaches such as Francis, Bompa, Kreis, Verkoshansky, Rahn Sheffield, and others.

Other studies were performed with the use of EEG (electroencephalogram; measurement of brain activity). When subjects fatigued, the EEG revealed a gradual appearance of what is known as an alpha-rhythm. The alpha-rhythm normally appears when we are at a lowered state of arousal. It usually appears when we close our eyes and disappears when we open our eyes. When different activities were introduced to the subject with the fatigue and alpha-rhythm, the alpha-rhythm disappeared.

In other words, the brain would allow other activities to take place, but it would not allow for the same activity to keep occurring over and over again. This is precisely the reason that multicomponent training is necessary. Taking time and energy away from ongoing skating practices will allow for better-quality training, better overall conditioned athletes, and better performance. Active rest falls into this category as well. Active rest is frequently a welcome component in training by the athlete.

Coach Francis says that CNS fatigue is caused by three major points:

1. high-intensity work occurring too frequently in the training cycle
2. too high a volume in a single session of high-intensity work
3. attempting to introduce high intensity too rapidly into the program when residual fatigue still exists

Francis says that the CNS is stressed by sprints at maximum or 100 percent intensity from 30 to 120 meters, heavy weight training of only two to five repetitions, bounding, stair running, explosive plyometrics, and medicine-ball work.

Francis continued with coaching advice: "The athlete must be monitored during the warm-up for changes in the actual performance of CNS-related work. The athlete should stop the workout when the personal best or near personal best is performed, or the intensity or technique is visibly degrading."

Coach Francis says that 48 hours are needed to recover from the CNS work. The recovery methods that Francis suggests employing during that time include massage, contrast bath, calcium supplementation, and relaxation techniques. (We recommend that if an injury has taken place, a correct diagnosis must be made, and, if indicated, soft-tissue mobilization that is specific to the diagnosis should be utilized.) During one of my (JMH) conversations with Coach Francis, he pointed out that a 95 percent effort by an elite athlete may require 48 hours of recovery while a 100 percent effort at world-record level may require up to 10 days of recovery. Similar conversations with Coach Debus revealed that a 100 percent effort may require nine days to recover. It is interesting to note that elite coaches working independently have arrived at the same information and conclusions. Francis emphasized, "Coaches rise or fall by the capacity to adjust. One's greatness is demonstrated by one's athletes. The failure to recognize and adjust to the superior output will end (limit) the athlete's capacity to exceed or even equal the same level of output again." An additional key point by Francis is, "If there is any degradation or deterioration in training, stop. If there is any doubt about one more rep or run, don't do it. If you are trying to learn with reps, you won't get it later if you haven't already. Leave it and come back to it. For example, if I hear a track athlete's feet hit heavier on the track, that's enough (for the workout). Top athletes need to be controlled from overmotivation. Don't listen to just anybody. If you are left in doubt, don't do it. The idea is to apply correct and appropriate training at the right time."

As previously discussed, fatigue can be in a local muscle, the motor nerve, motor end plate, or the central nervous system. According to Tudor Bompa, Ph.D., one of the leading strength-training authorities, the nerve impulse is what causes the muscle contraction. The higher nerve impulse creates a greater contraction, and the nerve is very sensitive to fatigue. Bompa noted: "If the level of fatigue is increasing, the force of contraction is decreasing." This is the reason that Bompa

feels rest periods for CNS recovery in a training session should be between four and seven minutes. The motor end plate (junction where the motor nerve attaches to the muscle) releases chemical transmitters to stimulate the muscle and can be slowed if enough time to return the end plate to a normal state is not allowed.

Several factors need to be considered in recovery:

- age of the athlete
- fitness or training level—the more fit and better trained the athlete is, the better the recovery will be
- nutritional status—balance of diet, dehydration level
- emotions—negative emotions such as problems with spouse, parents, or fear or even established stressors such as a change of environment or team, school, etc.
- overtraining—on-ice, too much speed-strength training, added bodybuilding movements that the coaches don't know about, too much plyometric training, etc.
- lack of sleep

A short-term remedy for overtrained athletes is to give them a three- to five-day break from their speed-strength training and intensive sport training/practice. Short-term recovery applies to overreaching (short-term overtraining). More time than that is usually not necessary. It must also be noted that Bompa feels a general rule of thumb is one week of missed training will require two weeks of training to regain the previous level of conditioning. As you may see by now, the program must be carefully applied and balanced. This is one of the reasons we wrote this book—to help the sport of hockey apply these principles and methods.

The most obvious signs of overtraining include the following, and the coaches must watch and listen for these changes:

- decreased sports performance (especially if increased effort to improve physical performance or strength has failed)
- insomnia or sleep disturbances
- decreased appetite
- decreased desire to train
- irritability and mood swings
- fatigue
- injuries

If these changes are happening with your athletes, they are already overtrained or are reaching CNS fatigue, and you must alter the training immediately to allow them to recover.

You can refer to Chapter 2 on program planning to learn about other factors such as a principle known as variability of load. The planned change, or variance, of the overall training load allows for an athlete to recover. Kreis phrased a question about the status of an overtrained athlete as: "How big a hole has he dug himself into?" The more overtrained the athlete is, the "deeper in the hole" he is, and therefore it will take more recuperative efforts to "get him out of the hole." An overtrained athlete has exceeded his or her ability to recover. Significant discipline must now be applied to reduce the athlete's training—on and off the ice—so that his or her performance will improve by reducing fatigue. It is like being overdrawn at the bank—you can't keep writing checks until you make deposits. The fatigued, overtrained athlete will not perform well late in the game or in back-to-back games. This is even worse when the playoff schedule starts. The playoffs are usually scheduled to have games every other day. If the athlete is overtrained and dehydrated from the games and dehydrated from flying, his or her performance will continue to decline.

There are other theories of recovery that have had empirical success but have had little study in the Western world. Reports of recovery methods from Eastern Bloc coaches for decades have included relaxation techniques, visualization, cold baths, alternating warm and cold baths, massage, nutritional supplements, and electronic muscle stimulation. A few of our Western coaches in track and field and weight lifting swear by these methods. However, these methods have not been fully evaluated with a truly scientific eye, so the jury is still out on their effectiveness. The difficult point is that most scientists are still trying to determine which factors are to be researched. At this point, we really don't know how to evaluate and measure these methods of recovery. But just because we don't know how to measure them, it doesn't mean they don't work.

PART TWO
CONDITIONING

8

ANAEROBIC AND AEROBIC CONDITIONING

"Inconsistent performance has come from a lack of a predictable training program for a given level of performance and for a predictable peak. The athlete frequently does not know the 'whys and wherefores' of such theories."

—Charlie Francis

The conditioning component of training—both preseason and in-season—is often not used to its fullest extent. For many years, conditioning has simply meant more skating during practice. Regrettably, long practices are often used as punishment for poor play. Punitive workouts need to become a thing of the past. Instead of long practices that may produce more fatigue, practice time would be more effective if used to improve weak points in the players' performance. There are a variety of conditioning methods and plans available. We will present a few of these methods and then give a plan that we feel is realistic and specific.

Anaerobic Conditioning

The anaerobic conditioning of a hockey player comes from strength training, dry-land and on-ice speed work, repeat speed work (which produces speed endurance), plyometric training, overspeed training, and explosive/ballistic training. Each one is addressed in this book. This chapter serves as an overview of direction, philosophy, and combination of these components.

The stamina and endurance of a player may be significant in avoiding injury. Some researchers feel that in ice hockey, anaerobic variables may reflect performance more accurately than aerobic variables. We agree with this point. As Bompa noted in his books, if an athlete is made to train aerobically for an anaerobic sport, the aerobic training actually moves the athlete away from the desired anaerobic performance. The demands on the muscle, CNS, and nutritional status from anaerobic training are significant.

The program design for anaerobic conditioning is important. The adding, deleting, and changing of exercises, drills, intensity, and volume require very careful attention to

165

detail by the coach. All of the various components of training should be included in the program and are most effective when varied throughout the year, according to Charlie Francis. Coach Francis commented, "If you change the components in training [add or delete], then you are constantly stiff and you must retrain constantly. What good is that? You must do all the components simultaneously." Francis developed a system known as "vertical integration" to monitor his athletes' training.

This method avoids a very common error and source of injury in the training of athletes. For example, many coaches keep track of various portions of the athletes' training on separate pages in a training log or notebook. If each component is analyzed separately, or in a "horizontal" manner, then all that the coach will see is the improvement in each category. If the athlete's weight-training percentages are going up and the speed work is increasing and the intensity and volume of various drills are increasing and explosive power work is increasing and tempo work is increasing, then the coach may feel that all is well with the athlete—everything is increasing. Therein lies the problem. Everything cannot keep going up without the body's ability to recover being compromised.

The Vertical Integration System

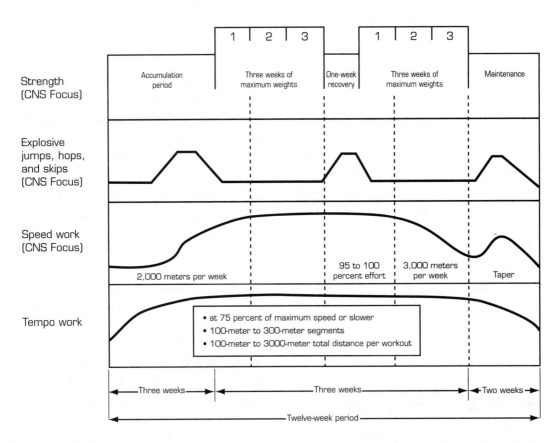

All components are being performed at all times; only volume varies

Reprinted with permission from Charlie Francis.

If all components of training keep going up, then in a matter of weeks, a "point of no return" is reached. Injuries occur commonly at this point of no return. This idea exemplifies the need for the idea of variability of load. This is precisely what Francis wished to convey. The vertical integration method allows the coach to see, on one graph, each aspect of training stacked on top of the others. This allows the entire training program to be quickly evaluated and adjusted. If the weight training is increasing, then the speed work may need to be decreased in volume. If explosive power work and speed drills are increasing, then weight training and other drills are decreased. The general principle is: increase and decrease the training components, but never eliminate. This allows the athlete to always be accustomed to all the aspects of training and to always be ready to increase the intensity without significant fear of soreness, injury, or recovery problems.

Francis stated that his sprinters were "never far from strength and speed." This same principle can apply very easily to hockey, especially once the players in the major and minor leagues of a particular team are past the novice stage of training. This is precisely what we want. Francis concluded: "Application and recovery from application are equal, which is why we train. Train smarter, not harder. The weight training is not specific. It is general to the organism. I wanted my athlete to train the highest percentage of muscles in his body with the fewest lifts, and I wanted it well balanced." The entire system was trained in a functional manner that was applicable to the event. The central nervous system, key muscles, reaction, speed, and conditioning were all addressed.

If time is spent developing speed, then the players will have a higher speed reserve to use in the game. Simply put, the greater the speed, the greater the submaximal speed. No one cares how long a player can skate slowly around the rink. Everyone cares how fast the player can get from one end of the ice to the other. Speed is developed via appropriate anaerobic training.

More coaches in hockey are beginning to see the anaerobic nature of the sport and are beginning to train in that direction. Sthair feels that sprint training should consist of sprinting distances of 30 meters to 60 meters at full recovery; technique improvement; and reaction training. Speed-endurance training should consist of running three to five sets of eight reps at 50 to 120 meters with one to two minutes between reps and four to five minutes between sets; speed bounding 30 to 60 meters with two to three minutes of recovery between sets; repetitive slap shots of three to five sets of 10 to 15 shots; and jump training.

On-Ice Conditioning Analysis

Hockey has used few established, reproducible tests and drills to analyze player performance. This is an area that will come into the forefront as hockey continues to develop and salaries grow accordingly.

A study was performed to evaluate ice hockey skill tests (Merrifield and Walford). Six skill tests were chosen:

1. forward skating speed at a distance of 120 feet
2. backward skating speed at a distance of 120 feet
3. skating agility
4. puck carry
5. shooting
6. passing

The results of these skill tests revealed that the puck carry, forward skating speed, and skating agility tests were found to correlate quite well with the players' overall ability as judged by the coach prior to the performance of the tests.

The 40-yard dash is one of the key components in analyzing the speed of a football player. There is no such landmark in hockey, and this is truly unfortunate because it creates a handicap for the scouts, coaches, general managers, and players. While working with the Long Beach Ice Dogs (IHL team), I (JMH) developed a standard of two sprints to analyze players' speed and ability to maintain their speed. They are the goal-line-to-near-blue-line sprint and the goal-line-to-far-blue-line sprint.

Although the distance between the blue lines varies from arena to arena, the goal line to near-blue line is a fixed distance of 60 feet (20 yards). An acceptable goal-line-to-near-blue-line time would be 2.75 to 3.00 seconds, and an acceptable goal-line-to-far-blue-line time would be 4.60 to 5.00 seconds, depending on the size of each rink. The times mentioned here have been obtained with infrared timers. Hand times are faster than electronic times. The standard adjustment used to convert a hand time (from an experienced person) to an electronic time in track and field is to add 0.18 second to the hand time.

You can use these sprint times to evaluate the success of your off-season and in-season speed-strength and conditioning programs. The test can be performed periodically during the season. If the times for the sprints are slowing, then the speed-strength coach must evaluate the situation and ask these questions:

1. Are the players performing enough non-hockey practice training?
2. Are the players skating too much and/or undergoing punitive practices?
3. Are the players overtrained and displaying fatigue?
4. Is the in-season strength training not sufficient to maintain speed?
5. Has too much strength training been done?
6. Has there been a poor selection of exercises for speed development?

A few examples of improvement in speed development are illustrated by several players. The Ice Dogs as a team improved in speed, and our most notable improvements were by Dave Smith and Mike Matteucci. Smith had a decrease of 0.29 second from the goal line to near-blue line. This occurred from March 1996 (beginning of instruction in a speed-strength program) to September 1996 (training camp). A decrease of 0.29 second would be considered excellent improvement in a 40-yard dash, but the goal line to near-blue line is only 20 yards. Matteucci lowered his time from 3.32 seconds to 2.62 seconds over the same distance over a two-year period. It is important to realize the change in speed and how this translates: 3.32 seconds for 20 yards is a velocity of 18.1 feet per second; 2.62 seconds for 20 yards is 22.9 feet per second. The difference in distance covered in one second is 4.8 feet. At 90 percent effort, Matteucci covered 20.8 feet per second. At 80 percent effort (which is a very easy speed), he moved at 19.1 feet per second. His new speed allowed him to move faster at 80 percent speed than at 100 percent two years prior and with obviously far less effort.

Speed increases in NHL hockey players can be further illustrated by Luc Robitaille's improvement in speed. Robitaille decreased his goal-line-to-near-blue-line time by 0.33 second during his 1998 off-season strength and conditioning program. By the 2000 training camp, he was fourth fastest on the team.

Speed can be improved, and every track coach and NFL strength and conditioning coach is aware of this. Some hockey coaches still believe that speed can't be improved. Speed can be improved with proper training.

If a player has trained for endurance only, then it is unreasonable to expect the player to become faster. Some individuals will be faster than others, but all players can improve their speed. This is part of the purpose of this book. As coach Kreis states, "Speed is at a premium today in sports. Everybody wants it and will pay for it."

The information about the condition of the players must then be shared with the head coach and assistant coaches. It is important that the coaches realize that this is vital information about the performance parameters of their players and is of great use to them. This information will help the coaches vary and manipulate the on-ice training loads to produce a better performance and therefore more wins. The information from the strength and conditioning coach about the fatigue state of the players should not be seen as criticism, second-guessing of the coach, or an attack. It is additional information that may not have been considered. It is as useful as having the head of a department give the chief executive officer of a corporation data that he or she needs to know about the status of the business or company.

Dry-Land Training Principles

"Today, sprint training methods are totally different from the traditional methods in that they stress the importance of high-intensity CNS-related work, and the development of explosive power throughout the entire training year."

—CHARLIE FRANCIS

The speed of today's players has certainly been a factor in the increased injury rate. Large players who are moving fast can produce a high degree of collision force. A smaller player can generate significant force if he or she has speed. Senior amateur hockey players have been measured at 30 miles per hour by high-speed cinematography. Peewee players skate at approximately 20 miles per hour. The fastest track athletes run at approximately 29 miles per hour.

While there is certainly a difference between dry-land sprinting and skating, it is advisable to incorporate sprints on land with sprints on the ice for supplementary training. The dry-land carryover effect is one of increased speed via an increased ability to recruit the hip flexors and extensors and therefore have a faster turnover (stride rate) and shorter ground contact time. The body will have an increased ability to handle the by-products of anaerobic muscle metabolism (lactate buildup). Running certainly requires much more athletic ability than riding the traditional stationary bike. Agility drills will increase the balance and coordination of the athlete's movement. Carefully planned plyometric training is well documented to increase the vertical jump, which indicates that the player has learned to recruit and coordinate the muscles of the leg and hip more effectively and is therefore quicker and more explosive. Many coaches each year state, "We need to increase the foot speed and quickness of the players." Dry-land training is one way to make these changes along with the speed-strength program. A recent published study noted a positive correlation between the vertical jump and skating speed in ice hockey. Those with the highest vertical jump demonstrated the fastest on-ice speed. Another article noted a positive correlation between the snatch pull and the vertical jump. Our research has verified the same findings. Do you see how these factors begin to work together?

A variety of drills described in Chapter 6 on plyometrics will supply a good base for off-season training. A grass field would be ideal for maximum force absorption during dry-land training drills. One hour to one and one-half hours each week of these drills is adequate to achieve the reaction time that is desired. This should be combined with runs ranging from 30 meters to 400 meters. These drills and runs should be performed on the same day as the weight-training exercises. If you perform plyometric and agility drills and sprints on your "off days" and then perform the quick lifts in the gym on the speed-strength-training days, you never give the muscle and central nervous system a chance to recover, and the glycogen stores in muscle may not replenish enough. Some strength coaches advise athletes to perform a high volume of work on light training days. Many strength coaches (including the authors of this book) disagree with the low-intensity, high-volume "light days." Renowned biomechanist and Olympic weight-lifting coach John Garhammer, Ph.D., of California State University, Long Beach, tells his students that if light training days have a very high volume, the total work of the "light days" may have the same total work as the "heavy days" (reps × weight = total tonnage lifted). If this happens, then the body doesn't get the chance to recover. So, by combining training components and allowing rest days and making "light days" actually light in intensity and volume, the athlete will recover. If you perform this off-season program (speed-strength and the conditioning aspects) four days per week, you will have three complete days of rest each week for recreational activities such as golf, swimming, and fishing.

Here is a tip for speed-strength coaches: be careful prescribing the number of runs you have the player perform. Speed work cannot be performed in high volume. As soon as high volume occurs, the velocity will decrease.

Planning a Conditioning Program

"The task faced by a coach is to comprehend the interplay between playing factors, and based on that understanding, prescribe what your athletes need—when they need it."

—CHARLIE FRANCIS

In-Season Program

In-season conditioning is primarily dominated and controlled by the specificity of playing hockey in game conditions and also by practice. Historically, riding the stationary bike was one of the first methods of supplemental training in hockey. Some form of training is usually better than none. Players improved on the stationary bike and, unfortunately, it became a pillar of hockey training. Riding a stationary bike, using a treadmill, or performing similar aerobic activities may still serve some purpose for those players with minimal ice time during a game. However, if a player has a role on a team that allows for only five to six minutes per game, the strength coach may decide that it is in this player's best interest to maximize his or her anaerobic capacity instead of making the player try to adapt to a higher aerobic level that he or she will never use. The players who play a few minutes have an opportunity to have a more comprehensive speed-strength program than those players with 25 to 32 minutes per game.

The program should have a few key components during the season. Two to three key strength-training exercises can be used each workout. These key lifts include a pull, squat, overhead lift, or bench press and Romanian dead lifts (see Chapter 4). These can be supplemented with a few drills with a medicine ball, limited plyometrics, agility drills, balance work, and/or dry-land training. The most important point is to avoid inducing fatigue in the players. Simply maintain stimulus to the CNS with the drills and exercises. The change of pace in training will still carry over to the physical needs of the player without simply having the player skate more. The player will be more ready to play on a physiological and psychological level.

Off-Season Program

The off-season program will consist of strength, agility, speed, and plyometric drills.

These will facilitate improved coordination, faster running/skating, and quicker reaction times. A combination of 10- to 20-meter, 40- to 60-meter, 100- to 120-meter, 200- to 250-meter, and 400-meter runs is advisable. These will be performed after a thorough warm-up and agility drills, medicine-ball throws, and plyometric drills. A good rule of thumb for a player is to keep the total meters in a single workout between 240 and 700 for speed work. This can be achieved in a variety of ways. For example, a week of early off-season, dry-land training may look something like this:

Sample Off-Season, Dry-Land Training Schedule

Day One

warm-up—jog 1,600 meters (four laps around a track or up and down a grass field)
stretching
jog 400 meters
agility drills
  backpedal running, four sets of 20 meters
  skating jumps, four sets of 30 meters
  carioca, four sets of 10 meters
  double-leg hops, two sets of 15 meters
medicine-ball drills (various) four sets of six reps (total)
run, four sets of 60 meters, four-minute recovery between runs
10-minute break (walk, jog, stretch, sit-ups, push-ups, rest)
run, four sets of 60 meters, four-minute recovery between runs
cooldown—walk 400 meters
stretching

Day Two

warm-up—jog 1,600 meters
stretching
jog 400 meters

(continued)

Day Two (continued)

agility drills

   jump-turn-jump, four sets at 20 seconds

   carioca run, four sets of 30 meters

   four-corner run, three sets

medicine-ball drills (various) four sets of six reps (total)

run 600 meters, three-minute recovery

run 400 meters

cooldown—walk 400 meters

stretching

Day Three

warm up—jog 800 to 1,600 meters (two to four laps around a track)

stretching

jog 400 meters

agility drills

   backpedal running, four sets of 20 meters

   skating jumps, four sets of 20 meters

   carioca, four sets of 10 meters

   single-leg hops, two sets of 10 meters

medicine-ball drills (various) four sets of six reps (total)

run, four sets of 75 meters, five-minute recovery between runs

10-minute break (walk, jog, stretch, sit-ups, push-ups, rest)

run, four sets of 75 meters, five-minute recovery between runs

cooldown—walk 400 meters

stretching

Day Four

warm-up—jog 1,600 meters

stretching

jog 400 meters

agility drills

   jump-turn-jump, four reps at 20 seconds

   carioca run, four sets of 30 meters

   four-corner run, three sets

   hopping over low hurdles or cones, four sets of 10 meters

run 800 meters, five-minute recovery

run 500 meters

cooldown—walk 400 meters

stretching

Later during the off-season, once the base is built, the speed work will become more specific and jumping drills will be included. This represents traditional speed periodization planning. Gradually over the off-season, the speed days will drop to 20-meter sprints, and the longer distance days will be 150 to 200 meters. You should always take the medicine ball to the track or grass field and have a friend, teammate, or training partner perform a few passes with you. The medicine-ball drills should not total more than approximately 30 minutes per week. Do not overdo the medicine ball or underestimate the amount of work that the body is performing with it.

I (JMH) have had young professional players for a few weeks in the summer who have never run for their hockey training. These young athletes have very poor judgment of their running speed, so they often run much too fast regardless of times that were requested or target split times being called out to them on the track. So, to reduce the risk of hamstring injuries in exuberant, novice athletes, you may need to have them perform tempo work on days two and four. Tempo work is low-intensity (slower-paced) running interspersed with walking. Tempo work serves as a method to improve recovery.

Speed Variation

Another very effective variation of speed development is used by Coach Francis, who says that the traditional periodization training doesn't allow for enough time spent on the development of speed. Francis believes that speed must be trained year-round. By following this method, enough time and volume of speed work will have occurred to improve the speed of the athlete. The athlete must develop speed first and then make the speed last longer

(build endurance). This is contradictory to the old notion of "building a base" of endurance (aerobic base) and developing speed later. Often, there isn't enough time left to develop speed in the traditional periodization, and excessive aerobic training is counterproductive to speed development. Coach Francis is writing a book about this training, so I will not try to cover all he has to say about speed development in a few pages. I (JMH) will note that I have utilized Francis's speed-development training method with athletes in a variety of sports, and it has been very successful. The athlete would have speed days beginning with short runs (30-meter runs in a very relaxed manner) in the early off-season. The distance would remain relatively short, but the volume (number of sets) would increase over weeks. The distance is also pushed out, or increased, as time passes. A speed-endurance day is used, and slightly longer distances are used. There are also easy days (tempo days) in which the athlete will run at 75 percent speed or less, the volume is high, and the rest is short. These tempo days serve as active recovery for the speed-training days.

Aerobic Conditioning

As previously noted, despite the fact that hockey is a game that appears to go without stop, time-motion analysis reveals that it is primarily an anaerobic sport. However, this does not mean that aerobic conditioning should be avoided. Nor should it be overemphasized.

The main emphasis on aerobic conditioning in hockey should be for the recovery process between shifts. Because hockey is played in 30- to 60-second shifts with an average of two to three minutes between shifts, the main energy pathways in the game center around the anaerobic systems. Better aerobic conditioning will allow for more intense anaerobic training. The game of hockey is played under sprint conditions or an interval-type sprint performance.

Sthair states that both aerobic and anaerobic conditioning are important because forwards and defensemen will skate between two and four miles in a game. (Note: international rinks are larger than NHL rinks at this time.) However, this distance is covered in explosive breaks at high speed using anaerobic pathways.

Verkoshansky has noted that in ice hockey and European football, a problem exists in annual training cycles that begin with intensive training. The cardiovascular system has frequently not been prepared for this intense work. Hockey players could begin with mild levels of work (400- to 800-meter runs) in June or early July. I (EJK) have found repeated speed training to yield speed endurance. The 800-meter and 400-meter runs during off-season training will also help develop aerobic conditioning.

Elite male sprinters will run 400 meters in 44 seconds or less, and elite female sprinters will run the same distance in 51 seconds or less. However, this is continuous running. Sixty seconds would be an excellent time for a hockey player in the 400-meter run. A hockey shift is 45 to 70 seconds but has an average of 33 seconds of skating and the rest is nonskating time. The 200-meter run more closely resembles the 33-second time of skating. If the training program has runs and sprints including 600 meters, 400 meters, 300 meters, 200 meters, 150 meters, 100 meters, 60 meters, 40 meters, and 10 meters, then all facets of the aerobic and anaerobic conditioning will be met. Of course, these are not all included in one workout. In addition, don't forget the significant contribution that the speed-strength program, agility drills, and plyometric drills will make to speed and speed endurance.

One has to be careful with the use of longer, aerobic-based runs so that they don't take too much from the speed work. The aerobic training can be what is referred to as "tempo days" in track, in which the runs are light (i.e., 75 percent speed or less), and these days are used to enhance recovery. This way, the aerobic work is easily woven into the program. Alternating the tempo days and speed days is the construct of Coach Francis.

I (JMH) have come across several hockey players who have been advised, or coached in off-season training, to perform 20 to 24, 400-meter runs at approximately 70-second pace, with one- to two-minute rests between runs. This is a total distance of 8,000 to 9,600 meters for one workout. This method is severe overtraining. Track athletes who compete in the 400-meter sprint do not train like this. The logic that was given for this method of training is a hockey shift lasts about one minute and there may be seven shifts per period; because a 400-meter run is about one minute, the player should run 20 to 24 400-meter distances. Please recall that a shift may last 45 to 70 seconds but contains only about 33 seconds of skating, not 60 to 70 seconds. Also, if you continually train at 70 seconds per 400-meter speed, you will not improve your speed. When will you ever reach 55 seconds or 52 seconds for the same work? If the nerves and the muscles have never had to fire at 52 seconds, then you have never achieved this speed, and it will not be there for you. You will be a 70-second runner. Also, noted strength authorities, such as Bompa, and track coaches have indicated that too much aerobic training will take away from speed and explosive performance. This is the last effect we want for a hockey player. Who cares how long a hockey player can skate slowly around the rink?

If hockey players have knee, hip, or back injuries that prevent them from running, then there are other methods. Deep-water running with a flotation belt is a good alternative for aerobic work. Some types of elliptical running machines can have a similar movement to running, but without the impact forces. And of course, the stationary bike can be used.

Flexibility

Like athletes in most sports, hockey players tend to use certain muscles over and over again. This can cause certain muscles to become overused and injured and can cause other muscles to tighten. It is important to address these muscles during the stretching portion of your training, which should follow a general warm-up. The general warm-up elevates your body temperature, and this makes the muscles, tendons, joint capsules, and other connective tissue more pliable and ready to be stretched. Stretching cold muscles is a bad idea. A rule of thumb is that if you begin to perspire, then you are warm. The brain has recognized the increase in the core temperature and is beginning to cool the body. Muscles that need to be stretched include the hip flexors, hip adductors (groin muscles of the inner thigh), hamstrings, low back, and shoulders.

It is difficult to stretch the hip flexors without placing too much stress on the low back. A simple hip flexor stretch is one in which the player is standing in a position similar to a lunge exercise. The leg that is placed behind you allows the hip flexors on the same leg to be stretched. This knee should be kept fairly straight. It is important to keep the abdominal muscles tight during this stretch. This keeps the pelvis from tilting forward during the stretch, which would cause you to lose the stretch. Another stretch is similar. You can kneel on one knee and have the other foot flat on the ground in front of you. Keep the abdominal muscles tight, keep your upper body upright, and shift your body forward so that the hip flexors in the front of your thigh and hip are stretched on the leg on which you're kneeling. Again, leaning backward does not help the back, nor does relaxing the abdominal muscles.

All athletes have performed a stretch for the hamstring muscles. However, a slight modification from what has traditionally been done should be used when stretching the hamstrings. We were usually told to touch our toes or bring our head toward our knees. This does stretch the hamstring, but it also stretches the back. If the athlete rounds his or her back too much, then the hamstring muscles are understretched and the back muscles are overstretched. Dance instructors correctly advise their students to bring their stomach toward their thighs. This keeps the back flat and allows the hamstring to be stretched. So, keep the back flat, keep the chest out, and bend forward from the hip only. As soon as you feel the tightness in the hamstring muscle, hold that position for at least 15 seconds and up to 60 seconds as you progress over weeks.

The sacrum (central portion of the pelvis where the spine joins the pelvis) moves five to six millimeters when a person bends forward and straightens. This forward bending in hockey is a common position and may place stress on the joint between the sacrum and the remainder of the pelvis (sacroiliac joint or SI joint). The SI joint is a common place of pain in hockey players. If the athlete stretches the adductor muscles, hamstring muscles, and hip flexors, then the SI joint will be allowed to move better as well. The adductor (groin) muscles can be stretched by the standard adductor stretch in the standing position, while performing a side lunge–type movement so that the knee bends on the side you are leaning toward and the other knee stays fairly straight. This will help stretch the adductor muscles. Also, the old standby of sitting on the floor with the bottoms of your feet against each other and letting the knees move toward the floor will stretch the adductor muscles.

An added bonus to all of this is if you stretch the hamstring muscles, adductor muscles, and hip flexor muscles, you will strengthen the back muscles and have less low-back pain.

Skating

Analysis of Skating Forces

The use of force-plate analysis (method of measuring the amount of force someone applies to the ground during a running, walking, or skating stride) of skating strides has demonstrated that during the push-off phase of skating, the vertical reaction force measures one and one-half to two and one-half times the player's body weight. The posterior push force measures 150 pounds but is dependent on the player's skating style. The lateral force is approximately 80 pounds, and the vertical twisting movement between the skate and the ice surface is 40 to 80 inch-pounds. Daly and his colleagues say this may be the reason that groin injuries are so common in hockey. You can certainly see from these force measurements why the need for proper strength training exists for ice hockey.

Starts and Stops

One area where performance can be improved is skating. Without question, technique and motor skills are developed over time, particularly in one's youth. However,

certain elements of skating can be enhanced by increased strength. This is most evident in the aspect of starting and stopping, which is a critical part of hockey.

Unfortunately, skating techniques in ice hockey have not been extensively studied. However, there has been a study (Naud) comparing the effectiveness of three different stop, reverse, start (SRS) techniques. They were divided into the following categories:

1. "feet in line, crossover"—The subject skated from the finish line to the starting line; stopped (18-inch stopping area) with both feet heel to toe and parallel to the starting line; then reversed direction; made use of one or two crossover steps; and skated forward as quickly as possible to the finish line.

2. "feet parallel, crossover"—The subject skated from the finish line to the starting line, stopped with both feet side by side approximately 12 to 18 inches apart and parallel to the starting line, reversed direction by using one to two crossover steps, and skated forward as quickly as possible to the finish line.

3. "feet parallel, thrust and glide"—The subject skated from the finish line to the starting line, stopped with feet together approximately 12 inches to 18 inches apart and skate blades parallel to starting line, and reversed direction by making use of the "thrust and glide," which is the process of stopping with the back leg and immediately thrusting laterally with the same leg while the front leg is rotated outward and gliding forward. After executing this reversal of direction, the subject skated forward as quickly as possible to the finish line.

This study used professional, junior "B," college varsity, and bantam hockey players. They were all trained in these techniques twice per week for eight weeks. Each player in the study performed each of the three methods 10 times during the test. The conclusion was that method 3, "feet parallel, thrust and glide," was the most effective stop, reverse, start technique. Methods 1 and 2 tended to drift or glide sideways during the stop.

Method 3 requires strength in the quadriceps, hamstrings, adductor, and gluteal muscles to stop the momentum and reverse the direction. If this method is in fact the most effective SRS technique, then the hockey player must have adequate power-generating capability to execute it properly.

Powerskating

Hockey players are frequently believed to have ineffective strides on the ice. This has led to the use of "powerskating" instruction. Powerskating provides general improvement in skating technique and ability. A number of players have sought out skating coaches like Laura Stamm, and they have reported good results.

Clinically, those who work on their strides at a younger age tend to benefit the most. There is a population of hockey players who may require special consideration when it comes to powerskating. Those who are 30 years of age and older and have always played and skated in a certain way have become set in their motor patterns. These players have performed hundreds of thousands of strides on the ice, and they have specifically adapted to the range of their stride length. When their stride length is suddenly and consciously lengthened, there may be a risk of hamstring, groin, and hip rotator injury. This can also be seen in long-distance runners (who have a high volume of a given stride) who suddenly add speed work with a longer stride length to their training. The hamstring tears in these groups usually occur high in the hamstring at the origin of the muscle at the ischial tuberos-

ity (bone where the hamstrings attach). Caution must be used in these veteran athletes.

Supplemental Skating Training

In the past, some hockey players developed their leg strength by pushing various types of ice-cleaning equipment around the arena. This is comparable to football players' pushing cars not only to develop their leg and hip power but to learn to keep their feet moving against resistance. A resistance machine for powerskating was developed in the mid-1970s (Hermiston). This resistance machine was utilized in research at that time. It would be interesting to know how many coaches ever heard of this equipment or this study. Three groups of 15-year-old hockey players were used for the research. All subjects were timed in a sprint from the goal line to their own blue line before the training program. The first group served as a control and did not have resistance training or start-and-stop-skating training. The second group did not have resistance training but performed 25 starts and stops lasting a total of two to three minutes during each practice. The third group used the powerskating resistance machine and did not perform any start-and-stop training. This experiment was conducted three times per week for eight weeks. The results revealed that the third group (which had resistance training only) was significantly faster than the other two groups, and the second group (which had start-and-stop training) was no faster than the control group. Another aspect of this study is the use of 15-year-old subjects. Most 15-year-old athletes will respond to any training load. Even though this study is 20 years old, it warrants further testing and investigation.

This study shows the results of resistance training and the positive effect that was pro-

Coaches John Van Boxmeer and Brian McCutcheon behind the Long Beach bench

duced. Hockey performance can and will improve dramatically in the next five years with increased resistance training.

Overspeed Training

Overspeed training usually involves running on a slight downhill grade or making use of assistance equipment to increase the velocity of the athlete. I (JMH) have used tubing for overspeed training on the ice with the Ice Dogs players late in the season in an effort to increase their speed prior to the playoffs. The tubing consists of a harness that the player wears. This harness is attached to a thick bungee cord. Another person takes the cord

to a specific tension (determined by the distance it is stretched). The player maintains his or her position until the tension is set. The player then sprints toward the near-blue line while the tubing is pulling him or her faster than he or she could normally skate.

For example, our assistant strength coach, Dave Good, would go on the ice with a player. The player would go to the goal line, and Dave would vary the stretch from the faceoff circle to the far-blue line or a little farther (the length of the stretch each time is critical). The player would then sprint from the goal line to the near-blue line. Track coach Chuck Debus adds: "The player should try to outskate the pull force and not go along for the ride by being pulled." Also, the player should not try to stop suddenly as this can cause muscular soreness. The manufacturer of the harness and bungee cord recommends that goggles be worn. Both the player and the coach or trainer would wear goggles during this drill. The cord should also be inspected regularly for defects. If the cord has been slightly cut by a skate, it should be replaced so that it doesn't break at full tension.

The players must have built a base from their training—clean pulls, snatch pulls, hypers, glute-ham-gastroc raises, and squats—during the season before they could participate in overspeed training. If they missed any significant time from their strength program during the season, then I (JMH) would not have them perform this drill. The tubing will make the athlete contract the hamstring faster than it has ever contracted. Only a well-prepared athlete should perform this drill. The volume should be low (a few sprints per session) for this drill, and it should not be performed if the players are exhausted. The recovery period between overspeed sprints should be seven minutes or more. Overuse of the tubing could easily lead to injury of the hamstrings, adductors, or hip flexors.

Some track coaches do not like overspeed work because it can cause the athlete to over-stride and have braking action. I readily see the track coaches' point in regards to over-striding and braking on the track or grass, but I (JMH) have had good results of overspeed training on the ice. Skating has longer ground contact time and also has a glide effect of the skate blade on the ice. The glide effect keeps the body moving forward.

Parachutes

I (JMH) usually do not use parachutes in training because the chute slows the athlete during its use. The chute may have a place in rehabilitation, however. The theory is that added resistance during a specific speed movement will make for a faster athlete. This theory is not always valid. I (JMH) try to use exercises that will teach the CNS to fire faster. This concept is one that I (JMH) have learned from elite track coaches over the years. Overspeed training with tubing accomplishes this. Much research reveals that if resistance is used during speed training, athletes change their mechanics so that they become more efficient with the resistance. But as soon as the resistance is removed, their mechanics do not change and there is no improvement in speed. Remember, too much of anything is not good, so don't overdo the overspeed training. If you do, you will have nothing but injuries to show for it.

9

DEHYDRATION AND REHYDRATION

G. Douglas Andersen, D.C., D.A.C.B.S.P., C.C.N.

"The Long Beach players were quite receptive to the hydration protocols set forth in this program. As the hydration study unfolded, their eyes opened to a part of the game they had long ignored. Once convinced of the benefits of rehydration, they were extremely conscientious about monitoring their loss and intake of fluids. The incidence of cramping due to dehydration was almost nil and the weight lost during a game or practice was usually regained in two days or less. Again, the players believed we had an advantage over our opponent."

—RICK BURRILL, A.T.C.; ASSISTANT ATHLETIC TRAINER, LOS ANGELES KINGS; FORMER HEAD ATHLETIC TRAINER, LONG BEACH ICE DOGS

One of the most overlooked aspects of a hockey player's conditioning is hydration. Even though competition is in a cool environment, because of the intensity of the game and the amount of equipment worn, hockey players can lose a great deal of fluid. Virtually all experts on sports nutrition and exercise performance agree on how important adequate hydration is for an athlete. Contrast this to disagreements on virtually every other aspect of sports nutrition (amino acids, vitamins, minerals, herbs, proteins, carbohydrates, and fat), and one quickly realizes how important hydration is.

Water and the Body

Muscles are 80 percent water. Blood is more than 90 percent water. If you do not have enough water, your performance will suffer. Water is the main transport medium to deliver nutrients into your cells and to remove cellular waste products. Water is essential for biological and chemical reactions in all types of athletes participating in all types of sports. It is mandatory for proper joint lubrication as well as waste removal. It is also the body's most important nutrient for homeostatic temperature control. A properly hydrated athlete will be able to play longer and with greater intensity than a dehydrated one. The risks of injury from repetitive microtrauma are reduced in the athlete who has ample fluid to lubricate his or her joints. The risks of injury or illness are also reduced in the athlete who has adequate fluid to prevent the body from overheating.

In a hot environment, athletes in intense competition can lose more than two liters of fluid per hour. Even in moderate conditions, it is not uncommon for sweat losses to be greater than one liter (33 ounces) per hour. Conversely, most people can comfortably consume only 9 to 15 ounces per hour and may exceed 50 ounces per hour during vigorous practices or games. I (GDA) have personally observed NHL players who have lost eight to ten pounds during the course of a game or practice. At one pint per pound, this is 160 ounces of fluid over a three-hour period.

To complicate matters, athletes in competition do not get thirsty until they have already lost 2 percent of their bodily fluids. At this level of dehydration, performance will noticeably suffer. A 4 percent loss of fluid, which is only 6 pounds for a 150-pound athlete, will result in a 30 percent decrease in physical work capacity! In a game like hockey, the loss of one step or a reaction time that is a second or two slower can make the difference between winning and losing.

Fluid Loss

Adequate hydration will prevent the three major problems a fluid shortage can create: dehydration, overheating, and mineral (electrolyte) imbalances.

1. **Dehydration.** Numerous studies have shown that when an athlete is even mildly dehydrated, performance will suffer. A hockey player will have less strength, less stamina, a longer reaction time, and a loss of quickness. Due to fluid loss, a dehydrated athlete's blood is thicker. Thicker blood requires the heart to pump harder and faster thus putting a greater strain on the heart. This in turn reduces the length of time it takes for the athlete to reach an exhausted state. To make matters worse, once an athlete is dehydrated it will take longer to rehydrate because in the body's effort to conserve fluids, dehydration slows down the rate that the stomach empties fluid into the intestine.

2. **Overheating.** The body's normal temperature is 98.6 degrees plus or minus a few 10ths of a degree. Hard exercise like hockey increases heat production in the muscles, which in turn increases internal body temperature. As internal heat increases, the blood is used to transport this heat to the skin, where it is then released into the air as sweat is evaporated. The loss of fluid from sweating reduces the volume of blood, which in turn means there is less blood available to deliver oxygen and other nutrients to the muscle. This results in muscular fatigue. As fluid losses during exercise continue, the rate of overheating accelerates. Energy normally utilized by the muscles must instead fuel the cooling process. With less available energy, muscle strength, power, and endurance are reduced.

3. **Electrolyte imbalances.** Electrolytes are minerals. They include sodium, potassium, chloride, magnesium, and calcium. All these minerals are in sweat, and exercising athletes will lose these minerals and others such as chromium and zinc when they are performing rigorous activity. Experts agree that adequate amounts of minerals are critical for optimum athletic performance. The most important electrolytes for athletic performance based on the amount lost in sweat are sodium and chloride. Low sodium levels can

cause cramping and weakness and lead to excessive sweat loss; excessive sweating in turn results in dehydration.

Sport Drinks

Sport drinks are big business. They were invented in Florida in the late 1960s. Since then, scores of companies are marketing sport drinks for athletes to give them "an edge." Sport drinks have three primary goals. The first is to hydrate and rehydrate. The second is to provide simple carbohydrates for quick energy. The third is to replace electrolytes lost in sweat.

The main ingredient in sport drinks is water. They also contain carbohydrates, which may be referred to as sugars, and minerals that are sometimes called electrolytes. The carbohydrate sources in sport drinks include glucose, sucrose, fructose, glucose polymers, or maltodextrin. There is general agreement among experts that the amount of carbohydrates in a sport drink should be in the 5 to 8 percent range. (Some experts have even narrowed this down to between 6 and 7 percent.) This works out to approximately 13 to 18 grams of carbohydrates per eight ounces, or 50 to 75 calories per eight ounces. Fluids with more than 75 calories in an eight-ounce serving are OK to drink after an event, or two or more hours before an event, but not during an event. This is because a higher percentage of carbohydrates will slow the absorption of water from your stomach and intestines into your bloodstream and muscles. When fluid stays in your stomach too long during exercise, this can cause gas, burping, and an upset stomach. Sport drinks in the recommended carbohydrate ranges leave the stomach almost as quickly as water leaves the stomach. When they reach the intestine, the carbohydrates and electrolytes in the sport drink actually stimulate intestinal fluid absorption.

Types of Carbohydrates in Sport Drinks

There is no consensus as to the best types of carbohydrates a sport drink should include. Although the type of carbohydrates is debatable, the inclusion of multiple carbohydrates as opposed to a single type is preferred by most experts. Using at least two different carbohydrate sources will activate different uptake and transport mechanisms, which lead to faster absorption. For example, a sport drink that contained a mixture of glucose and sucrose would be superior to a sport drink that contained just glucose or sucrose alone, even though the amount of calories and carbohydrates are the same. When used during competition, there appears to be little difference among glucose, sucrose, glucose polymers, and maltodextrin. However, when fructose is the only sugar or carbohydrate used in a sport drink, problems can arise. Research has shown that because the absorption of fructose is slower than other sugars, some individuals are prone to gastrointestinal (GI) upset if they have only fructose. If a sport drink does have fructose, make sure that another carb source (glucose, sucrose, maltodextrin, glucose polymer) is listed ahead of fructose on the label. When fructose is not the main sugar in a sport drink, GI problems generally do not occur.

Types of Minerals in Sport Drinks

The types and amounts of minerals in sport drinks is another area of controversy. We do know that in their sweat, athletes lose sodium, chloride, potassium, magnesium, chromium, and zinc. The amounts of these minerals lost can be quite small with the exception of sodium in some athletes. Therefore, the most important electrolyte that a sport drink should contain is sodium. Sport drinks that advertise they are salt free are not recommended for athletes in competition. There is no consensus on the correct amount of minerals, the number of minerals, and the ratios of minerals needed in a sport drink. Research in this area is ongoing. The American College of Sports Medicine does recommend that in events lasting longer than one hour, sport drinks should contain 125 to 175 milligrams of sodium per eight-ounce serving. This exceeds the amounts of sodium in most commercial sport drinks.

Heat Illness

As previously mentioned, fluid loss, also known as dehydration, can negatively affect performance by shortening the time it takes to fatigue. As dehydration, overheating, and electrolyte losses progress, the result is heat illness.

Risk Factors for Heat Illness
- inadequate fluid intake prior to and during exercise
- high rate of sweating (varies greatly among individuals)
- high temperature (greater than 80 degrees)
- high humidity (greater than 70 percent)
- a combination of high temperature and high humidity (when the temperature in degrees and the humidity in percent add up to 140 or greater)
- long exercise (the longer the workout, the greater the risk)

- intense exercise (intense sports like hockey)
- out-of-shape athletes (should start physical conditioning before training camp)
- underconditioned athletes (have returned from injury or illness with inadequate reconditioning)
- overweight athletes (will run hotter when they exercise and thus will lose more fluids)
- heat-trapping clothing (a definite risk factor in hockey due to the amount of protective equipment that hockey players require)

Symptoms of Heat-Related Illness
- thirst
- lack of urine
- small amounts of urine
- dark-colored urine
- dizziness
- feeling chills and goose bumps when your teammates are comfortable
- cramping, especially in the legs, calves, and stomach
- low blood pressure
- fatigue
- headache

Management of Heat Illness

Athletes should be removed from competition and instructed to drink water or, if available, sport drinks until their symptoms subside and they are able to urinate a large amount of clear-colored urine. Before allowing the athlete to return to competition, make sure he or she is medically cleared.

Symptoms of Very Serious Heat-Related Illness
- very hot and dry skin
- cessation of sweating

- high blood pressure
- rapid pulse and respiration
- confusion
- high temperature
- weakness

Management of Serious Heat-Related Illness

If an athlete has the previously listed signs and symptoms, it is a medical emergency. The athlete should be immediately removed from competition, and paramedics should be called. Make sure the athlete is out of the sun (which is not an issue for hockey players in game and practice situations), and encourage him or her to drink as much fluid as possible. Cool the athlete with cold moist towels on the legs, arms, and trunk. Put an ice pack on the back of the neck and under the arms while you wait for emergency medical personnel. Reassure and continue to cool the athlete, even if he or she complains of chilling, as long as the body temperature is high.

Prevention of Heat Illness

The best way to prevent heat-related illness is to drink enough fluid. This includes fluid preloading prior to the game or practice and drinking as much as you comfortably can during competition. Other ways to help prevent heat-related illness include eating a diet high in complex carbohydrates the day before the game and at the pregame meal. Each gram of stored carbohydrate (glycogen) requires the body to retain almost three grams of water. Thus, by "carbing up," you will not only have more energy reserves, you will also have more fluid available.

Alcohol and caffeine can contribute to dehydration. Because they weaken the body's fluid-retaining hormone, urine volume can increase. This means you retain less fluid than you would with a nonalcoholic, noncaffeinated beverage. Drinking a beer the night before a game and a cup of coffee or some ice tea on game day should not affect most healthy, well-trained, well-rested, fully hydrated individuals. However, sensitivity to alcohol and caffeine does vary. Practice is the best time to rehearse proper drinking techniques and to experiment with other beverages to find individual levels of tolerance.

If possible, choose loose-fitting clothing that breathes, thus allowing heat to escape.

Drinking Guidelines

There are wide physiological differences in the amounts of fluids that athletes require. Sweat rates vary considerably and are affected by the physical condition of the athlete, acclimatization of the athlete, weather conditions, and the athlete's pre-event fluid levels. Carbohydrate intake prior to competition tops off glycogen reserves and stimulates fluid retention. Athletes should practice hydration during training. This will improve their ability to hydrate during competition.

The hydration guidelines on page 186 will keep the athlete hydrated before, during, and after competition.

For a morning competition, follow the "day before competition" protocol. On the day of the competition, drink 20 ounces of a carbo-load beverage as soon as you wake. Drink a sport drink (one ounce per 10 pounds of body weight) 60 minutes before competing.

A sport drink should contain no more than 75 calories per eight-ounce serving. A carbo-load beverage should contain no fewer than 150 calories per eight-ounce serving. You can make your own carbohydrate-loading bever-

Guidelines for Hydration

Day Before Competition	one-fourth ounce of water per pound of body weight[1] over and above normal intake divided evenly throughout the day (multiply your body weight by .25)
Four Hours Before Competition (optional)	if dehydration is a problem, one ounce of sport drink[2] per 10 pounds of body weight[3] (divide your body weight by 10)
Three Hours Before Competition	one ounce of sport drink[2] or water per 10 pounds of body weight[3]
Two Hours Before Competition	one ounce of sport drink[2] or water per 10 pounds of body weight[3]
One Hour Before Competition	one ounce of water per 10 pounds of body weight[3]
During Competition	sport drink—consume as much as comfortably possible
Recovery	beverage: water or sport drink (sport drink if competing within 24 hours) amount: 16 ounces per pound of body weight lost (or 24 ounces per pound of body weight lost if competing within 24 hours)

[1] Example: 160 pounds × .25 = 40 ounces extra above your normal consumption
[2] Use a sport drink if:
  • it is the second game in two days
  • it is the third game in four days
  • you feel flat or fatigued
  • you are sick or have been sick in the previous 72 hours with a cold or flu
  • you have cramped within 72 hours
  • you have missed time due to injury and are deconditioned
[3] Example: 160 pounds ÷ 10 = 16 ounces

age from powdered sport drink mixes by making them stronger.

Remember that when athletes prehydrate, approximately 50 percent of the fluid they consume will be lost in the urine. For example, in the hours before a game, if an athlete has consumed 60 ounces, 30 ounces will be lost in urine leaving the athlete with a net gain of 30 ounces. Although it does not seem like much, having 30 ounces more fluid in your body than your opponent has will give you both a physiological and psychological advan-

tage. Between periods, drink as much as you comfortably can. Shoot for between 10 and 20 ounces depending on how much you played and how much you weigh. (The more you play and the more you weigh, the greater your fluid needs.)

Pre-Event Drinking

In the guidelines for hydration, notice that sport drinks are not recommended in the hour before competition, yet they are recommended two hours prior to, during, and following competition. These are the reasons:

1. Prior to competition the carbohydrates in sport drinks can top off your stored-sugar (glycogen) level in your muscles, essentially filling your tank before battle.

2. In the hour before competition, water is recommended because when carbohydrates are ingested, insulin is released. Insulin is a hormone that shuttles glucose (which is broken down from carbohydrate) from the blood to the muscle. When we exercise, two things happen that affect insulin: (1) The action of the rapidly contracting and relaxing muscles makes membranes more permeable to glucose; thus, much less insulin is needed for uptake and absorption. (2) The hormones epinephrine and norepinephrine are released at the beginning of exercise; one of their many functions is to reduce the amount of insulin secreted.

3. "Hypoglycemia" is the term for low blood sugar. Low blood sugar can cause fatigue. Ingesting simple carbohydrates in the form of sport drinks will raise insulin levels. If exercise is initiated and insulin levels are high, the combination of elevated insulin and increased membrane permeability can lead to hypoglycemia in some individuals, which in turn will cause early exhaustion. Therefore, in the hour prior to practice or a game, drink water so you will not have high insulin at the onset of activity.

4. During exercise, rebound hypoglycemia from sport drinks is not an issue because insulin levels are lowered by hormonal action as previously explained. Following exercise, insulin is also not an issue because the low stored-sugar (glycogen) levels in your muscles need to be replenished. After exercise, certain enzymes are temporarily elevated, and if you consume simple carbohydrates like the ones in sport drinks, your muscles will recover the glycogen used during exercise faster.

Drinking During Exercise

There is ample evidence that consuming sport drinks during activities leads to improved exercise capacity, increased length of time to exhaustion, and improved performance. For years this has been true in endurance sports, and recent research is pointing to the fact that sports that are high intensity and intermittent in nature, such as hockey, also benefit from the use of sport drinks versus water. Not only do sport drinks provide carbohydrates for energy and replace electrolytes, they taste good. And the fact is that to prevent fluid losses and heat-related illness, athletes must drink *before* they are thirsty. Many studies have shown that people will consume greater amounts of flavored beverages than water, especially when they are not thirsty. If people wait to drink until they are thirsty, they are already dehydrated. The bottom line: if it tastes good you will drink more, and the more fluid you drink, the better your performance will be and the lower the risk of illness you will have.

Drinking Following Exercise

To maximize recovery, drink 16 to 24 ounces of fluid per pound lost. Sport drinks are preferred for three reasons:

1. They provide simple carbohydrates to replace muscle losses.
2. They provide sodium to help fluid retention and rehydration.

3. Their ingredients improve taste and stimulate the drive to drink.

Hydration Review

Drinking

- Drink throughout the day.
- Drink one ounce for each 10 pounds of body weight per hour starting three hours before practice.
- Drink as much as you comfortably can during practice.
- Drink *before* you are thirsty.
- Drink 16 to 24 ounces of fluid per pound of body weight lost after practice.

Dos and Don'ts

- Do weigh yourself before and after each practice.
- Do observe the color of your urine (dark urine means you need to drink more).
- Do watch the volume of your urine (small amounts indicate you need to drink more).
- Do tell your coach or trainer if you are on *any* kind of medications.
- Don't consume beverages containing alcohol and caffeine (they reduce the power of your water-holding hormone).
- Don't come to camp or preseason workouts out of shape.
- Don't practice or play if you are sick or injured (unless you are medically cleared).

Warning Signs of Heat Illness

- headache
- nausea
- weakness
- excessive thirst
- dizziness
- fever
- cramps
- poor performance or fatigue
- feeling chills in hot weather
- feeling hot without sweating
- dark-colored urine
- decreased urine output

Be Smart

Every year young athletes decide to be "tough" instead of smart, and every year unnecessary tragedies occur. Heat illness can progress from simple headaches and weakness to catastrophe within minutes! If you do not feel well, be smart—*tell your coach and trainer*. It could save your life!

Dr. Andersen's Home Sport Drink Recipe

Ingredients

30 ounces of water
10 ounces of 100 percent fruit juice
3 level tablespoons of sugar
¼ rounded teaspoon of salt

Shake or blend all ingredients together until sugar and salt are not visible on the bottom.

Approximate Nutritional Values of Individual Ingredients

- Ten ounces of juice provide approximately 36 to 41 grams of carbohydrate, equaling approximately 145 to 165 calories, depending on the type of juice used.
- Three level tablespoons of sugar provide 36 grams of carbohydrates, approximately 139 calories. (Sucrose is 3.85 calories per gram.)
- One-quarter rounded teaspoon of salt provides approximately 600 to 700 milligrams of sodium.

Approximate Nutritional Value of Homemade Sport Drink

- Recipe makes five eight-ounce servings.
- Each serving has approximately 6 percent carbohydrate solution.
- Two sources of carbohydrates (juice and sugar) provide around 14 to 15 grams.
- Each serving contains approximately 120 to 140 milligrams of sodium.
- Potassium will vary depending on the type of fruit juice used.

Our Hockey and Fluid Studies

Two dehydration/rehydration studies were performed with the Long Beach Ice Dogs during the 1996–97 season. The first study had the players drink fluids on their own accord (no formal instruction), and they were given performance scores for each game during the study. The results were most interesting. The top-five-rated players lost approximately three pounds of fluid per game. The bottom-five-rated players lost close to four pounds per game. When left on their own, players took longer to regain their body weight; in fact, five players took between five and seven days to regain their body weight, and three players did not regain their body weight over the nine-day period of the study. Of the five players who took a week to regain their fluid, one was ranked in the top five, but the other four were in the bottom five. For example, one player went from 180 to 171 pounds during the first game. At the beginning of the second game his weight was 175. Thus, he started the second game with five fewer pounds than the first game, which is a 2.7 percent loss. Remember that studies have shown that a 3 percent loss can cause a 20 to 30 percent decrease in performance. Needless to say, this top five player was in the bottom five in a performance ranking during this study, but he was by no means a bottom five player. I (GDA) was asked to consult for the next study, which was performed with players given the hydration protocol previously mentioned. When the team followed the pregame, postgame, and during-game instructions, players lost one pound less per game on average (23 percent less). All the players gained their body weight back within two days, except one player who required three days. Performance ratings were higher in the next study when the players were fully hydrated. Most important, players reported that they felt better when they followed the drinking guidelines.

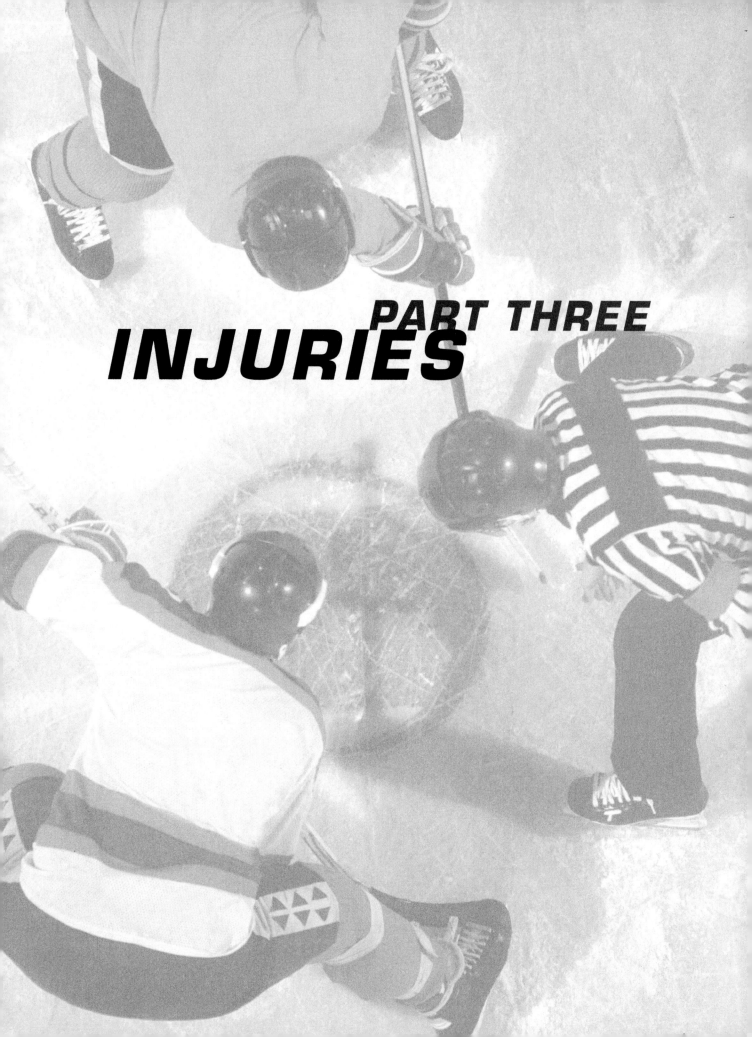

PART THREE
INJURIES

10

INJURY PATTERNS

Studies of Injury Patterns

It is important to have a very brief overview of the overall injury rate and understand what can be done about these injuries—this is the reason for this book. The following pages highlight various studies of hockey injuries from several countries, leagues, and ages that were published over a number of years.

A third-division Swedish amateur ice hockey team was evaluated to determine if injuries could be prevented. Twenty-three players had 68 injuries, 62 of which were minor. Data throughout the season revealed that quadriceps and hamstring muscles were found to decrease in strength, and oxygen uptake did not change during the season.

Another study found that 76 percent of injuries occurred in games; 73 percent of injuries were from legal checking!

In a study published in the article "Ice Hockey Injuries: Incidence, Nature, and Causes," Tegner and Lorentzon found that most injuries were minor, but 8.8 percent were major (causing the player to miss more than 30 days, including one case of quadri-

plegia from a fracture-dislocation of the cervical spine). Of the injuries, 74 percent occurred during a game, and 26 percent occurred in practice.

A Danish study found that the injury incidence rate per 1,000 hours was 1.5 in training and 38.0 in games. Fifty percent of the injuries occurred to the head and lower extremities. Knee and elbow injuries required the longest time to resolve (knee—mean of 31 days; elbow—mean of 33 days). The pathology of injuries included: contusions, 46 percent; sprains, 26 percent; fractures, 14 percent; and strains, 14 percent.

An older Czechoslovakian study of hockey injuries found that the accident rate was 29.6 per 1,000 ice hockey players. The main causes of injury were found to be from personal physical contact (82.1 percent). Sixty-four percent of the injuries were located in the upper half of the body; 36.7 percent were on the head.

Further delineation of injuries by Park and Castaldi found that professional hockey players have an injury rate that is twice that of players on the junior "B" team. Forwards sustained 67.5 percent of the injuries, and defensemen had 30 percent. Goalies had the remaining 2.5 percent of the injuries. The body check was the major cause of injury. The check from opponents accounted for 48 percent of the injuries. The puck caused 17 percent of the injuries; the stick caused 12 percent, with 8 percent intentional and 4 percent unintentional; falling caused 7 percent; and skating caused 6 percent. (The last 10 percent were from other causes.) The thigh pad usually became displaced during contact. The majority of the strains were to the groin; the groin injury can be a frustrating, disabling injury. Specific conditioning methods allowed continued competition for athletes burdened with acute and chronic problems.

Injury Prevention

Numerous coaches, athletic trainers, and strength coaches have noted the empirical evidence of decreased injuries associated with the initiation of a strength program that is supervised by a strength and conditioning coach. For example, one college team noted that from 1971 to 1976, their injuries and recovery time grew by 60 percent. Since adding a full-time strength coach in 1978, that number decreased by 20 percent. In 1973 the team had 12 surgical knee cases; since 1978 they average two per year (Wathen). Another college team noted similar statistics: prior to having a strength coach, the team had 11 serious knee injuries, and since they added a strength coach they also average two per year. Remember, the muscles around the knee give it dynamic stability while the ligaments prevent excessive motion. The stronger the muscles surrounding the knee, the more stable the knee.

As mentioned previously, the Ice Dogs had a substantial decrease in injuries once their strength-training program was initiated. Among NHL and AHL (and now-defunct IHL) players, we see a marked decrease in groin injuries once the power squat was introduced. Preventable injuries in the man–games lost column have reduced significantly. The abdominal strengthening program also greatly reduced the incidence of abdominal tears.

Overtraining has been found to be a significant contributor to injury, particularly of the musculotendinous junction. If a layoff from strength training has occurred, then one must allow for the physiologic adaptation of the muscle and tendon to return. The neurologic recruitment of the muscle fibers may occur quickly, but the musculotendinous structures may not be ready. This can be seen in hockey when a player who is performing poorly is "bagged" (told to skate in high volume at high speed). "Bagging" a player can also occur after he or she returns after an injury and is deconditioned. The thought behind "bagging" the player is to get him or her into shape again quickly because he or she is "out of shape." We cannot expect a deconditioned player to perform the workload of a well-conditioned player. The result is usually groin injuries and sometimes even injury to the abdominal muscles. If a player is performing poorly, please make sure the player is not overtrained, dehydrated, ill, or injured and not reporting the injury to anyone. If a player is just returning after a layoff of a few weeks, give the player a chance to increase the training volume and intensity. Also, be careful on the third day after the athlete returns to play. This is the point that fatigue and delayed-onset muscle soreness can cause the player to perform even worse.

It is important to realize the dollar value that is associated with injury prevention. The players have contracts in which they are paid regardless of time and games missed due to injuries. The healthier players are, the more game time they will have and the more they will produce. If players are healthy and accumulate higher season totals, their position at the time of contract negotiation will be stronger.

Some coaches have tried to make rehabilitation so difficult and miserable that the players try to return to play sooner than they should. This approach is not only unwise rehabilitation, it is absolutely abusive.

Head Trauma

Ian I. T. Armstrong, M.D.

Head injuries constitute the most frequent cause of death in sports-related events and accidents.

Ten percent of college football and 20 percent of high school football players suffer from significant head injuries and/or concussions. Approximately 85 percent of deaths in football are a result of significant head or neck injuries. Modification of tackling techniques has decreased head injuries. Despite proper equipment and technique, however, significant head injuries do occur. Head injuries must be fully evaluated on the sideline by trained personnel. Inappropriate return to play with a reinjury can result in the sudden death of the athlete.

Head trauma and hockey are becoming common sports news items. In the recent past, the news has reported the cases of Tony Granato and his brain surgery resulting from a head trauma suffered playing hocky; the mandatory retirement of Brett Lindros from five concussions over a one-and-a-half-year period; the retirement of Pat Lafontaine because of repeated head trauma; Paul Kariya's concussion after a cross-check to his head; Eric Lindros's career-interrupting concussions after being checked into the boards;

and the playoff-ending concussion of Ron Francis.

Anatomy

The brain is certainly one of the most delicate structures in the body and one of the most critical. Hence, it has been carefully protected by the surrounding bony structure of the skull. A thick covering called the dura surrounds the brain. The brain floats in a lake of cerebrospinal fluid. This anatomic configuration offers maximal protection for the brain.

Mechanisms/Types of Brain Injury

Head injuries can occur as a result of a direct blow to the skull causing local trauma to the skull. This may manifest as a contusion or fracture and cause injury to the brain. A sudden acceleration or deceleration, without a direct blow to the head, can make the brain strike against the surrounding hard skull causing a brain injury. A player can receive a blow to one side of the head but actually sustain a brain injury on the opposite side of the head. In this type of trauma, the brain will strike the opposite side of the skull and result in a brain injury on the side opposite the direct blow. This is known as a contra-coup injury. Another type of brain injury is called a diffuse axonal injury. Rotary forces, or tangential forces, cause a shearing effect in the deep substance of the brain causing confusion or bleeding within the brain.

Concussion

A concussion is an alteration of mental status or mental function as a result of trauma to the brain. It may be the result of a direct blow, acceleration and deceleration forces, or a contra-coup injury. The hallmark signs of a concussion are confusion and amnesia. An athlete does not have to have loss of consciousness to have a concussion.

Classic Characteristics of a Concussion

The classic characteristics of a concussion include the following: blank stare; delayed verbal response to questions; delayed ability to follow instructions; inability to focus attention; apparent distraction by the patient; inability to follow a conversation; disorientation; walking (or skating) the wrong direction; loss of awareness of place, time, or date (not knowing who the opposing team is or at which rink they are skating); slurred speech; poor coordination with stumbling; poor balance; and inability to walk a straight line (drunk test or heel-to-toe test). More subtle signs include emotionality (i.e., crying for no apparent reason), memory loss, and poor intellectual function.

Early complaints by the athlete with a concussion may include headaches, dizziness, lack of awareness of surroundings, nausea, and vomiting.

Later complaints include persistent low-grade headaches, light headaches, inability to concentrate, memory dysfunction, excessive fatigue, irritability, intolerance to bright lights, intolerance to loud noises, or ringing in the ears. Some of these symptoms may develop that were not present during the early complaint stage. As an example of this, the newspapers reported that Tony Granato's headaches were becoming intolerable. He arose from bed due to pain from the headaches. As he walked around downstairs, he looked at framed photographs of family and friends, which were placed on the piano. Tony did not recognize half of the people in the photographs and realized that he was in

trouble. Tony was lucky to recognize his deficit. Many times, the athlete with the concussion is completely unaware of his or her deficits.

Classification of Concussion

There is not an absolute standard of grading and managing concussions. However, there are three guidelines that are referenced most frequently. The first is the American College of Sports Medicine (ACSM) Guideline, which is sometimes referred to as Cantu's Guideline. The second is somewhat more conservative and is known as the Colorado Guideline. The third is the American Academy of Neurology (AAN) Guideline. I will refer to the AAN Guideline. Concussions are defined as mild (grade I), moderate (grade II), or severe (grade III). I also utilize my own clinical experience in neurosurgery, so at times my opinions may be even more conservative.

• **Grade I Concussion.** A grade I concussion is the most common type of concussion and is certainly the most difficult to recognize and diagnose. The athlete does not have any loss of consciousness or amnesia but has a brief period of confusion. The confusion can present as inattention or as the inability to maintain a coherent stream of thought and carry out goal-directed movements. Most players who have a grade I concussion refer to this as having their "bell rung." There may be minimal evidence for the grade I concussion. It is only after careful observation and questions to the athlete by sideline medical personnel that this diagnosis will be evident. The symptoms usually resolve in 15 minutes.

• **Grade II Concussion.** A grade II concussion will also exhibit transient confusion and amnesia but will not have loss of consciousness. The patient may have amnesia for the events following the injury (posttraumatic amnesia or anterograde amnesia) or amnesia for events that preceded the injury (retrograde amnesia). A thorough neurological evaluation must be performed. The player may not return to the game.

• **Grade III Concussion.** Any loss of consciousness will automatically be defined as a grade III concussion. Loss of consciousness even for only a few seconds is still considered a loss of consciousness according to the AAN Guideline. A grade III concussion requires immediate removal from the game, and the athlete must be transported to a hospital for evaluation. A CT scan or MRI of the brain must be performed on any athlete rendered unconscious for any period of time.

AAN Guidelines for Return to Competition Following a Concussion

• **Grade I Concussion.** An athlete must be removed from the game and examined immediately and every five minutes for postconcussion-syndrome symptoms. If the athlete is symptomatic, he may not return to the game. Symptoms may include headache, dizziness, impaired orientation, impaired concentration, or memory problems. In order to return to play, symptoms must resolve while at rest and with exertion. Exertion or provocation testing is usually done on the sidelines in football and may be done in the locker room/training room for hockey. Again, return to play is allowed after a grade I concussion only if amnesia does not appear and the athlete is asymptomatic (without symptoms) during rest and exertion within 15 minutes.

If the player has a second grade I concussion in the same contest, this player is eliminated from competition for the day. A CT scan or MRI scan is recommended in all incidences in which a headache persists. These players should be given a head injury precaution information sheet for them to follow at home. The patient should be evaluated

over the next 24 hours for signs of evolving intracranial problems. The family needs to have explicit, written information about warning signs and instructions to follow if the athlete becomes worse. The patient is removed from contact sports until he or she is asymptomatic for one week at rest and with exertion. A CT scan or MRI is recommended for those who have headaches or symptoms for more than one week. The AAN recommends that after a second grade I concussion, the player should be pulled from contact sports and returned only after having been asymptomatic for one week. I believe that it is not inappropriate to wait even longer for return to play, perhaps at least one month, and termination of the season should be considered. There is a problem known as second-impact syndrome that needs to be avoided if possible. I believe that termination of the season is mandated after a third grade I concussion. The athlete with three grade I concussions in a season must have a formal neurological evaluation before being considered for return to play.

• **Grade II Concussion.** The player with the grade II concussion may not return to play, and frequently repeated reexaminations in the locker room need to be performed. The athlete needs to be examined the following day. I believe that a CT scan should probably be performed. Two grade II concussions in a season keep the player out until the athlete is asymptomatic for two weeks. I would consider terminating the season for the player, and he or she should have a follow-up MRI or CT scan. The player should have a complete neurological examination prior to returning to play the next season.

• **Grade III Concussion.** Any loss of consciousness necessitates removal from the game, transfer to a hospital, neurological examination, and CT scan or MRI of the brain. The AAN Guideline indicates an athlete should be held from contact sports until he or she is asymptomatic for two weeks after a grade III concussion. I believe it would not be inappropriate to wait one month or to terminate a season.

A second grade III concussion requires the athlete to be asymptomatic at least one month and perhaps longer, based on the physician's opinion. It is never wrong to err in the conservative direction, so it would not be unreasonable to terminate the season for a second grade III concussion. The player must have a full neurological exam prior to the next season.

Sideline Evaluation of Concussions

History

1. Check the orientation of the athlete to person, place, time, and purpose. For example, ask the athlete these questions: What is your name? Where are you? Why are you here? Whom are you playing? A few years ago, one NHL player scored a game-winning goal in overtime against the Calgary Flames. Two days later, he received head trauma while playing the Edmonton Oilers. He was removed from the game. His teammates reported that in the locker room after the game, when he was asked where he was, he replied, "We're in Calgary and I just scored the game-winning goal." This player lost two days of memory preceding the trauma (retrograde amnesia).
2. Concentration may be evaluated with a counting test such as counting backward or naming the months of the year in reverse order, or a memory test such as naming the president of the United States or remembering three words or objects right away and five minutes later.
3. Ask the athlete about the events in the game and his or her own trauma.

Neurological Testing

1. Check the pupils for asymmetry and reaction to light.
2. Test coordination by asking the athlete to walk heel-toe (drunk-driving test) or to rub one heel up the opposite shin. This also helps determine if the athlete can follow directions.
3. Ask the athlete to touch his or her finger to the nose with eyes closed.
4. Ask the athlete to hop on one foot.

If the athlete passes these tests and does not have headaches or dizziness and has clear mental function, then this is a grade I concussion. The examiner should test the athlete with exertional movements. An easy battery of exertional tests in a training room for a hockey player could include five sit-ups, five push-ups, five knee bends, and a short (few steps) maximum sprint effort. If a headache, nausea, dizziness, or other mental changes reappear, the athlete may not return to play.

The following covers other terms that those involved in trauma sports such as hockey should be familiar with.

Diffuse Axonal Injury (DAI)

Diffuse axonal injury takes the form of a prolonged traumatic brain coma with loss of consciousness lasting more than six hours. Residual neurological, psychological, or personality deficits often result because of the structural disruption of numerous axons in the white matter of the cerebral hemispheres and brain stem.

Postconcussive Syndrome

Postconcussive syndrome refers to the constellation of signs and symptoms that characterize the period of recovery from acute brain injury. Headache, dizziness, tinnitus, memory disturbance, and difficulty with concentration are hallmarks described by most victims. While these sequelae invariably follow moderate or severe brain injury, they have also been shown to result from minor head trauma. Willberger reported that more than half of high school football players complained of fatigue, dizziness, poor attention, or memory disturbances after minor head injury. Approximately 8 percent of the athletes suffered mild head injuries identified by the team physician or head trainer over the four-year testing interval. Only 4.7 percent of the injuries involved a positive loss of consciousness, none longer than five minutes. The head-injured players had more complaints of headache and dizziness than their middle-age-matched controls at one and five days after injury, while complaints of difficulty with memory persisted to ten days posttrauma.

Intracerebral Hematoma and Contusion

Intracerebral hematoma and contusion occur in patients with a significant intracerebral (within the brain) pathologic condition who have not suffered loss of consciousness or focal neurologic deficit but who do have persistent headache or periods of confusion after head injury and posttraumatic amnesia. As with any patients who have suffered head injuries, athletes with such symptoms should undergo a CT scan to permit early differentiation between solid intracerebral hematoma and hemorrhagic (bleeding) contusion with surrounding edema (swelling).

Epidural Hematoma

Epidural hematoma results when the middle meningeal artery tears as a result of a skull fracture. Because the bleeding in this instance is arterial, accumulation of clot continues under high pressure and, as a result, serious brain injury can occur. The classic description of an epidural hematoma is that of loss of consciousness at the time of injury, followed by a recovery of consciousness in a variable period after which the patient is lucid. This is followed by the onset of increasingly severe headache, decreased level of consciousness, dilation of one pupil, and decerebrate posturing and weakness.

Acute Subdural Hematoma

Acute subdural hematoma raises the image of a large collection of clotted blood in the intracranial cavity, compressing the brain substance and causing compromise due to the space occupied by the hematoma. This is not an infrequent consequence of closed head trauma, but this type of subdural hematoma is more common in adults who have a degree of cortical atrophy. Athletic head injuries result from inertial loading, which is lower than that of serious head injuries caused by vehicular accidents or falling from heights. Patients with an acute subdural hematoma typically are unconscious, may or may not have a history of deterioration, and frequently display focal neurological findings. It is necessary to obtain a CT or MRI scan to diagnose an acute subdural hematoma.

Second-Impact Syndrome

Multiple injuries have been noted to increase the duration and magnitude of postconcussive syndromes. It was found that headache, dizziness, and memory deficit persisted longer in head trauma victims with a history of previous concussions. Many isolated case reports detailing malignant brain swelling following relatively minor blows in the setting of recent mild head injury have been documented. The pathophysiology of this entity is believed to involve subclinical brain swelling from a traumatic insult that makes the brain more susceptible to further injury. It is postulated that the first insult disturbs the brain's autoregulatory mechanisms, with consequent vascular congestion and poor brain compliance.

Emergency Management of Head and Cervical Spine Injuries

Although all athletic injuries require careful attention, the evaluation and management of injuries to the head and neck should proceed with particular consideration. An intracranial hemorrhage may initially present with minimal symptoms yet follow a significant downhill course, whereas a less severe injury, such as a neuropraxia of the brachial plexus ("stinger") that is associated with alarming paresthesias (tingling and numbness) and paralysis may resolve swiftly and allow for quick return to activity.

Individuals responsible for athletes who may sustain injuries to the head and neck should consider several principles:

1. The team physician or trainer should be designated as the person responsible for supervising on-the-field management of the potentially serious injury. This person is the "captain" of the medical team.
2. Prior planning must ensure the availability of all necessary emergency equipment at the site of potential injury. At a minimum, this should include a spine board, stretcher, hard collar, and equipment necessary for the initiation and mainte-

nance of cardiopulmonary resuscitation (CPR).
3. Prior planning must ensure the immediate availability of a properly equipped ambulance as well as a hospital equipped and staffed to handle emergency neurological problems.
4. Prior planning must ensure immediate availability of a telephone for communicating with the hospital emergency room, ambulance, and other responsible individuals in case of an emergency.

Managing the unconscious or spine-injured athlete should not be done hastily or haphazardly. Being prepared to handle this situation is the best way to prevent actions that could convert a repairable injury into a catastrophe. A means of transporting the athlete must be immediately available in high-risk sports such as hockey and football and "on-call" in other sports. Having the proper equipment is essential! A spine board is necessary and is the best means of providing a supporting splint. By splinting the body, the risk of aggravating a spinal cord injury is reduced.

On-Site Management

Properly trained personnel must know who is the person in charge; CPR; proper procedures for movement and transportation of the injured athlete; how to use emergency equipment; and procedures for activating the emergency support system.

Prevention of further injury is the single most important objective. Do not take any action that could possibly cause further injury. The first step should be to immobilize the head and neck by supporting them in a stable position. If the victim is breathing, maintain the airway. If not, the airway must be established. If the athlete is facedown when the ambulance arrives, change his or her position to faceup by log rolling him or her onto a spine board. Once the athlete has been moved to a faceup position, quickly evaluate the breathing and the pulse. The jaw-thrust technique is the safest first approach to opening the airway of a victim with a suspected neck injury. If the jaw thrust is not adequate, the head tilt–jaw lift should be substituted. The transportation team should be familiar with handling a victim with a cervical spine injury, and they should be receptive to taking orders from the team physician or trainer. It is extremely important not to lose control of the care of the athlete; therefore you should be familiar with the transportation crew being used. Lifting and carrying the athlete requires five individuals: four to lift and the leader to maintain immobilization of the head. The leader initiates all actions with clear, loud verbal commands.

In summary, any athlete who has suffered loss of consciousness from head injury for more than one minute, or who has persistent headache with confusion or any disorientation that persists longer than one hour after trauma, or who has had more than one episode of unconsciousness, however momentary, during any one playing season, should be referred for neurological examination and a CT scan.

New data are always emerging on the management of concussions. Research presented at a medical conference by Dr. Hovdaa, neurophysiologist at UCLA, involving PET (positron emission test) scans indicated that complete rest may be the most effective method to manage a significant concussion case. PET scans revealed that there was decreased uptake of glucose (blood sugar) in the area of the brain that received the concussion. Studies with rats that were given concussion revealed that if they were kept physically active, the recovery was delayed.

So, the concept of preventing deconditioning in the concussion athlete may be erroneous.

Dental-Facial Injuries in Ice Hockey: Mouth Guards and Concussion Prevention

A. Patric Cohen, D.D.S.

Ice hockey is a fast-paced game involving both finesse and controlled aggression. Eighty percent of hockey injuries are related to direct trauma, with high puck velocities, aggressive stick use, and body checking (collisions) accounting for most of these. Unfortunately, injuries to the face and mouth in hockey are all too common. They often result in long absences from participation and significant morbidity for the rest of the player's life.

As in all of sports medicine, decisions involving emergency treatment of facial injuries have components. Unlike injuries to the extremities, which may affect function, facial injuries involve cosmetic as well as functional considerations.

Dental-facial injuries can be life-threatening by themselves or by virtue of their association with other structures such as the airway or nervous system. As with injuries of the extremities, dental-facial injuries can involve other structures such as muscles, tendons, and bones. Because the dental-facial complex is associated with the airway, spine, and brain, management of injuries must involve a systematic review, prioritization of treatment, and consideration of other trauma.

This section is designed to give an overview of the types of dental-facial injuries that occur in hockey and their treatment. I will also discuss ways to prevent some of these injuries using state-of-the-art protective equipment.

Types of Injuries and Their Treatment

There are a variety of types of injuries that can affect the teeth and surrounding structures. The first of these is trauma to the tooth without any visible damage. This often results in what is termed "tooth concussion"—damage to the blood vessels supplying the nerve of the tooth. The tooth may become discolored over time, or the nerve in the tooth may die. The player may experience soreness or sensitivity with pressure or biting. Initial treatment is not necessary. The player should avoid direct stress on the tooth. If symptoms persist or get worse, a visit to the dentist with appropriate x-rays is indicated.

The next type of dentoalveolar injury is a fracture of the crown or root of the tooth. These come in a variety of shapes and sizes depending upon the severity of the blow. Uncomplicated fractures or "chips" are generally asymptomatic or may be sensitive to temperature change or touch. This type of fracture is easily repaired by smoothing or recontouring the tooth. More moderate fractures may require the dentist to "bond" some resin material to the tooth. Severe fractures generally involve the front teeth, often resulting in involvement of the nerve. This type of injury generally requires root canal therapy. If there is no nerve involvement, then conventional bonding or porcelain veneers can be used to replace the damaged tooth structure. Fracture of the root of the tooth can be confirmed by dental x-ray. Treatment of root fracture depends on the type of fracture. Generally, stabilization of the tooth by splinting it to adjacent teeth is the treatment of choice. The bite is adjusted so there is no biting force on the tooth. Follow-up visits are necessary to monitor any possible abscess or infection.

The third type of dentoalveolar injuries are periodontal luxations. A blow is absorbed by the tooth and supporting structures without any apparent fracture or loss of tooth structure. There are four types of luxations. First, there is a concussion-type injury. In this type of luxation there is no displacement or movement of the tooth. The surrounding structures may be sensitive or bruised. No treatment is necessary. The second type of luxation is a subluxation. Subluxations show minor movement of the tooth, but the tooth is not displaced from the alveolus. No specific treatment is indicated unless the symptoms persist for more than a few weeks.

The next type of luxation is a displacement luxation. This is a true luxation in that the tooth is physically displaced from the socket. There are three directions in which a displacement can occur: lateral displacement; intrusive or inward displacement, which is rare; or outward displacement. Treatment for a minor displacement (less than than five millimeters) is to simply reposition the tooth with or without splinting for two to eight weeks. If the displacement is major (greater than five millimeters), there is a good chance of neurovascular and periodontal injury with possible nerve damage. Treatment consists of splinting the tooth for four to eight weeks. If the vitality of the tooth does not return in 8 to 12 weeks, then a root canal is required.

The last type of luxation injury is an avulsion. This is a complete displacement of the tooth (i.e., the tooth is knocked out). The prognosis in this type of injury is better the less time the tooth is out of the mouth. Acting quickly can make the difference between retaining or losing the tooth. Studies show a 90 percent success rate with reimplantation occurring within 30 minutes of injury. After two hours, the chance for success drops to 5 percent. Careful handling of the tooth is imperative to prevent abrasion and dryness of the root and to minimize bacterial contamination. The treatment is as follows: the avulsed tooth should be rinsed off but not scrubbed to remove any dirt or foreign debris. It is preferable to use sterile water or milk to rinse with. The tooth should then be replanted into the socket using minimal pressure. If immediate reimplantation is not possible, gently wrap the tooth in gauze and place in Hank's Save-A-Tooth solution or a container of milk and transport it to the dental office as quickly as possible. Treatment in the dental office will consist of reimplantation and splinting with stabilization for 7 to 14 days. Antibiotic therapy should be started the day of injury. The success of reimplantation is inversely proportional to the length of time the tooth is out of the mouth.

Preventative Measures to Reduce Facial Trauma

There are three preventative measures to reduce the incidence of facial trauma in hockey. The first is the use of properly fitting headgear and face masks. Today, headgear is required at all levels of ice hockey. However, face masks or shields are not required at the professional level. All face masks and headgear should fit properly, meaning that the face mask or shield should be securely fastened to the headgear and the headgear should fit snugly on the player's head and not flop around. The next preventative measure is to teach athletes the proper techniques at all levels of play. This means reinforcing good hockey techniques and the avoidance of illegal checking. The third and most important preventative measure is the use of properly fitted mouth guards.

Mouth Guards: The Ultimate Preventative Measure

In the 1960s and 1970s, mouth guards were used primarily in boxing and football. Today they are used in a variety of sports including football, field hockey, ice hockey, wrestling, soccer, basketball, gymnastics, lacrosse, the martial arts, volleyball, boxing, and weight lifting. Many of the mouth guards used today are almost 100 percent effective in preventing oral injuries. In this section we will be discussing the types of mouth protectors available, how they are made, the differences among them, and the benefits they provide in addition to protecting the mouth.

Today there are basically three types of mouth protectors: the ready-made or stock mouth protector, the mouth-formed protector, and the custom-made protector. The first type, the stock mouth protector, is intended to fit any mouth. They are available in a limited number of sizes and can be found in sporting goods stores and pharmacies. The stock mouth protector is the least expensive of the four and doesn't involve any type of fitting. Stock mouth guards are usually made of rubber, polyvinyl chloride, or polyvinyl acetate-polyethylene copolymer. Although the physical properties of these materials are excellent, the design of these protectors is the least desirable due to their poor fit. They interfere with speech and breathing, and the mouth must remain closed for them to stay in place. As the public becomes better educated, fewer athletes are using them.

The second type of mouth protector is a thermoplastic mouth-formed protector commonly known as a "boil and bite." It is made of polyvinyl acetate. This mouth guard is preformed by the manufacturer in standard sizes. To fit, the athlete immerses it in boiling water for about one minute, then puts it in cold water for one second, and then immediately places it in his or her mouth. The advantages of this system are that it can be refitted if not properly fitted the first time, the cost is relatively low, and all fitting procedures can be accomplished at one sitting. The disadvantages include decreased retention over time and hardening of the material from continued exposure to oral fluids. Studies have shown that because the occlusion (bite) is unbalanced when these are made, the stability of these guards is poor and cannot withstand the forces that can cause facial trauma.

The third category of mouth protector is the custom-fitted mouth guard. This can be divided into two subcategories. First is what is known as the type 1 custom mouth guard. This is the type of custom mouth guard that we dentists have made in the past. It is one sheet of ethyl vinyl acetate copolymer three millimeters thick that is vacuum formed over a cast of the athlete's teeth. The problem with this type of mouth guard is that because there is such variety in the types of vacuum forming machines and the heat they produce, the thickness of the guard can vary in different parts. There is no way of knowing if you will end up with the two- to two-and-one-half-millimeter range of thickness in the back teeth that is needed to protect against concussion and other trauma. The advantages of these types of custom guards are that they are better than the stock or boil and bites as far as retention, they are relatively inexpensive, and they can be used for children who are in braces whose bites are changing every few months.

The second subcategory of custom-fitted mouth guard is the type 2. It can be bi- or tri-laminated, and it is a thermal-pressure-molded material that can be two to five millimeters thick. For hockey, we prefer to use four to five millimeters of material. By multi-laminating these guards, we are ensuring the necessary thickness to help prevent trauma. There is a uniform thickness throughout the guard as a result of the pressure used in forming them. These can also be used for players who have missing teeth to give them a true custom fit. The major advantages of this type of protector are that it has the best fit and the most retention, is least bulky, and causes the least amount of interference with breathing. (Most players think that mouth guards interfere with breathing, but Drs. Balikov and Holland did a ventilation study at Cal State Northridge that showed there was no actual difference in breathing between athletes wearing mouth guards and the control group.) In summary, comparing custom mouth guards with stock or boil-and-bite-type mouth guards reveals significant differences. The custom-fitted guards fit more accurately, are more comfortable, and protect the athlete better. It is my opinion that non-custom mouth guards should not be worn by any athlete playing hockey.

Let's talk about the benefits of mouth guard protection. As mentioned, there is a much lower incidence of oral injuries when mouth guards are used. Studies have shown that the incidence of fractured jaws and soft-tissue injuries decreases significantly when mouth protection is used. A study by Hickey in 1967 used cadavers to show that when a blow to the chin was received, the mouth guard reduced the amplitude of intracranial pressure wave and decreased the amount of bone deformation by 50 percent. This study shows that proper use of mouth guards can reduce the amount of trauma to the brain, decreasing the chance of concussion. Finally, the psychological benefit of players knowing that there is a lower chance of their being hurt while wearing a mouth guard allows them to do what they are supposed to, which is focus on playing.

In conclusion, there are many types of oral-facial injuries that occur in hockey, some obviously more severe than others. Many of these injuries can severely limit or end an athlete's career. This is a risk that should not be assumed at any level of play. Proper immediate diagnosis and treatment is essential to minimizing potential damage. The use of high-quality protective equipment is a must if the players are going to perform at optimum levels in the safest manner possible.

Spinal Injuries

ROBERT S. BRAY JR., M.D.,
WITH CONTRIBUTIONS BY
JOSEPH M. HORRIGAN, D.C.

The spine is divided up into three areas: cervical, thoracic, and lumbar spine. The cervical spine involves the first seven vertebrae (bony segments) from the base of the skull to the upper chest. The thoracic spine has twelve vertebrae stabilized by the ribs of the chest wall. The lumbar spine has five lumbar vertebrae and attaches into the sacrum and pelvis. Each section of the spine has unique characteristics and is subject to different types of injuries by different mechanisms.

The spinal cord starts at the base of the skull and runs to the lower thoracic area. Below this (in the lumbar spine) is a collection of nerve roots that is known as the *cauda equina* ("horse's tail"). True spinal cord injuries can therefore occur with either cervical or thoracic injuries. With lumbar injuries, a nerve root injury can occur. Injuries to any portion of the spine can be of the following types:

1. soft-tissue injuries to the supporting muscles and ligaments around the spine

2. injuries to the disks, which are the shock-absorbing cartilage-like plates between the bony vertebrae

3. injuries to the neurological structures at the level of injury with spinal cord involvement in the cervical or thoracic region and with nerve root involvement at any of the spine regions

Fractures of the bony elements of the spine often lead to compromise, or injury, to the associated nerves or spinal cord at this level. By far the most common of these injuries is the soft-tissue strain or sprain. A strain is generally used as a term describing a "pulled muscle" or an overstretched muscle, and it usually has a relatively short recovery with rest followed by proper muscle conditioning. A sprain is a more severe stretch injury usually resulting in overstretching and microtears of the ligaments or joint capsules as well as the muscular injury. This often requires six to twelve weeks for recovery and can lead to prolonged problems unless properly rehabilitated (e.g., a chronic strain injury of the low back resulting in persisting low-back pain).

Injuries of the soft-tissue type are common in the cervical region and are known as "whiplash" injuries. They are very uncommon in the thoracic region because of the stabilization of all the surrounding musculature by the ribs. They are common in the low back, especially with lifting-type injuries when the muscles are not properly conditioned.

Pain is the primary symptom of injuries of soft tissue with focal muscle pain and pain on range of motion of the affected area of the spine. Specifically, there is no neurological deficit and no radiation of pain into the arms or legs. Radiation of pain, numbness, or weakness in an arm or leg indicates a disruption of the spine, more serious than a sprain or strain injury. The most common would be injury to the cartilaginous disks between the vertebrae. Again, the most common are disk injuries in the cervical and lumbar area, although thoracic disk injuries do occur on rare occasions.

When radiating pain, numbness, or weakness is present, a disk injury must be suspected. In the cervical region, pain or numbness radiates from the neck, across the shoulders, down the arm, and possibly to the level of the hand. With thoracic disk injury, the pain will wrap around the chest and under the armpits into the front of the chest and mimic a bruised or broken rib. In the lumbar region, low-back pain with pain in the buttocks and/or back of the thigh, side of the thigh, and calf with numbness in the foot is the hallmark presentation.

When disk injury is suspected, proper diagnosis, usually with magnetic resonance imaging (MRI) and evaluation by a spinal specialist is important. Many disk injuries can be treated conservatively as most represent a bulging or protrusion of the disk and not a complete tear or rupture. Up to 80 percent of disk injuries can be handled with nonsurgical intervention. Proper conditioning and range of motion both help to prevent disk injuries as well as rehabilitate them once they have happened. This condition should be taken seriously and not ignored as proper treatment can prevent progression. More serious injuries such as fractures are fortunately a rare occurrence. The incidence, however, especially of cervical spine fractures has been on the rise for a variety of reasons and will be considered in detail. Thoracic and lumbar fractures are very rare because of the large stabilizing musculature of the back and ribs in the thoracic area. If a fracture is suspected by severe incapacitating pain immediately at the time of injury, appropriate precautions need to be taken when moving the patient.

"Burners" and "stingers" represent an acute, sudden, hot burning or stinging pain usually related to the cervical area but sometimes occurring in the lumbar spine. They are the sudden onset of a burning, stinging pain following an impact, usually a hyperextension injury of the neck. The neck is in a neutral position when we are standing straight. Tucking the chin forward and bending the head downward is flexion. Lifting the chin upward and rotating the head backward is hyperextension. Hyperextension causes a compromise or pinch of the nerves as they exit from the spinal cord. The impact of a check, or contact, with another player affords sudden forcing of the chin and head upward and back, thus causing a hyperextension injury. If burners and stingers occur, the player should be immediately removed from the ice and should not be allowed to continue playing until appropriate evaluation by a spinal expert has been performed. This is often the first sign of a condition known as spinal stenosis or narrowing within the spine. It is potentially dangerous because subsequent hyperextension injuries could cause damage to the spinal cord itself or even quadriplegia. Further criteria for spinal stenosis will be reviewed later in this section. A more severe form of transient nerve deficit from a similar mechanism is direct spinal cord bruise, also most commonly from hyperextension injuries. This results in electric-like feelings radiating down the back or a feeling of ice and heat sensations running down the body from the neck region. Even if transient or mild, this is a warning of a potentially serious or devastating injury to the spinal cord. It is known as Lhermitte's sign and again requires immediate cessation of play and full spine evaluation by a specialist. It commonly means the patient has cervical spinal stenosis, which may require further treatment.

Finally, degenerative joint disease (wear and tear injury) to the joints of the spine is common in any athletic sport that has repeated impact and trauma to the spine. It is by no means unique to hockey. Degenerative joints result in stiffness, aching pain in the neck or back, and decreased range of motion. As a player ages, it becomes increasingly important to maintain proper range of motion and conditioning of the musculature to prevent the progression of degenerative joint disease as well as more serious injuries because of the natural loss of range of motion by the degenerative joints.

Neck

Neck or cervical spine injuries are on the rise in hockey. A review by Tator of two Toronto-area hospitals from 1948 to 1973 revealed 55 patients with acute cervical spinal cord injury were reported. None were from hockey. Subsequent to that date, however, increasing numbers of spinal cord injuries from hockey have been documented. At one Toronto hospital alone, six were reported from 1977 to 1980, and six further from 1980 to 1981. Rates of injury have been rising since that time at a continued and rather alarming rate.

Tator's opinion regarding the increasing cervical spine injury rate involves a variety of factors:

1. Players are taller, heavier, and skating faster with greater forces on impact.
2. There is an increasing emphasis on full contact by major-league scouts.
3. Improved pads worn from a young age upward promote a feeling of invincibility to the player.
4. There is a lack of enforcement of the current rules as well as a need for further rules on types of contact.
5. There is a lack of knowledge among coaches and trainers about the importance of neck muscle strengthening and protection.

6. There is a lack of knowledge about the mechanism of checking and receiving impact.
7. There is a lack of safety standards and shock-absorption capability of the boards and rinks.
8. There is increased friction between helmet and boards.
9. There is an increased incidence of impact or contact on small rinks because of less skating room.

Compilation of Cervical Spine Injuries by Tator

Year	Number of Cases
1966	1
1975	1
1976–79	12
1980	7
1981	12
1982	14
1983	16
1984	15
By April 1985	7
1986	19

Castaldi reported three mechanisms that he felt were most common for injuries:

1. Playing rules are not being uniformly enforced by game officials, especially pertaining to body checking on opponents or from behind or tripping into the boards.
2. The size and strength of the players have increased significantly, and they are skating faster and checking harder while the hockey rinks remain the same size.
3. There is a lack of safety standards for hockey rinks.

Mechanisms of Injury

There are two most common mechanisms for injury to the cervical spine. The first is a hyperflexion axial loading injury. This simply means the head is bent forward in a chin tuck position and receives an impact to the top of the head. Here are the most common ways this happens:

1. from an unsuspected check from behind while the player has his or her head down
2. spearing with the head or chin down, into an opponent
3. sliding headfirst into the boards and trying to tuck the chin or head to avoid impact
4. from any contact that results in a blow to the top of the head with the chin tucked down

The hyperflexion axial loading injury is the most severe type of injury because it often results in both fracture of the cervical spine and injury to the cervical spinal cord.

In the six cases of acute cervical spinal cord injury reported to the Toronto hospital during the 1980 to 1981 period, five of the six cases resulted from hyperflexion axial loading injuries. In all six of the cases, the players wore helmets. Four struck their heads against the boards in flexion. One struck his head against another player. One that struck the board in hyperextension instead of hyperflexion resulted in a milder version of injury to the nervous system instead of a severe spinal cord injury. The key point that comes from this is to keep your head up.

The second mechanism for injury to the cervical spine is hyperflexion or hyperextension of the neck without an axial load (blow to the top of the head). This results in the so-called whiplash-type injury. The most common is the soft-tissue injury to the muscles and ligaments of the neck resulting in the sprain- or strain-type injury; although painful, these injuries rarely result in neurological deficit. If this type of whiplash injury, the "burners" or "stingers," occurs or there are electric, icy feelings running down the back, then there is usually compromise of the size of the spinal canal (cervical stenosis), and full evaluation of the cervical spine is necessary. Rarely does hyperflexion or hyperextension alone result in fracture.

Prevention

Prevention of cervical spine injuries desperately needs to be addressed by coaches, trainers, and referees. There is nothing sadder than seeing a young player or rising star rendered quadriplegic for life by an injury that should be preventable in the majority of cases.

The first step is the recognition of dangerous signs or symptoms that require ceasing all contact in play and getting an appropriate spinal evaluation by a fully trained spinal specialist. Symptoms of radiating pain or numbness, burners, stingers, radiation of electric sensations down the back or spine, or persisting or unrelieved muscular pain in the neck should be thoroughly evaluated.

The second step to injury prevention is the proper enforcement at the referee level of the rules of the game. Checking from behind into the boards and tripping into the boards are the two most common infractions that result in serious spinal cord injuries. These should be considered intent-to-injure infractions with automatic game misconduct penalties to firmly ingrain in younger players that this type of infraction cannot occur. There is another penalty that can be added to hockey.

If an infraction such as previously described occurs late in the third period as "payback" or intimidation, then the player should be suspended for the next game instead of drawing a minor, major, and game misconduct penalty with less than two minutes to go in the game. At that point, the player does not suffer any real penalty. Meanwhile, the other player may be severely injured.

From a coaching point of view, several important techniques need to be taught. Most important is not promoting an attitude of invincibility among the players. Current hockey padding, although it has improved in quality over the years, does not in any way prevent cervical spine injuries. Proper techniques of checking and observing impact need to be taught. Blind entrance into corners with the head down to dig a puck out can lead to serious injury. A "heads-up" attitude must be promoted so that any contact of the head against the boards is in a neutral or extended position, which is far safer than the head-down, axial-loaded (blow to the top of the head) position. This is perhaps the single most important point that a player can be taught.

Hockey coaches can take a lesson from football, where high school players are taught to hit with a "bull neck" or play "heads-up football." This is a verbal cue to remind players to keep the neck in extension pending any impact or collision. The tragic lessons that have been learned from football do not need to be repeated in hockey, and appropriate coaching for this type of contact needs to be promoted. In any instance where a player is going to suddenly contact the boards, tucking the head forward and thereby allowing the impact to come on top of the helmet can be a fatal mistake.

The athletic trainer or strength coach can have significant impact on proper neck conditioning, which is extremely important and completely ignored at most levels—even up to the NHL. Proper training techniques including cervical spine stabilization by increasing musculature with isometrics and flexion/extension exercises, proper range of motion, and proper development of the shoulder musculature are extremely important to neck conditioning to prevent injury.

Finally, redesign of equipment—especially helmet changes to prevent friction contact between the top of the helmet and the boards—needs to be reviewed by equipment companies. Helmets designed with flat tops promote the axial-loading component of the hyperflexion injury and can actually increase the risk of cervical spine injury. I (RSB) am investigating the possibility of developing a new hockey helmet that will offer significantly more protection than the current helmet. Additional weight will not be an issue due to the fact that we are using lightweight materials such as those in the design of fighter pilot helmets. This will provide a strong, durable, and light helmet for hockey.

Treatment of Cervical Spine Injuries on the Ice

When cervical spine injury is suspected in a situation on the ice with sudden, severe neck pain, radiating pain to the arms or legs, or inability to move, proper care and treatment are extremely important. Do not attempt to remove the player's helmet. All movement should be done using a method known as log rolling. This method keeps the head and neck aligned with the body during the turning. The injured player should be placed on a spine board. The neck should be stabilized using sandbags or rolls of towels placed on each side of the head and neck to prevent movement. Preferably, movement of any type should be done by appropriately trained emergency medical technicians or with a physician in attendance. Appropriate movement is critical to avoid further injury.

Cervical Spinal Stenosis

There has been much controversy over how to deal with players with documented cervical spinal stenosis. The term *spinal stenosis* describes a narrowing of the spinal canal in the bony canal where the spinal cord passes. The spinal cord is normally bathed by cerebrospinal fluid, front and back, for protection in any form of contact with the spinal cord floating freely in the fluid. If the spinal canal is narrowed below a certain critical diameter, any subsequent injury to the neck results in compromise or injury to the spinal cord much easier than with normal anatomy. There is no set criteria in professional athletes that spinal specialists have yet agreed upon as to the absolute critical level of stenosis that should prohibit a player totally from further contact or collision sports. A normal spinal canal measures 17 to 20 millimeters, a mildly stenotic canal measures from 10 to 15 millimeters, and a canal is considered severely stenotic at 9 millimeters or less. A ratio was developed by a spine specialist named Joseph Torg. This ratio is called Torg's ratio. A ratio is obtained from x-rays of the cervical spine, and the measurement that Torg has deemed critical is 12 millimeters. He believes that athletes with this measurement or less should usually not participate in contact sports. Another spine specialist, Robert Cantu, described "functional spinal stenosis," a condition in which patients have a narrow canal and are displaying symptoms of this. He believes that these are the athletes that we should be concerned with rather than with those who do not have symptoms. I (RSB)

believe that nine millimeters represents an absolute measurement for eliminating a player from contact sports. A clear-cut clinical judgment call is always difficult. Several years ago, a hockey player was brought to the Soft Tissue Center during the third round of the Stanley Cup playoffs. This player had developed neck pain and pain radiating down both arms when he was checked by large, aggressive defensemen. MRI scans revealed that the player had an 11-millimeter canal and had narrowing of the space where the nerve root exits (foraminal stenosis). The team sought six opinions from various noted doctors around the country about his condition, and the opinions certainly varied:

> **Opinion 1 (team physician):** "Wait and see how much you improve."
> **Opinion 2:** "Your career is over. We can reevaluate in six weeks, but don't count on anything."
> **Opinion 3:** "You can return to play."
> **Opinion 4:** "Let's wait and see how you respond. You could probably play again in six weeks."
> **Opinion 5:** "You cannot play in the playoffs, and you should have another neurosurgical opinion to weigh your options about your future status."
> **Opinion 6:** "You have played with this mild stenosis all of your life, so you can probably return to play." A surgical procedure to open the narrow nerve exits was suggested to reduce the symptoms.

These six opinions included those of very well known spine specialists, and you can see the confusing dilemma the team and player were in. The player sat out during the rest of the playoffs and also opted to rest during the summer and strengthen his neck. He played in the NHL for five more years without having surgery.

The athlete with severely stenotic canals with no cerebrospinal fluid production around the cord who presents with symptoms of spinal cord compromise during minor contact is at increased risk of neurological injury if he or she is allowed to continue to play. Appropriate, skilled opinions from neurologic or orthopedic surgeons or doctors of chiropractic specializing in spinal treatment need to be reviewed before any player with a canal of this small dimension can be allowed to return to any type of contact or collision sport.

Low-Back Injuries

The low back consists of five lumbar vertebrae (bony segments) starting below the ribs and attaching into the sacrum. About 85 percent of the motion of the low back comes from the lowest two vertebrae at L4-5 and L5-S1; therefore most of the injuries occur at these levels. The low back is supported by strong muscle groups:

- the large erector spinae and paraspinous muscles (collectively known as erector spinae muscles)
- the psoas (the large muscle running down internally in the abdomen in the front of the spine)
- the anterior abdominal wall musculature—the rectus abdominus ("abs") and obliques

The majority of the stability of the low back comes from the musculature surrounding it, not from the bones and ligaments and disks. It is therefore absolutely essential that proper conditioning of the back musculature be a part of the workout program. It is also the most commonly ignored area during training. There is an old adage that "you can't fire a cannon from a canoe," implying that the essential nature of the supporting structure provides the base of support. This truism can be simply stated with hockey: you can't fire a good shot (or check) from a weak abdomen and back.

If the coaches and trainers could learn one point to both prevent injury and improve performance of the players, it would be to develop a strong abdomen and back program during their training course. The results would be dramatic in the speed and power of the shooting as well as injury prevention.

The anatomy of the back is very similar to the neck with the exception of being a larger structure. There is an intervertebral disk between each vertebral body, which acts as a weight-loading shock absorber and allows motion between the joints. There are facet joints on the posterior (back portion) on both sides of the vertebrae, which allow for flexion and extension motion and a small degree of rotation.

Important characteristics of the back should be noted in examining every player as simple corrections in posture or muscular balance can make a dramatic difference in performance. Small degrees of scoliosis are very common.

Scoliosis is a curvature of the spine that is usually a developmental condition during adolescence. Slight curves of 5 to 10 degrees are very common and may result in abnormal weight bearing with one leg shorter than the other. Careful observation by a spinal specialist or an appropriately educated trainer can pick up these subtle differences. I (RSB) have seen professional hockey players in my office with as much as half an inch discrepancy in leg length that was completely unnoticed even years into playing. Correction with a heel lift or custom skate can even out weight bearing, thus making a dramatic difference. One professional hockey player I saw strongly favored turning to the left because the right leg was half an inch longer, bearing weight on the outside of the right leg during a right stepover. It was difficult for him to turn in the other direction. Correction of weight bearing with a heel lift within a few weeks corrected this problem and relieved the stress on his low back, removing his chronic pain.

Again, degenerative conditions of the lower back are common, especially among professional athletes. Such conditions include degenerative changes of the facet joints with bony spur formation and drying and desiccation of the intervertebral disk causing collapse of disk height; these can lead to a chronically painful low back. There are many conservative treatments that will help including physical therapy, soft-tissue mobilization, joint manipulation, therapeutic and rehabilitative exercise, anti-inflammatory medications, or steroid shots. New microsurgical techniques exist if the condition becomes severe enough. Moderate techniques of surgery do not preclude a player from returning to play, often in as little as three to four months.

Fractures are very rare in the lumbar spine because of the tremendous sporting musculature strength; most fractures are reported in the cervical region. Occasionally seen are thoracolumbar fractures at the junction of the thorax and lumbar spine, but these require a high-speed injury where the player is flexed dramatically forward. They can occur in a high-speed collision with the goalpost or when a player in a bent-forward position slides into the wall, but this is rare. Modern goalposts that dislodge have essentially eliminated this type of injury. Occasionally seen are transverse process fractures from a direct blow to the low back with a cross-check. These do not result in neurological damage and do not represent a dangerous injury as they heal with conservative care. However, transverse process fractures will be painful for three to six months and therefore often disable a player for this period. Checking-

style or hard-hitting players would be well advised to wear a back plate or kidney plate, which essentially alleviates this type of injury.

Mechanisms of Injury

The most common form of injury to the lower back is the strain or sprain injury. This lumbar injury is similar to the corresponding neck injury. A low-back strain is a pull of a muscle, which results from overstretching a muscle that is improperly conditioned. It may sideline a player from days to weeks, and it is the single most common form of low-back injury. It should be nearly preventable with a proper conditioning program during training (as outlined in this book). Because it represents one of the most frequent reasons for lost ice time during a professional season, in these days of large contracts in professional sports, it is an extremely costly and often unnecessary injury.

A more serious sprain injury involves ligament and/or capsular fibers around the joints and has a more lengthy recovery course, often sidelining a player for six to twelve weeks. In years past, low-back injuries of this nature were treated with bed rest and medications. This has now been well demonstrated to be the wrong approach even in a layperson much less a professional athlete.

Disk injuries represent the next most common injury. Disk injuries typically occur from a lifting-type injury. This is commonly seen when players go into a corner to dig out a puck and someone comes in on top of them, pinning them in a forward-flexed position. As the players attempt to stand erect by pushing the opposing player off, they are lifting tremendous weight with the lower back. If we examine this in more detail, we will see a defenseman going into the corner to get the puck. An opposing player, weighing from

200 to 240 pounds, may jump up and lean the body weight across the shoulders of the defenseman. The personality profile of a defenseman is usually one that is aggressive, and the defenseman will push back against this opposing player in a very quick, explosive response. So the player is lifting the opposing player (200 to 240 pounds) and doing so explosively, thus increasing the force the low back is exposed to. Now, if this is a player that does not have a proper training program and therefore has a weak lower back, then the injury is quite predictable. In this forward-flexed position, the weight to the lumbar disk is magnified by a factor of 10, and rupture is common. Disk injuries in up to 80 percent or more cases represent a tear of the annulus (fibrous outer lining) of the disk with a bulge of the inner nuclear material, which is a soft cartilaginous jelly, through the outer rings. The hallmark sign is immediate severe back pain at the time of the annular tear, often followed by radiating pain to the buttocks or legs within a day or two of the injury. A spine specialist should be consulted to determine the nature and extent of the injury. If surgery is suggested as the immediate form of treatment, a second opinion is often warranted as most disk protrusions are treated conservatively unless there is dramatic nerve deficit or damage developing quickly. Short periods of rest with anti-inflammatory medications are appropriate for the initial pain, but rapid progression into an exercise protection program is essential to prevent deconditioning. Again, lengthy periods of rest even with a disk injury are unnecessary and cause additional harm.

Unfortunately, some disk injuries fail conservative management and continue with persisting pain or the progression of neurological deficit (weakness or numbness) in the leg on a persisting basis. This is common in disks that are quite large (eight millimeters or more). Surgical intervention in this case may be necessary. Older surgical techniques that involve laminectomy as the approach for disk removal have usually resulted in a career-ending operation for the professional athlete. Newer microsurgical techniques are available that preserve the laminar arch, the interspinous ligament, and the facet joints and microsurgically remove the disk fragments. While full recovery may take six to eight months, often a player can be back to skating and conditioning in as early as eight weeks, with active exercises starting in as early as two to three weeks. This prevents excessive deconditioning and leads to a return to play in as many as 90 percent or more of most professional athletes.

Proper coaching and training need to occur to teach players to receive a pass in the heads-up posture, avoiding direct contact in the head-down position. This prevents cervical spine hyperflexion and axial weight-loading injuries as well as lumbar injuries. Proper coaching and actual practice drills for entering a corner in a heads-up position or turning to the side as impact with the boards occurs can again prevent both neck and back injuries. It is essential that coaches caution athletes against lifting themselves out of a pinned position with the head down and flexed forward at the waist. It is far easier to temporarily drop to the knees to straighten the upper body and then arise from the legs rather than try to lift from the low back. Again, current rules with avoidance of cross-checking (which can result in transverse process spinal fractures and lumbar contusion to the soft tissues) or checking into the boards need to be strictly enforced.

Most important for prevention is a proper training program. Proper range-of-motion and stretching exercises need to be incorporated into the daily workout routine for back, hips, and groin musculature. In practice up to

NHL level that I (RSB) have observed, I have rarely seen an adequate stretching program incorporated into the preskate workouts. The players are usually left to stretch out on their own, with players usually having several simple routines that they may have picked up on their own along the way. These routines are rarely adequate to properly condition all of the directions that are necessary for proper range of motion. A simple 5- to 10-minute program incorporated into preskating or even stretching routines worked out on ice can prevent most strain or sprain injuries.

Abdomen- and back-strengthening programs need to be properly balanced with a program developed to both strengthen and balance the posture of the athlete. I (RSB) have commonly seen professional athletes come in with chronic back pain. When I ask about their workout programs, they will typically tell me they have a strong abdomen (performing 150 to 200 sit-ups or crunches per day). When I inquire about which exercises they are doing for their low back, the usual answer is, "Nothing" or, "I don't know how to do that." This book provides the answers.

In the lumbar spine, the erector spinae muscles of the back should be 20 to 30 percent stronger than the abdominal muscles. Pure strengthening of the abdominal musculature, which is very common among athletes, leads to increased weight in a forward-flexion position on the lumbar disk, and this can exacerbate or cause a disk injury. The oblique muscles on the sides of the waist and the erector spinae muscles of the back are the most important musculature to prevent injury as well as to develop a strong base for shooting and stick handling. Dramatic results will be observed with the addition of this type of program. Rotary strength is of equal importance and needs to be properly conditioned. I (RSB) agree with Dr. Horrigan's recommen-dations of avoidance of rotary torso–type machines, which can place shearing forces on the lumbosacral junction. Proper rotary conditioning needs to be addressed for development of this musculature.

Treatment immediately on the ice is rare for lumbar injuries as most strains or sprains are not noticed until the day after injury. If a player experiences sudden or severe incapacitating low-back pain on the ice, it must be considered a fracture until proved otherwise. Again, immobilization of the player and proper log rolling techniques by a highly experienced trainer or physician are important to prevent further injury. More common than a fracture, this severe pain represents a serious disk injury but needs to be treated to prevent possible increases in neurological damage. Severe direct contusions to the lumbar spine area result in muscle trauma and should be treated initially with ice followed by professional evaluation.

The thoracic spine is an important rotary structure that has often been ignored because of the rarity of injuries in this area. In fact, most injuries to the thoracic spine are misdiagnosed as rib contusions or intercostal muscle sprains. In recent years, widespread interest in thoracic injuries in hockey became apparent with the much-publicized injury of Wayne Gretzky. Gretzky had a ruptured thoracic disk that fortunately, with good conservative care, resolved. The thoracic spine is a rotary structure that allows a significant degree of twisting and turning. It allows very little motion in the flexion or extension planes.

Very little has been written about spinal injuries in hockey, yet overall they represent between 15 and 30 percent of injuries received on the ice and are a leading cause of disability time (and career-ending injuries) during a professional career. To avoid spinal injuries, all of the participants in the sport have a role to play. The referees need to understand the mechanisms of injury so that when they see infractions of the rules that have a high risk of injuries, they impose appropriate penalties. Players at a very young age will then learn that these are game misconduct activities, and they will carry this knowledge into professional play in later years. Coaches need to emphasize the importance of proper training and incorporate drills on the ice, especially with younger players where little control is seen in off-ice activities. At a professional level, control and incorporation of the proper training programs need to be emphasized. Trainers need to become more educated in the importance of proper range-of-motion and strengthening exercises and the critical role they play in the prevention of injury. Finally and most important, the players—whether juvenile, amateur, adult, or professional—need to develop proper training programs for spinal conditioning of the neck, thorax, and lumbar spine; the results will be not only improved performance on the ice but also the prevention of serious and disabling injuries.

Injuries Other than to the Spine

Joseph M. Horrigan, D.C.

Shoulder

The shoulder is a complex joint and is commonly injured in hockey. It actually comprises several joints between these areas:

- the head of the humerus (ball) and the glenoid fossa (socket), known as the glenohumeral joint

- the clavicle (collarbone) and the acromion (top of the shoulder), known as the acromioclavicular joint
- the clavicle (collarbone) and the sternum (breastbone), known as the sternoclavicular joint
- the scapula (shoulder blade) and the thorax (middle back), known as the scapulothoracic joint

The ball and socket joint (glenohumeral joint) contains several key anatomical structures that can be injured. The shoulder socket is a very shallow joint, and this gives the shoulder its tremendous range of motion. There is a cartilage rim (glenoid labrum) around the socket to give it more depth and support. There are ligaments that form the capsule that encloses the joint. The middle and lower portions of these ligaments are vital for shoulder stability. There are four important muscles in the shoulder that are known as the rotator cuff. These muscles attach near the ball, and they pull it into the socket to assist in stability of the shoulder.

One of the most common injuries to the glenohumeral joint is dislocation that occurs from direct trauma. When this occurs, several structures are damaged. The most common direction of dislocation of the glenohumeral joint is anterior (forward). This affects the ligaments in the shoulder (particularly the middle and inferior glenohumeral ligaments), which become stretched; depending upon the severity of the dislocation, they may not provide stability properly again. As the ball dislocates from the socket, the ball overrides the glenoid labrum and tears it. The rotator cuff muscles may become torn as well during the trauma.

Interesting research has revealed a deeper insight into the management of these dislocations. Hovelius noted that the amount of time that a dislocated shoulder is immobilized does not have any significant importance for recurrence. This goes against much of the common train of thought. Age, however, may be an important factor if not the key factor. Recurrences were noted in 90 percent of players who first dislocated at less than 20 years of age, whereas those who dislocated for the first time at over 25 years had a recurrence rate of 50 percent. If the shoulder repeatedly dislocates, then a surgical procedure is relatively unavoidable. However, there are usually times when athletes are made to play in a brace. The brace used previously for this condition usually confined the player excessively. Fortunately, a few years ago, a new shoulder stabilizer was developed by Dr. Tim Brown. This stabilizer has already been used by NHL teams and major-league baseball teams. Dr. Brown is the former director of sports medicine for the Association of Volleyball Professionals (AVP), and he is the current director of sports medicine for the Pro Surfing Tour. The shoulder stabilizer can be used dynamically to support an unstable shoulder and to reinforce the rotator cuff. This shoulder stabilizer is, without doubt, the most advanced shoulder stabilizer on the market.

The acromioclavicular joint, more commonly referred to as the AC joint, is located between the clavicle (collarbone) and the acromion (top of the shoulder). This is a simple joint with relatively little motion. It usually suffers a great deal in hockey. The problems that can arise include separation of the AC joint, arthritis, fractures, and a wearing away or thinning of the bone after injury (posttraumatic osteolysis).

Aggressive checking causes shoulder and AC joint separations. One study demonstrated that 45 percent of the players examined had abnormal findings on x-rays of their acromioclavicular joint even though they did not have any symptoms (Daly, Sim, and Simonet). Another study (Norfray et al.) reviewed shoulder x-rays of 77 professional hockey players. Forty-five percent of the players were found to have abnormalities of the clavicle that could be recognized on x-ray. The average age of those players with clavicular abnormalities was 31.4 years, and the average age of those players with normal clavicles was 23.3 years. Clavicular changes occurring 10 to 15 years later would be of great interest as well.

One key point to remember is that the acromioclavicular joint is strengthened by the trapezius from above and from the deltoid muscles from below. The inferior (underneath) surface is in direct contact with the subacromial bursa (fluid-filled sack) and supraspinatus (rotator cuff muscle). AC joint problems can affect these structures, thus causing more shoulder pain. If several of these structures are painful at the same time, it can make accurate diagnosis a difficult task.

There is a particular type of problem that can occur between the scapula (shoulder blade) and the back (thorax). This problem is known as winging of the scapula. We have seen this in hockey players, including atypical cases. The most common cause of winging of the scapula is the compression of the nerve (long thoracic nerve) to a muscle underneath the shoulder blade (serratus anterior). This compression is usually from direct trauma (checking or falls). If this problem is caused by the nerve compression, it will usually resolve over time (many months to one year). Tears of the rotator cuff muscles can also produce a winging of the scapula. Either way, this injury requires a thorough examination of the shoulder by a doctor.

Wrist and Hand

The wrist is commonly injured in hockey due to slashes, slap shots, fights, and the countless falls that occur on an outstretched hand. It is also a highly mobile joint comprising the two long forearm bones (radius and ulna) and eight small bones in the wrist itself (carpals). Although anything can happen with trauma, the wrist bone known as the scaphoid is the most commonly fractured, and the lunate is the most commonly dislocated. The scaphoid fracture is frequently difficult to diagnose and may not be visualized on the initial x-rays. Persistent pain over the central back of the wrist (dorsal and proximal wrist) may require a follow-up x-ray a few weeks later to rule out a fracture. Advanced diagnostic tests such as MRI, arthrogram, and bone scan may be required to evaluate this complex set of joints. Another common wrist injury in hockey is known as a TFCC (triangular fibrocartilage complex) tear. The TFCC is a small but important network of cartilage and ligaments in the wrist. The pain from a TFCC tear does not usually resolve. The pain is usually located on the backside of the wrist and toward the outer part of the wrist (dorsal, ulnar aspect). The pain may occur from supinating and pronating your wrist (turning your palm up and down). There may be a painful click associated with the movement. The vibration from contact on a slap shot may cause pain. An MRI or arthrogram may be required to confirm the diagnosis of the TFCC tear.

"Gamekeeper's thumb" is an injury to a ligament in the thumb (ulnar collateral ligament of the metacarpophalangeal joint). A key reason for this injury in hockey players is that the players do not bend their thumbs when wearing the gloves and do not bend their thumbs when throwing off the gloves to fight. A fist that does not have the thumb closed in the common manner exposes the thumb to being bent backward (hyperabduction). The stability of this joint is critical to stick handling. One study (Rovere et al.) of

seven hockey players in the mid-1970s revealed that all cases had partially or completely ruptured the ligament and all were from fighting. A special type of splint was utilized for four weeks with good results, and the players did not miss any games with the splint. It must be kept in mind that there are always varying degrees of injury and a severe injury may require surgery.

There are numerous combinations of both common and uncommon injuries to the wrist and hand. Falling, slashing, checking, and fighting can produce these injuries. The hands of a hockey player must be carefully examined by the medical and sports chiropractic staff.

Groin

Groin injuries are becoming more common in hockey than ever before. This category of injury includes several muscles and areas. Strains of the inner thigh (adductor muscles), hip flexor muscles located in the abdomen (iliopsoas) and thigh (rectus femoris), as well as abdominal muscles (rectus abdominus) are included in the definition of groin injuries. The groin injury is a disabling injury, and it can cause significant playing time to be lost. However, the groin injury is a difficult case to diagnose, and this can be frustrating for the player, coach, general manager, and team owner. The groin injury often cannot be identified by definitive diagnostic measures. For example, x-rays frequently do not reveal any abnormal findings. If an MRI is performed in an early enough time frame, it may demonstrate pathology. The MRI may otherwise be negative. Bone scans and CAT scans may be normal. Athletes may have normal range of motion and adequate strength in the hip yet be unable to play due to pain.

Bartolozzi, Horrigan, Mink, and Deutsch performed a four-year groin injury study of professional hockey players. The purpose of this study is to identify causative factors and common denominators of the injury, most accurate diagnostic methods, and treatment of groin injuries. While it is too soon to draw any conclusions from this study, there is preliminary data to suggest that too much stretching of the groin muscles may predispose players to groin injuries. The groin muscles may not require any extra effort or time in stretching. The final results of this study will shed light on this topic.

Abdominal Muscle Injuries

Abdominal injuries also fall into the category of groin injuries. One type of injury is pain occurring at the insertion of the rectus abdominus muscle ("abs") at the pubic symphysis (middle portion of pubic bones). This condition is known as osteitis pubis. Osteitis is an inflammation of the bone, and this particular condition occurs at the insertion of tendon into the bone. It is actually quite similar to a more common condition known as tennis elbow, or lateral epicondylitis/extensor tendinosus, in which the extensor muscle on the top of the forearm becomes inflamed at the insertion into the bone (epicondyle) by the elbow. The onset of osteitis pubis is believed to be an overuse syndrome. The pull of the rectus abdominus muscles and also the powerful pull of the adductor muscles of the inner thigh contribute to this problem. The pain may be local to the pubic symphysis, and it may radiate into the lower abdomen and inner thighs. X-rays and a bone scan are used to diagnose this problem. The treatment usually includes rest, anti-inflammatory medication, and appropriate stretching; soft-tissue mobilization of the rectus abdominus tendon is useful in some cases.

Another form of injury that is rapidly increasing in hockey is tearing of the rectus abdominus muscles. This injury is usually located low in the abdomen and off to one side or the other. Its symptoms are commonly mistaken at first to be a hernia. The tear, or overstretch, is usually only a few centimeters in length, and it can be anatomically close to the location of an inguinal hernia. The injury's symptoms do not usually resolve; it may get better, and then it returns right back to where it was before. This injury is extremely difficult to diagnose, and the tear is identified through a clinical examination. The effective clinical examination consists of a battery of functional tests that reveal the defect or weakness in the abdominal muscles. MRIs and ultrasound tests usually fail to visualize this injury. This injury commonly requires surgery to resolve it. When the tear requires surgery, there are a very few doctors that are familiar with the injury, and one of them is Ross Davidson, M.D., in Vancouver. Dr. Davidson coined the term "hockey hernia" to describe this injury. Bill Myers, M.D., in Boston, Massachusetts, has performed a significant number of these repairs and often includes an adductor release (surgical cutting of the groin muscles). Craig Smith, M.D., in Los Angeles, California, is performing the repair with an endoscope as well as an open procedure if necessary. Dr. Smith has performed more than 75 endoscopic repairs of the abdominal muscle, and my patients have had excellent outcomes. The return-to-play rate has been quite successful for the players with this diagnosis after the surgical procedure.

I have seen 45 cases of rectus abdominus tears; 1997 was an unusual year because that was the first year I saw athletes other than hockey players with this injury. The other athletes were one Olympic beach volleyball player, two elite NBA players, one NCAA basketball player, one NFL player, one Olympic weight lifter, two NCAA soccer players, and four recreational athletes. The rest were all hockey players.

One reason for this injury may be the tremendous load that the abdominal muscles take during the game, particularly during aggressive checking. It is the powerful muscles such as the quadriceps, hamstrings, glutes, erector spinae, trapezius, and even serratus anterior that deliver a check against an opponent. Once contact with the other player is made, the abdominal muscles must contract to keep the spine from bending backward, and this allows the power of the check to continue to be delivered. If the abdominal muscles are weak, then the sudden loading and overpowering and forced lengthening of the abdominal muscle while it is attempting to contract (eccentric loading) can produce an injury. This can happen if one player is overpowering the other player or if one player gets under the opposing player and therefore has better leverage.

It is statistically established that injuries usually occur during the eccentric portion of a movement (Shellock). The preventative resolution for this injury is to have good abdominal strength, not just endurance. Weighted sit-ups, pulley crunches, and medicine-ball exercises will help. This injury is far less common in professional football players, and this may well be due to the fact that the football players are better prepared for contact than the hockey players have been traditionally.

Treatment for hip adductor muscle strains include soft-tissue mobilization, ice packs, electric muscle stimulation, ultrasound, gentle strengthening programs, reduced stretching program, gentle skating, anti-inflammatory medication, and rest. All of these methods have produced results for various groin injuries in various individuals. I have found that these injuries, particularly those that are not responding adequately, respond best to appropriate soft-tissue mobilization.

Knee

Injury of the knee is common in hockey. The stress on the knee during turns, sudden stops, falls, and unintentional clipping–type movements can injure the knee. The unique anatomy of the knee gives us insight into the types of injuries that can occur.

The knee is a type of hinge joint in that it does bend back and forth (flexion and extension), but the lower leg bone (tibia) has an ability to rotate somewhat and glide forward and back. The bony structure of the knee consists of the upper thighbone (femur), the major weight-bearing bone of the leg (tibia), and the kneecap (patella). The other lower leg bone (fibula) provides a place of attachment for some of the knee ligaments. The low end of the femur and the upper end of the tibia are covered in a smooth cartilage that is known as articular cartilage. Another type of cartilage is also found in the knee and these are C-shaped structures called menisci that sit on top of the tibia. The one on the inner portion of the tibia is called the medial meniscus, and the outer one is called the lateral meniscus. Meniscal tears are common in most sports. Some patients are able to rehabilitate their meniscus injuries so well that surgical intervention is not necessary. If joint pain becomes intolerable or unacceptable, or if the knee begins to lock, then an arthroscopic partial meniscectomy is in order.

There are two ligaments that cross each other in the knee, and these are known as cruciate ligaments. One begins in the front of the tibia and inserts into the back of the femur, and it is known as the anterior cruciate ligament (ACL). The other starts from the back of the tibia and inserts into the front of the femur, and it is known as the posterior cruciate ligament (PCL). There are two major ligaments on the outer portion of the knee, one on the inside (medial) of the knee and one on the outside (lateral). These are known as collateral ligaments with one being the medial collateral ligament (MCL) and the other being the lateral collateral ligament (LCL). There are other supportive ligaments of the knee that are thickened areas of the capsule surrounding the knee. The MCL is commonly injured in hockey. MCL injuries used to be surgically repaired, but the outcomes were similar with or without surgery. Brace technology has improved so much that athletes will wear a specific type of brace during the healing process and upon return to play. Conservative care assists in reducing the inflammation in the injured ligament. ACL injuries are not uncommon. The clinical diagnosis is important as it is difficult to fully visualize the entire ACL on MRI. The first stage after the injury is to reduce inflammation, and then rehabilitation may begin. Many athletes are able to rehabilitate so successfully that a surgical reconstruction of the torn ACL isn't necessary. If rehabilitation fails, then the patient has several options of ACL repair.

The main muscle groups surrounding the knee include the quadriceps muscle in the front of the thigh, the hamstring muscle in the back of the thigh, the popliteus muscle behind the knee, and the gastrocnemius (calf) muscle. The outer area (lateral aspect) of the knee is also supported by a thick band of connective tissue (fascia) known as the iliotibial band.

The quadriceps is composed of four muscles: vastus medialis, vastus lateralis, vastus intermedius, and rectus femoris. These muscles draw a great deal of attention today, particularly regarding the movement of the patella (kneecap) up and down the lower end of the femur (thighbone). This movement is called tracking. The patella may have an abnormal movement or tracking pattern. This can be due to a muscle imbalance in the quadriceps muscles. The vastus medialis, when developed, is called the "teardrop" muscle in the gym due to its appearance. The vastus medialis has two parts—really two distinct directions of muscle fibers. The muscle fibers in the lower portion are more oblique in direction, and the upper portions are more vertical. This lower portion is commonly called the VMO (vastus medialis oblique). The VMO pulls the patella toward the medial or inner area of the thigh. The vastus lateralis pulls the patella toward the outside (lateral aspect) of the knee. If the VMO is weak, then there is a stronger pull toward the lateral aspect of the knee, and this abnormal tracking causes inflammation as well as wear and tear of the cartilage lining the back of the patella and the groove in the femur that it tracks in. This can lead to a problem known as a patellofemoral pain syndrome (PFPS). This does not usually occur in normal, healthy hockey players, but the muscle imbalance is quite common after knee surgery. There are other causes of this syndrome such as excessive tightness of the connective tissue (retinaculum) surrounding the patella. This can cause the patella to track laterally or, as recent research has indicated, it can also track medially (Shellock).

Another key point is the quadriceps muscles support the posterior cruciate ligament (PCL). If you have had a significant injury to the PCL, you must strengthen the quadriceps muscles.

The hamstring muscle group consists of three muscles: biceps femoris (long and short head), semimembranosus, and semitendinosus. The hamstring muscles serve to generate power and speed in your stride as well as during checking.

We usually hear about the hamstring with regard to injury (such as "pulling a hamstring"). There are numerous causes of hamstring injuries. Here are just a few of the most common:

- Weakness of the hamstring when compared to the quadriceps. It is generally accepted that if the hamstring is less than 60 percent as strong as the quadriceps, then this is a high predictor of pending hamstring strain. The percentage is frequently expressed as a ratio of hamstring to quadricep (0.6:1.0). The percentages are usually measured on isokinetic equipment such a Lido or Cybex.
- Other muscle imbalances have been implicated. These include imbalance between left and right hamstring and/or quadriceps muscles as well as imbalance between left and right hamstring-to-quadriceps ratios.
- Tightness of the hip flexor muscles. The tightness of the opposing hip flexor may not allow the hamstring to function over a full and normal range without experiencing resistance.
- Fibrotic adhesions or scar tissue from previous tears or injury. The adhesions do not allow the muscle to lengthen and contract normally.

Another critical point regarding the hamstring is that it supports the anterior cruciate ligament (ACL). If you have had a partial tear, overstretch, or complete rupture of the ACL, you must make your hamstring muscles as strong as possible. I advise that you restrict your quadriceps training (do not eliminate, but significantly reduce it) and carefully increase both the volume and intensity of your hamstring training. The better the hamstring-to-quadriceps ratio becomes, the more stable an ACL-deficient knee will become. In fact, if the hamstring becomes

strong enough, then is it very possible that surgery to repair the ligament will not be needed.

The large calf muscle (gastrocnemius) does not have a large degree of movement at the ankle during skating due to the limited ankle movement from the boot. The training of the calf is more important during a rehabilitation program for the knee or ankle. The gastrocnemius helps to stabilize the knee due to the fact that it crosses the back of the knee joint.

Tears of the MCL (medial collateral ligament) require that the entire knee be strengthened. Additionally, the use of an inner-thigh machine can be helpful in that one of the adductor muscles (gracilis) crosses over the MCL and helps to support it. The inner-thigh machine allows a pad to be placed against the knee for resistance. This is correct. Do not use a cable with a strap around your ankle to perform a similar movement. This method places a great deal of torque on the MCL, and that can aggravate a partially torn or overstretched MCL. The Romanian dead lifts, glute-ham-gastroc raises, hypers, good mornings, various cleans, and snatch pulls will strengthen the hamstring muscles as well and will help support the MCL. An MCL brace should be worn during the healing phase and during the initial loading of the knee (squats, pulls, etc.).

Ankle

The ankle and foot do not have a preponderance of injuries in ice hockey. This is primarily due to the nature of the hockey boot. The boot provides a great deal of stability, thus reducing the stress on the ankle ligaments. Additionally, the same support of the boot does not allow for strain on the various ankle muscles because they are not put through the range of motion and associated force production that one would see in football or track.

Many of the foot and ankle injuries that do occur are due to high-velocity impacts from the puck. The result of these impacts can be very painful and can disable a player for a few weeks. Even well-established professional hockey defensemen move out of the way when Al MacInnis fires his 100-plus-mile-per-hour slap shot. Every NHL player remembers when MacInnis fired a shot at the Kings' net and the puck went high and shattered the glass behind the net. A player will be disabled if struck by a puck moving with that magnitude of force.

Another uncommon but devastating injury is the laceration of the Achilles tendon by a skate blade. The absence of Temmu Selanne was quite obvious after he suffered one of those few Achilles tendon lacerations. The rehabilitation that has been published (Kelly and Ryan) is promising; Selanne's recovery is evidence to that fact. Other sources of violent trauma can produce unique ankle injuries. One must always watch for the injury following unique and unusual trauma. Alexander Mogilny suffered from an ankle fracture when he received a cliplike injury. Luc Robitaille received an ankle fracture when he

was taken into the boards and his ankle was forced in an unusual direction (up and out—dorsiflexion and eversion). Tears of the ankle ligaments can be expected as well from this type of trauma.

Other Injuries

Myositis ossificans is another uncommon injury, but it is still seen in hockey. There were two well-publicized cases among NHL All-Stars over the past several years. Myositis ossificans follows an impact or similar source of contusion or bruising. The bruising does not have to be visible. The most common sites of this malady are the front and side of the thigh. The occasional end result of contusions is the formation of calcium (component of bone) in the muscle that was bruised. There is usually painful swelling, local tenderness, and heat over the site of injury for the first 24 hours. Early x-rays usually show a soft-tissue mass, and the calcification is not usually seen until the second to fourth week after injury. The size of the calcification usually stabilizes after three to six months to a painless state, and some of it will reabsorb (Tredget).

CONCLUSION

Strength and conditioning for hockey serve many purposes. Common injuries can be reduced and speed, quickness, and agility can be improved. Strength can be significantly increased. These improvements can occur for young players as well as professional veterans.

Sid Gillman and Tom Landry were the first coaches in the NFL to realize the potential benefits of strength training for their players. They were the first ones to develop strength programs and invest in proper equipment. Needless to say, they became coaching legends. Their legendary reputations were earned because of their coaching skills and strategy. Their insights in scouting and talent recognition, and their recognition of the value of the proper tools to assist the players and their team were also key factors in their success. The first coaches in the NHL to realize the value of proper supplementary training will be known as coaches with insight and will also become coaching legends.

The Ice Dogs head coach and general manager John Van Boxmeer recognized the need for an appropriate speed-strength and conditioning program. Coach Van Boxmeer encouraged the players and me (JMH)

throughout the initial stages of the program and reinforced the program with his support. Further support came from the assistant coach Mark Hardy; head athletic trainer Rick Burrill; medical director of the team Keith Feder, M.D.; owners Barry and Maggie Kemp; and Centinela Hospital and hospital liason Jill Sleight, A.T.C., also provided their support.

The speed-strength and conditioning program with the Ice Dogs began with technique instruction in the spring of 1996 when players were given an off-season program and were evaluated when they returned for the 1996–97 season training camp. An in-season program was initiated. After key players were traded, all new players were instructed in the lifts and joined in the in-season training. That season, the Ice Dogs went to the Turner Cup Finals for the first time.

When Kings' general manager Dave Taylor saw the results the Ice Dogs were having, as well as the results Kings' player Luc Robitaille and others, including U.S. women's hockey player Cammi Granato, were experiencing after training with me (JMH), Taylor asked us to bring the program to the Kings. Since the training, the Kings players are faster, jump higher, weigh more with less body fat, and lift more weight each year than they did the previous year. The Kings posted their first back-to-back 90-point seasons, followed by a third consecutive 90-point season.

The need for improved training in hockey is well recognized. We hope this book has given you a guideline to start your training in the right direction. Our goal is to assist in producing stronger, faster hockey players for a faster, harder game of hockey. We feel that this book has accomplished that goal and filled the void of hockey training material. Hockey is going through an enormous growth spurt and experiencing the "growing pains" that go with growth. It is important to see that these changes are a necessary part of progress and are good for the sport, the professional players, the college and junior players, and the youth hockey players. All fields grow and develop. Our ability to adapt determines our place in the future. This is a time of adaptation for hockey.

Hockey is a wonderful sport and has provided great moments, opportunities, memories, and friendships for us. We hope that hockey is as kind to you as it has been to us. We look forward to the next level of hockey performance.

REFERENCES

Articles

Arnett, M. G. "Effects of Specificity Training on the Recovery Process During Intermittent Activity in Ice Hockey," *Journal of Strength and Conditioning Research* 10, no. 2 (1996): 124–26.

Asmussen, E. "Muscle Fatigue," *Medicine and Science in Sports and Exercise* 11, no. 4 (1979): 313–21.

Baker, D. "Improving Vertical Jump Performance Through General, Special, and Specific Strength Training: A Brief Review," *Journal of Strength and Conditioning Research* 10, no. 2 (1996): 131–36.

Bartonietz, K. E. "Biomechanics of the Snatch: Toward a Higher Training Efficiency," *Strength and Conditioning* (June 1996): 24–31.

Bergsneider, M., et al. "Metabolic Recovery Following Human Traumatic Brain Injury Based on FDG-PET: Time Course and Relationship to Neurological Disability," *Journal of Head Trauma Rehabilitation* 16, no. 2 (2001): 135–48.

Bergstrom, J. L., et al. "Diet, Muscle Glycogen, and Physical Performance," *Acta Physiologica Scandinavica* 71 (1967): 140–50.

Bjornaraa, B. "Power Training for Hockey," *National Strength and Conditioning Association Journal* 3, no. 1: 24

Blackburn, T. A., et al. "EMG Analysis of Posterior Rotator Cuff Exercises," *Athletic Training* 25 (1990): 40–45.

Bompa, T. O. "Periodization of Strength: The Most Effective Methodology of Strength Training," *National Strength and Conditioning Association Journal* 12, no. 5 (1990): 49–52.

Bompa, T. O. "Variations of Periodization of Strength," *Strength and Conditioning* (June 1996): 58–61.

Borg, G., P. Hassmen, and M. Langerstrom. "Perceived Exertion Related to Heart Rate and Blood Lactate During Arm and Leg Exercise," *European Journal of Applied Physiology* 65 (1987): 679–85.

Bracko, M. R., and G. W. Fellingham. "Prediction of Ice Skating Performance with Off-Ice Testing in Youth Hockey Players," abstract in *Medicine and Science in Sports and Exercise*, supplement to vol. 29, no. 5 (1997): S172.

Briggs, R. C., P. H. Kolbjornsen, and R. C. Southall. "Osteitis Pubis, Tc-99 MDP, and Professional Hockey Players," *Clinical Nuclear Medicine* 17, no 11 (1992): 861–63.

Brittenham, G., et al. The Second Annual USOC/ACSM Human Performance Summit, "Overtraining: The Challenge of Prevention—A Consensus Statement," Medline search.

Brust, J. D., et al. "Children's Ice Hockey Injuries," *American Journal of Diseases of Children* 146 (1992): 741–47.

Buckley, W. E. "Concussion in College Football: A Multivariate Analysis," *American Journal of Sports Medicine* 16 (1988): 51–66.

Budgett, R. "Overtraining Syndrome," *British Journal of Sports Medicine* 24, no. 4 (1990): 231–36.

Canavan, P. K., G. E. Garrett, and L. E. Armstrong. "Kinematic and Kinetic Relationships Between an Olympic-Style Lift and the Vertical Jump," *Journal of Strength and Conditioning Research* 10, no. 2 (1996): 127–30.

Cantu, R. C. "Functional Cervical Spinal Stenosis: A Contraindication to Participation in Contact Sports," *Medicine and Science in Sports and Exercise* (1993).

Cantu, R. C., and R. V. Voy. "Second Impact Syndrome," *Physician and Sports Medicine* 23, no. 6 (1995): 27–34.

Carlssion, G. S., et al. "Long-Term Effects of Head Injury Sustained During Life in Three Male Populations," *Journal of Neurosurgery* 67 (1987): 197–205.

Castaldi, C. R. "Prevention of Craniofacial Injuries in Ice Hockey," *Dental Clinics of North America* 35, no. 4 (1991): 647–56.

Cerberich, S. G., et al. "Concussion Incidences and Severity in Secondary School Varsity Football Players," *American Journal of Public Health* 73 (1983): 1370–75.

Clark, C. R. "Hockey Helmets Instead?" letter in *Canadian Medical Association Journal* 146, no. 12 (1992): 2141.

Clement, D. B., et al. "Iron Status in Winter Olympic Sports," *Journal of Sports Sciences* 5 (1987): 261–71.

Covertino, V. A., et al. "American College of Sports Medicine Position Stand on Exercise and Fluid Replacement," *Medicine and Science in Sports and Exercise* 28, no. 1 (1996): i–vii.

Crouch, L. "Neck Injuries—Prevention to Avoid, Rehabilitation," *National Strength and Conditioning Association Journal* 1, no. 5: 29–31.

Crouch, L. "Neck Injuries—Prevention to Avoid, Rehabilitation, Part II," *National Strength and Conditioning Association Journal* 1, no. 6: 29–31.

Cunningham, D. A. "Characteristics of the Elite Minor Hockey Player," *Canadian Journal of Applied Sport Science* 4, no. 2 (1979): 123–25.

Cunningham, D. A., P. Telford, and G. T. Swart. "The Cardiopulmonary Capacities of Young Hockey Players: Age 10," *Medicine and Science in Sports* 8, no. 1 (1976): 23–25.

Daly, P. J., F. H. Sim, and W. T. Simonet. "Ice Hockey Injuries," *Sports Medicine* 10, no. 3 (1990): 122–31.

Davis, J. M., et al. "Carbohydrate Drinks Delay Fatigue During Intermittent, High-Intensity Cycling in Active Men and Women," *International Journal of Sports Nutrition* 7, (1997): 261–73.

Davis, J. M., and S. P. Bailey. "Possible Mechanisms of Central Nervous System Fatigue During Exercise," *Medicine and Science in Sports and Exercise* 29, no. 1 (1996): 45–57.

Durck, C. "Squat and Power Clean Relationships to Sprint Training," *National Strength and Conditioning Association Journal* 8, no. 6 (1986): 40–41.

Emmert, W. "The Slap Shot—Strength and Conditioning Program at Boston College," *National Strength and Conditioning Association Journal* 6, no. 2 (1984): 4–6, 68, 71, 73.

Enoka, R. M. "The Pull in Olympic Weightlifting," *Medicine and Science in Sports and Exercise* 11, no. 2 (1979): 131–37.

Everson, J. "University of Wisconsin Complete Hockey Conditioning," *National Strength and Conditioning Association Journal* 4, no. 3 (1983): 20.

Everson, J., G. Hunter, and J. Olson. "Improved Offensive Line Play Through Strength Conditioning," *National Strength and Conditioning Association Journal* 5, no. 1 (1983): 6–11, 58.

Fekete, J. F. "Severe Brain Injury and Death Following Minor Hockey Accidents," *Canadian Medical Association Journal* 99 (1968): 1234–39.

Foster, C. "Monitoring Training in Athletes with Reference to Overtraining Syndrome," *Medicine and Science in Sports and Exercise* 30, no. 7 (1998): 1164–68.

Fry, A. C., and W. J. Kraemer. "Resistance Exercise Overtraining and Overreaching: Neuroendocrine Responses," *Sports Medicine*, no. 2 (February 23, 1997): 106–29.

Fry, A. C., et al. "Performance Decrements with High-Intensity Resistance Exercise Overtraining," *Medicine and Science in Sports and Exercise* 26, no. 9 (1994): 1165–73.

Fry, A. C., et al. "Relationships Between Serum Testosterone, Cortisol and Weightlifting Performance," *Journal of Strength and Conditioning Research* 14, no. 3 (2000): 338–43.

Fry, R. W., et al. "Psychological and Immunological Correlates of Acute Overtraining," *British Journal of Sports Medicine* 28, no. 4 (1994): 241–46.

Gisolfi, C. V., and S. M. Duchman. "Guidelines for Optimal Replacement Beverages for Different Athletic Events," *Medicine and Science in Sports and Exercise*, 24 (1992): 679–87.

Garhammer, J. "Power—Kinesiological Evaluation," *Strength and Conditioning* (1984): 40, 61–63.

Goldstein, G. "Recommendations on Physical Development of Football Players," *National Strength and Conditioning Association Journal* 11, no. 1 (1989): 49–50.

Gotshalk, L. "Analysis of the Deadlift," *National Strength and Conditioning Association Journal* 6, no. 6 (1985): 4–5, 74–78.

Graves, J. E., et al. "Limited Range-of-Motion Lumbar Extension Strength Training," *Medicine and Science in Sports and Exercise* 24, no. 1 (1992): 128–33.

Green, H. J. "Metabolic Aspects of Intermittent Work with Regard to Ice Hockey," *Canadian Journal of Applied Sports Sciences* 4, no. 2 (1979): 29–34.

Green, H. J., and M. E. Houston. "Effect of a Season of Ice Hockey on Energy Capacities and Associated Functions," *Medicine and Science in Sports* 7, no. 4 (1975): 299–303.

Harman, E., and P. Frykman. "The Effects of Knee Wraps on Weightlifting Performance and Injury," *National Strength and Conditioning Association Journal* 12, no. 5 (1990): 30–35.

Hermanse, L. A., and E. Holtman. "Muscle Glycogen During Prolonged, Severe Exercise," *Acta Physiologic Scandinavica* 71 (1967): 129–39.

Hermiston, R. T. "Resistance Machine for Power Skating of Hockey Players," *Journal of Sports Medicine* 16 (1976): 233–36.

Hickey, J. C., et al. "The Relation of Mouth Protectors to Cranial Pressure and Deformation," *Journal of the American Dental Association*, 24, no 4: 735–40.

Holcomb, W. R., et al. "The Effectiveness of a Modified Plyometric Program on Power and the Vertical Jump," *Journal of Strength and Conditioning Research* 10, no. 2 (1996): 89–92.

Holger, H. W., et al. "Overtraining and Immune System: A Prospective Longitudinal Study in Endurance Athletes," *Medicine and Science in Sports and Exercise* 30, no. 7 (1998): 1151–57.

Holland, G. J. "Custom vs. Commercial Mouthguard Use: Effect on Exercise Metabolic-Ventilatory Response of Trained Distance Runners," *NSCA Journal of Applied Sports Science Research* 3 (1989).

Hooper, S. L., et al. "Markers for Monitoring Overtraining and Recovery," *Medicine and Science in Sports and Exercise* 27, no. 1 (1995): 106–12.

Hornof, Z., and C. Napravnik. "Analysis of Various Accident Rate Factors in Ice Hockey," *Medicine and Science in Sports* 5, no. 4 (1973): 283–86.

Horrigan, J. M. "Ben Johnson's Weight Training Connection: An Interview with Charlie Francis," *Ironman* (June 1990): 100–104.

Horrigan, J. M. "Resolution of a Groin Injury in a Professional Hockey Player: A Case Report," *Chiropractic Sports Medicine* 6, no. 4 (1992): 151–54.

Horrigan, J. M., and B. R. Mandelbaum. "Complications of Plyometric Depth Jumps: Patellar Tendon Injuries," *Journal of Sports Chiropractic and Rehabilitation*, acceptance pending, 2002.

Horrigan, J. M., et al. "Magnetic Resonance Imaging Evaluation of Muscle Usage Associated with Three Exercises for the Rotator Cuff," *Medicine and Science in Sports and Exercise* 31, no. 10 (1999): 1361–67.

Horrigan, J. M., et al. "Muscle Recruitment Patterns Associated with Different Shoulder Exercises: Assessment Using MRI,"

abstract in *Medicine and Science in Sports and Exercise*, supplement to vol. 26, no. 5 (1994): S20.

Horrigan, J. M., et al. "Changes in Bodyweight in Professional Hockey Players as an Indicator of Dehydration Compared with Performance Assessment: A Pilot Study," abstract in *Journal of Sports Chiropractic and Rehabilitation* 12, no. 3 (1998): 127–28.

Horrigan, J. M., et al. "Changes in Bodyweight in Professional Hockey Players as an Indicator of Dehydration Following Hydration Protocol Instruction Compared with Prehydration Instruction: A Pilot Study" abstract in *Journal of Sports Chiropractic and Rehabilitation* 12, no. 3 (1998): 122.

Horrigan, J. M., et al. "Jumps and Sprints in Hockey," abstract from Sixth IOC Congress on Sports Science, Salt Lake City, Utah, September 2001 (postponed).

Horrigan, J. M., S. P. Coughlin, and M.A. Lazar. "Winging of the Scapula Associated with Traumatic Anterior Glenohumeral Instability in Professional Hockey Players: A Two Case Review," *Journal of the Neuromusculoskeletal System* 2, no. 1 (1994): 28–32.

Hovelius, L. "Shoulder Dislocation in Swedish Ice Hockey Players" *American Journal of Sports Medicine* 6, no. 6 (1978): 373–77.

Howstill, T. A. "Effective Fluid Replacement," *International Journal of Sports Nutrition*, 8 (1998):175–95.

Jobe, F. W., and D. R. Moynes. "Delineation of Diagnostic Criteria and a Rehabilitation Program for Rotator Cuff Injuries," *American Journal of Sports Medicine* 6 (1982): 336–39.

Joesting, D. R. "Diagnosis and Treatment of Sportsman's Hernia," *Current Sports Medicine Reports* 1 (2002): 121–24.

Johansson C., R. Lorentzon, and A. R. Fugl-Meyer. "Isokinetic Muscular Performance of the Quadriceps in Elite Ice Hockey Players," *American Journal of Sports Medicine* 17, no. 1 (1989): 30–34.

Jolley, J. "Developing an Effective Training Program," *Weightlifting USA* 15, no. 1 (1997): 21–22.

Jones, A. M., T. Atter, and K. George. "Oral Creatine Supplementation Improves Multiple Sprint Performance in Elite Ice Hockey Players," *Medicine and Science in Sports and Exercise* 30, no. 5 (May 1998): S140.

Jordan B. D. "Neurologic Aspects of Boxing," *Archives of Neurology* 44 (1987): 453–59.

Jorgensen, U., et al. "The Epidemiology of Ice Hockey Injuries," *British Journal of Sports Medicine*, 20 (1986): 7–9.

Kelly, T. F., and J. B. Ryan. "Lacerated Achilles Tendon in a Collegiate Hockey Player—A Case Report," *American Journal of Sports Medicine* 20, no. 1 (1992): 84–87.

Kentta, G., and P. Hassmen. "Overtraining and Recovery: A Conceptual Model," *Sports Medicine* 1 (July 26, 1998): 1–16.

Kippers, V., and A. W. Parker. "Posture Related to Myoelectric Silence of Erector Spinae During Trunk Flexion," *Spine* 9, no. 7 (1984): 740–45.

Koutedakis, Y., R. Budgett, and L. Faulmann. "Rest in Underperforming Elite Competitors," *British Journal of Sports Medicine* 24, no. 4 (1990): 248–52.

Koutedakis, Y., et al. "Maximal Voluntary Quadriceps Strength Patterns in Olympic Overtrained Athletes," *Medicine and Science in Sports and Exercise* 27, no. 4 (1995): 566–72.

Kraemer, W. J., et al. "Acute Hormonal Responses in Elite Junior Weightlifters," *International Journal of Sports Medicine* 13 (1992): 103–9.

Kraus, J. F., B. D. Anderson, and C. E. Mueller. "The Effectiveness of a Special Ice Hockey Helmet to Reduce Head Injuries in College Intramural Hockey," *Medicine and Science in Sports* 2, no. 3 (1970): 162–64.

Kreis, E. J. "University of Colorado Speed-Strength and Conditioning Program—Linemen." Denver: University of Colorado Press (1993).

Kuipers, H. "How Much Is Too Much? Performance Aspects of Overtraining," *Research Quarterly for Exercise and Sport*, supplement to vol. 67, no. 3 (1996): 65–69.

Kuipers, H. "Training and Overtraining: An Introduction (Symposium: Training/Overtraining: The First Ulm Symposium)," *Medicine and Science in Sports and Exercise* 30, no. 7 (1998): 1137–39.

Lehman, L. B., and S. J. Ravich. "Closed Head Injuries in Athletes," *Clinics in Sports Medicine* 9, no. 2 (1990): 247–61.

Lehmann, M., et al. "Autonomic Imbalance Hypothesis and Overtraining Syndrome," *Medicine and Science in Sports and Exercise* 30, no. 7 (1998): 1140–45.

Lenhard, R. A., et al. "Monitoring Injuries on a College Soccer Team: The Effect of Strength Training," *Journal of Strength and Conditioning Research* 10, no. 2 (1996): 115–19.

Lorenzton, R., H. Wedren, and T. Pietila. "Incidence, Nature, and Causes of Ice Hockey Injuries: A Three Year Prospective Study of a Swedish Elite Ice Hockey Team," *The American Journal of Sports Medicine* 16, no. 4 (1988): 392–96.

Martin, B. J., and G. M. Gaddis. "Exercise After Sleep Deprivation," *Medicine and Science in Sports and Exercise* 13, no. 4 (1981): 220–23.

Martin, B. J., and H. I. Chen. "Sleep Loss and the Sympathoadrenal Response to Exercise," *Medicine and Science in Sports and Exercise* 16, no. 1 (1984): 55–59.

Martin, B. J., et al. "Effect of Warm-Up on Metabolic Responses to Strenuous Exercises," *Medicine and Science in Sports* 7, no. 2 (1975): 146–49.

Mascaro, T., W. L. Seaver, and L. Swanson. "Prediction of Skating Speed with Off-Ice Testing in Professional Hockey Players," *Journal of Orthopedic and Sports Physical Therapy* 15, no. 2 (1992): 92–98.

McClellan, T., and W. J. Stone. "A Survey of Football Strength and Conditioning Programs for Division I NCAA Universities," *National Strength and Conditioning Association Journal* 8, no. 2 (1986): 34–36.

McCunney, R. J., and R. K. Russo. "Brain Injuries in Boxers," *Physician and Sportsmedicine* 12 (1984): 53–67.

McLaughlin, T. M., and N. H. Madsen. "Bench Press Techniques of Elite Heavyweight Powerlifters," *National Strength and Conditioning Association Journal* 6, no. 4 (1984): 44, 62–65.

Meleski, B. W., and R. M. Malina. "Cortical Bone, Body Size, and Skeletal Maturity in Ice Hockey Players 10 to 12 Years of Age," *Canadian Journal of Applied Sports Science* 6, no. 4 (1981): 212–17.

Merrifield, H. H., and G. A. Walford. "Battery of Ice Hockey Skill Tests," *Research Quarterly* 40, no. 1 (1968): 146–52.

Metivier, G. "Changes in the Total Blood Serum Cholesterol Level, Cardiovascular Condition, and Adiposity of Adult Males Following One Season of Ice Hockey," *Medical Services Journal, Canada* (June 1966): 411–22.

Miller, J. "The Practical Use of Medicine Ball Drills," *National Strength and Conditioning Association Journal* (1985): 38–40.

Minardo, M. A. "Hemangioma of the Clavicle of a Hockey Player," *Journal of Sports Chiropractic and Rehabilitation*, 11, no. 1 (1997): 18–20.

Minkoff, J. "Evaluating Parameters of a Professional Hockey Team," *American Journal of Sports Medicine* 10, no. 5 (1982): 285–92.

Molsa, J., et al. "Spinal Cord Injuries in Ice Hockey in Finland," abstract in *Medicine and Science in Sports and Exercise*, supplement to vol. 29, no. 5 (1997): S191.

Monpetit, R. R., P. Binette, and A. W. Taylor. "Glycogen Depletion in a Game-Simulated Hockey Task," *Canadian Journal of Applied Sport Sciences* 4, no. 1 (1979): 43–45.

Moore, T. H., et al. "Quantitative Assessment of Longitudinal Metabolic Changes in Vivo After Traumatic Brain Injury in the Adult Rat Using FDG-microPET," *Journal of Cerebral Blood Flow Metabolism* 20, no. 10 (2000): 1492–501.

Morgan, W. P., et al. "Psychological Monitoring of Overtraining and Staleness," *British Journal of Sports Medicine* 21, no. 3 (1987): 107–14.

Morrow, L. J. "Single Leg Strength: Its Relationship to Speed Enhancement," *National Strength and Conditioning Association Journal* 8, no. 5 (1986): 64–65.

Mueller, F. O., and C. S. Blyth. "Fatalities from Head and Cervical Spine Injuries Occurring in Tackling Football: 40 Years' Experience," *Clinics in Sport Medicine* 6 (1987): 185–94.

Mueller, F. O., and R. D. Schindler. "Annual Survey of Football Injury Research 1931–1984," Orlando, Fla.: American Football Coaches Association, 1985.

Naessens, G., et al. "Clinical Usefulness of Nocturnal Urinary Noradrenaline Excretion Patterns in the Follow-Up of Training Processes in High-Level Soccer Players," *Journal of Strength and Conditioning Research* 14, no. 2 (2000): 125–31.

Naud, R. L. "A Comparison of Selected Stop, Reverse, and Start (SRS) Techniques in Ice Hockey," *Canadian Journal of Applied Sport Science* 5, no. 2 (1980): 94–97.

Norfray, J. F., et al. "The Clavicle in Hockey," *American Journal of Sports Medicine* 5, no. 6 (1977): 275–80.

Novkov, P. "Depth Jumps—Soviet Lecture Series #1," *National Strength and Conditioning Association Journal* 9, no. 5 (1987): 60–61.

Oakland, C. D. "Ice Skating Injuries: Can They Be Reduced or Prevented?" *Archives of Emergency Medicine* 7 (1990): 95–99.

Olson, J. R., and G. R. Hunter. "A Comparison of 1974 and 1984 Player Sizes, and Maximal Strength and Speed Efforts for Division I NCAA Universities," *National Strength and Conditioning Association Journal* 6, no. 6 (1985): 26–28.

Orvanova, E. "Physical Structure of Winter Sports Athletes," *Journal of Sport Sciences* 5 (1987): 197–248.

O'Shea, P. "The Parallel Squat," *National Strength and Conditioning Association Journal* 7, no. 1 (1985): 4–6, 78.

Palmieri, J., and R. Cope. "Conditioning the Defensive Football Player for the Last Two Minutes of the Game," *National Strength and Conditioning Association Journal* 11, no. 6 (1989): 24–25.

Park, R. D., and C. R. Castaldi. "Injuries in Junior Ice Hockey," *Physician and Sports Medicine* 8, no. 2 (1980): 81–90.

Parry-Billings, M., et al. "Plasma Amino Acid Concentrations in the Overtraining Syndrome: Possible Effects on the Immune System," *Medicine and Science in Sports and Exercise* 24, no. 12 (1992): 1353–58.

Pashby, T. J. "Making Hockey Safer" (letter), *Canadian Medical Association Journal* 142, no. 9 (1990): 934.

Paterson, D. H. "Respiratory and Cardiovascular Aspects of Intermittent Exercise with Regard to Ice Hockey," *Canadian Journal of Applied Sports Sciences* 4, no. 1 (1979): 22–28.

Patterson, D. "Legal Aspects of Athletic Injuries to the Head and Cervical Spine," *Clinics in Sports Medicine* 6 (1987): 197.

Pauletto, B. "Periodization—Peaking," *National Strength and Conditioning Association Journal* 8, no. 4 (1986): 30–31.

Pedemonte, J. "Foundations of Training Periodization, Part I: Historical Outline," *National Strength and Conditioning Association Journal* 8, no. 3: 62–65.

Pelletier, R. L., G. Anderson, and R. M. Stark. "Profile of Sport/Leisure Injuries Treated at Emergency Rooms of Urban Hospitals," *Canadian Journal of Sport Science* 16, no. 1 (1991): 99–102.

Posch, E., Y. Haglund, and E. Eriksson. "Prospective Study of Concentric and Eccentric Leg Muscle Torques, Flexibility, Physical Conditioning, and Variation of Injury Rates During One Season of Amateur Ice Hockey," *International Journal of Sports Medicine* 10, no. 2 (1989): 113–17.

Reynen, P. D., and W. G. Clancy Jr. "Cervical Spine Injury, Hockey Helmets, and Face Masks," *American Journal of Sports Medicine* 22, no. 2 (1994): 167–70.

Reynolds, E. J., et al. "Pectoralis Major Tears: Etiology and Prevention," *Chiropractic Sports Medicine* 7, no. 3 (1993): 83–89.

Rovere, G. D., A. G. Gristina, and J. Nicastro. "Hockey Injuries—Three Season Experience," abstract in *Medicine and Science in Sports* 3, no. 4 (1975): 147–51.

Rovere, G. D., et al. "Treatment of 'Gamekeeper's Thumb' in Hockey Players," *Journal of Sports Medicine* 3, no. 4 (1975): 147–51.

Sale, D. G. "Neural Adaptation to Resistance Training," *Medicine and Science in Sports and Exercise* 20, no. 5 (1988): S135–45.

Sale, D., and D. MacDougall. "Specificity in Strength Training: A Review for the Coach and Athlete," *Canadian Journal of Applied Sports Science*s 4, no. 1 (1979): 87–92.

Sercl, M., and O. Jaros. "The Mechanisms of Cerebral Concussion in Boxing and Their Consequences," *World Neurology* 3 (1962): 351–57.

Shellock, F. G., et al. "Exertional Muscle Injury: Evaluation of Concentric Versus Eccentric Action with Serial MR Imaging," *Radiology* 179, no. 3 (1991): 659–64.

Shellock, F. G., et al. "Patellar Tracking Abnormalities: Clinical Experience with Kinematic MR Imaging in 130 Patients," *Radiology* 172, no. 3 (1989): 799–804.

Shellock, F. G., and W. E. Prentice. "Warming Up and Stretching for Improved Physical Performance and Prevention of Sports-Related Injuries," *Sports Medicine* 2 (1985): 267–78.

Shi, X., et al. "Effect of Carbohydrate Type and Concentration on Solution Osmolality on Water Reabsorption," *Medicine and Science in Sports and Exercise* 27 (1996): 1607–15.

Sim, F. H., and E. Y. Chao. "Injury Potential in Modern Ice Hockey," *American Journal of Sports Medicine* 6, no. 6 (1978): 378–84.

Snyder, A. C. "Overtraining and Glycogen Depletion Hypothesis," *Medicine and Science in Sports and Exercise* 30, no. 7 (1998): 1146–50.

Snyder, A. C., et al. "A Physiological/Psychological Indicator of Over-Reaching During Intensive Training," *International Journal of Sports Medicine* 14 (1993): 29–32.

Sthair, V. L. "United States Olympic Team Ice Hockey Conditioning Program," *National Strength and Conditioning Association Journal* 8, no. 3 (1986): 54–59, 74.

Stone, M. H. "Literature Review: Explosive Exercises and Training," *National Strength and Conditioning Association Journal* 15, no. 3 (1993): 7–15.

Stone, M. H., et al. "Training to Muscular Failure: Is It Necessary?" *Strength and Conditioning* (June 1996): 44–51.

Sullivan, P. "Sports MDs Seek CMA Support in Bid to Make Hockey Safer," *Canadian Medical Association Journal* 142, no. 2 (1990): 157–59.

Swain, R., and S. Snodgrass. "Managing Groin Pain," *Physician and Sport Medicine* 23, no. 11 (1995): 55–66.

Tator, C. H. "Neck Injuries in Ice Hockey: A Recent Unsolved Problem with Many Contributing Factors," *Clinics in Sports Medicine* 6, no. 1 (1987): 101–14.

Tator, C. H., et al. "Spinal Injuries Due to Hockey," *The Canadian Journal of Neurological Sciences* 11 (1984): 34–41.

Taylor, S. R., G. G. Rogers, and H. S. Driver. "Effects of Training Volume on Sleep, Psychological, and Selected Physiological Profiles of Elite Female Swimmers," *Medicine and Science in Sports and Exercise* 29, no. 5 (1997): 688–93.

Tegner, Y., and R. Lorentzon. "Evaluation of Knee Braces in Swedish Ice Hockey Players," *British Journal of Sports Medicine* 25, no. 3 (1991): 159–61.

Tegner, Y., and R. Lorentzon. "Ice Hockey Injuries: Incidence, Nature, and Causes," *British Journal of Sports Medicine* 25, no. 2 (1991): 87–89.

Torcolacci, M. "Rethinking Strength Training for Throwers," *National Strength and Conditioning Association Journal* 15, no. 6 (1993): 47–52.

Tredget, T., C. V. Godberson, and B. Bose. "Myositis Ossificans Due to Hockey

Injury," *Canadian Medical Association Journal* 116, no. 1 (1977): 65–6.

Triano, J. J., and A. B. Schultz. "Correlation of Objective Measure of Trunk Motion and Muscle Function with Low-Back Disability Ratings," *Spine* 12, no. 6 (1987): 561–5.

Twist, P., and T. Rhodes. "The Bioenergetic and Physiological Demands of Ice Hockey," *National Strength and Conditioning Association Journal* 15, no. 5 (1993): 68–70.

Twist, P., and T. Rhodes. "A Physiological Analysis of Ice Hockey Positions," *National Strength and Conditioning Association Journal* 15, no. 6 (1993): 44–46.

Valeriani, A. "The Need for Carbohydrate Intake During Endurance Exercise," *Sports Medicine* 12, no. 6 (1991): 349.

Verkoshansky, Y. V. "Explosive Power—Soviet Lecture #2," *National Strength and Conditioning Association Journal* 9, no. 6 (1987): 82–83.

Verkoshansky, Y. V. "Strength and Conditioning Considerations in American Football—Soviet Lecture Series #3," *National Strength and Conditioning Association Journal* 10, no. 2 (1988): 70–71.

Verkoshansky, Y. V. "Principles of Planning Speed and Strength/Speed Endurance Training in Sports," *National Strength and Conditioning Association Journal* 11, no. 2: 58.

Vermeil, A. "Periodization of Strength Training for Professional Football," *National Strength and Conditioning Association Journal* 4, no. 3 (1982): 54–55.

Vorobyev, A. N. "The Scientific Basis of Weightlifting Training and Technique," *Soviet Sports Review* 14, no. 1 (1978):1–5.

Wade, G. "Tests and Measurements: Meeting the Standards of Professional Football,"

National Strength and Conditioning Association Journal 4, no. 3 (1982): 23.

Walsh, R. M., et. al. "Compared High-Intensity Cycling Performance Time at Low Levels of Dehydration," *International Journal of Sports Nutrition*, 15 (1994): 392–98.

Warren, B. J., et al. "Performance Measures, Blood Lactate, and Plasma Ammonia as Indicators of Overwork in Elite Junior Weightlifters," *International Journal of Sports Medicine* 13 (1992): 372–76.

Waters, J. V. "Weight Room Motivation More than T-Shirts and Whistles," *National Strength and Conditioning Association Journal* 15, no. 6 (1993): 53.

Wathen, D. "Literature Review: Explosive/Plyometric Exercises," *National Strength and Conditioning Association Journal* 15, no. 3 (1993): 17–19.

Wathen, D., et al. "Prevention of Athletic Injuries Through Strength Training and Conditioning," *National Strength and Conditioning Association Journal* 5, no. 2 (1983): 14–19.

Welday, J. "Pittsburgh Penguins: Championship Strength and Conditioning," *High Intensity Training Newsletter* 4, no. 3 (1993): 2–4.

Wenger, H. "Los Angeles Kings High Performance Summer Program (unpublished)." Los Angeles: 1990.

Wheeler. "Sports Nutrition for the Primary Care Physician: The Importance of Carbohydrate," *Physician in Sports Medicine* 17, no. 5 (1989): 106.

Whiting, W. C. "Electromyographic Assessment of Lower Extremity Extensor Muscles in Response to Dynamic Fatigue," abstract in *Journal of Sports Chiropractic and Rehabilitation* 1, no. 3 (1996).

Widmeyer, W. N., and J. S. Birch. "The Relationship Between Aggression and Performance Outcome in Hockey," *Canadian*

Journal of Applied Sports Science 4 (1979): 91–94.

Widmeyer, W. N., and J. S. Birch. "Aggression in Professional Ice Hockey: A Strategy for Success or a Reaction to Failure?" *Journal of Psychology* 117 (1984): 77–84.

Wilk, K. E., et al. "A Comparison of Tibiofemoral Joint Forces and Electromyographic Activity During Open and Closed Chain Exercises," *American Journal of Sports Medicine* 24, no. 4 (1996): 518–27.

Yessis, M. "If the Soviets Had Football," *National Strength and Conditioning Association Journal* 4, no. 1 (1982): 4–7.

Yessis, M. "Glute-Ham-Gastroc Raises," *National Strength and Conditioning Association Journal* 6, no. 3 (1984): 54–57.

Young, P. "Optimal Strength Training in Speed-Strength Sports: A Theoretical Approach," *National Strength and Conditioning Association Journal* 7, no. 6 (1985): 44.

Young, W. "Training for Speed/Strength: Heavy vs. Light Loads," *National Strength and Conditioning Association Journal* 15, no. 5 (1993): 34–42.

Books

Aleves, W. M. "Football-Induced Mild Head Injury." In *Athletic Injuries to the Head, Neck and Face*, edited by J. S. Torg, 283–304. St. Louis: Mosby Year Book, 1991.

Bompa, T. O. *Periodization of Strength.* Toronto, Ontario: Veritas Publishing, Inc., 1993.

Bompa, T. O. *Power Training for Sport.* Gloucester, Ontario: Coaching Association of Canada, 1993.

Bompa, T. O. *Theory and Methodology of Training.* 2nd ed. Dubuque, Iowa: Kendall/Hunt Publishing Co., 1990.

Brunner, R., and B. Tabachnik. *Soviet Training and Recovery Methods.* Pleasant Hill, Calif.: Sport Focus Publishing, 1990.

Bucci, L. *Nutrients as Ergogenic Aids for Sports and Exercise.* Boca Raton, Fla.: CRC Press, 1993.

Buskirk, E., and F. Puhl. "Nutritional Beverages: Exercise in Sport." In *Nutrition in Exercise and Sport*, edited by Hickson and Wolinsky, 201. Boca Raton, Fla.: CRC Press, 1989.

Bylsma, D. *So, Your Son Wants to Play in the NHL?* Chelsea, Mich.: Sleeping Bear Press, 1998.

Cantu, R. C. "Criteria for Return to Competition After Closed Head Injury." In *Athletic Injuries to the Head, Neck and Face*, edited by J. S. Torg, 124–132. St Louis: Mosby Year Book, 1991.

Costello, F., and E. J. Kreis. *Agility Training for Athletes.* Nashville: Taylor Sports Publishing, Inc., 1994.

Croce, P., and B. C. Cooper. *Conditioning for Ice Hockey: Year Round.* Champaign, Ill.: Leisure Press, 1983.

Cushner, G. B., and F. V. Cushner. "Fluid Balance." In *Sports Medicine Principles and Primary Care*, edited by G. R. Scuderi, P. V. McCann, and P. J. Bruno, 568–77. St. Louis: Mosby, 1997.

Danzig, A. *The History of American Football.* Englewood Cliffs, N.J.: Prentice Hall, 1956.

Dintiman, G. B., and R. D. Ward. *Sport Speed.* Champaign, Ill.: Leisure Press, 1988.

Edwards, R. H. T. *Human Muscle Fatigue: Physiological Mechanisms.* London: Pitman Medical, 1981.

Francis, C., and P. Patterson. *The Charlie Francis Training System.* Ottawa, Ontario: TBLI Publications, Inc., 1992.

Freeman, W. H. *Peak When It Counts.* Mountain View, Calif.: Tafnews Press, 1991.

Hawley, J. A, S. C. Dennis, and T. D. Noakes. "Carbohydrate, Fluid, and Electrolyte Replacements During Prolonged Exercise." In *Sports Nutrition: Minerals and Electrolytes*, edited by C. Kies and J. A. Driskell, 235–65. Boca Raton, Fla.: CRC Press, 1995.

Horrigan, J. M., and J. Robinson. *The 7 Minute Rotator Cuff Solution.* Los Angeles: Health for Life Publications, 1991.

Huizenga, R. *You're Okay. It's Just a Bruise.* New York: St. Martin's Griffin, 1994.

Johnson, H. L. "The Requirements for Fluid Replacement During Heavy Sweating and the Benefits of Carbohydrates and Minerals." In *Sports Nutrition: Minerals and Electrolytes*, edited by C. Kies and J. A. Driskell, 215–33. Boca Raton, Fla.: CRC Press, 1995.

Jones, L. *USWF Coaching Accreditation Course, Club Coach Manual.* Colorado Springs, Colo.: U.S. Weightlifting Federation, 1991.

Kreis, E. J. *Speed-Strength Training for Football.* Nashville: Taylor Sports Publishing, Inc., 1992.

MacAdams, D., and G. Reynolds. *Hockey Fitness.* Champaign, Ill.: Leisure Press, 1988.

Nideffer, R. M., *Athlete's Guide to Mental Training.* Champaign, Ill.: Human Kinetics Publishers, 1985.

Payne, V. G., and L. D. Isaacs. *Human Motor Development.* Mountain View, Calif.: Mayfield Publishing Co., 1991.

Starr, B. *The Strongest Shall Survive.* Washington, D.C.: Fitness Products, 1978.

Tator, C. A., "Injuries to the Cervical Spine and Spinal Cord Resulting from Ice Hockey," 2nd ed. In *Athletic Injuries to the Head, Neck, and Face,* edited by J. S. Torg, St. Louis: Mosby Year Book, 1991.

The Training of a Weightlifter. Livonia, Mich.: Sportivny Press, 1988.

Torg, J. S. *Current Therapy in Sports Medicine,* 11–21. St. Louis: Mosby Year Book, 1995.

Verkoshansky, Y. V. *Fundamentals of Special Strength-Training in Sport.* Livonia, Mich.: Sportivny Press, 1986.

Verkoshansky, Y. V. *Programming and Organization of Training.* Livonia, Mich.: Sportivny Press, 1988.

Vorobyev, A. N. *Weightlifting,* translated by W. J. Brice. Budapest, Hungary: International Weightlifting Federation, 1978.

Wilmore, J. H., and D. L. Costill. *Physiology of Sport and Exercise.* Champaign, Ill.: Human Kinetics, 1994.

Yessis, M., and F. C. Hatfield. *Plyometric Training: Achieving Explosive Power in Sports.* Canoga Park, Calif.: Fitness Systems, 1986.

Videos

Kreis, E. J. *Speed Hurddles.* Nashville, Tenn.: Taylor Sports Publishing, 1977.

NOVA. "Can Science Make a Better Athlete?" Public Broadcasting System. Original broadcast February 16, 1993.

USA Hockey. *Checking.* Champaign, Ill.: Human Kinetics Publishers.

USA Hockey. *Designing a Practice.* Champaign: Ill.: Human Kinetics Publishers, 1992.

Ward, R., and G. B. Dintiman. *Speed and Explosion.* Dallas, Tex.: 1991.

INDEX

ABOUT THE AUTHORS

Joseph M. Horrigan, D.C., is the president of a sports medicine facility known as the Soft Tissue Center and Horrigan Sports Chiropractic in Los Angeles and Manhattan Beach, California. His postdoctorate certifications include the diplomate of the American Chiropractic Board of Sports Physicians and certified strength and conditioning specialist. He is also a certified club coach with USA Weightlifting. Horrigan is the developer and author of the monthly sports medicine column in *Ironman* magazine, and he created the magazine's upcoming strength and sport column. He also codeveloped and coauthors the sports medicine column in *Inside Kung-Fu* magazine. A previously published book by Horrigan is *The 7-Minute Rotator Cuff Solution*. He has served with the Long Beach Ice Dogs IHL hockey team as the chiropractic consultant for four years and as the director of speed-strength and conditioning for six years, and he still works as a staff physician. In addition, he now serves as the head strength and conditioning coach for the Los Angeles Kings. He has treated players from 17 NHL teams. Horrigan also serves on the postgraduate faculty in the sports medicine program at the Los Angeles College of Chiropractic and Northwestern College of Chiropractic. He served as the vice president of the American Chiropractic Board of Sports Physicians for four years, and he serves on the Sports Medicine Committee of USA Weightlifting. Horrigan was the medical director for Team USA at the 1999 Weightlifting Junior World Championships. He serves on the editorial board for the *Journal of Sports Chiropractic and Rehabilitation* and for *Biomechanics*. He is a member of the American College of Sports Medicine, the American Chiropractic Association Council on Sports Injuries and Physical Fitness, the International Sports Sciences Association, the National Strength and Conditioning Association, and USA Weightlifting. In 2001, Horrigan was named the Sports Chiropractor of the Year by the ACA Council on Sports Injuries and Physical Fitness and the American Chiropractic Board of Sports Physicians.

E. J. "Doc" Kreis, D.A., is the head speed-strength and conditioning coach and the assistant athletic director at the University of Colorado. He was previously the strength and conditioning coach at Middle Tennessee State University (MTSU) and Vanderbilt. Kreis received his doctorate at Middle Tennessee State University in 1989. He was named the National Collegiate Strength Coach of the Year in 1994–95 by the Professional Football Strength and Conditioning Coaches Society. Also in 1995, Kreis was the recipient of the Stan Jones Award from the International Sports Sciences Association for "excellence in multiple criteria of strength and conditioning." While at MTSU, Kreis won the National Strength and Conditioning Coach of the Year Award for 1991–92. In 2001 he was named one of ten "Strength Masters" by the Collegiate Strength and Conditioning Coaches Association. He has studied strength and conditioning in the Soviet Union, Bulgaria, East Germany, West Germany, and France. He is a member of the International Sports Sciences Association, the National Association for Speed and Explosion, and the National Organization of Speed-Strength and Conditioning. Kreis is the author of *Speed-Strength for Football* and *Sports Agility* and also coauthors the upcoming strength and sport column in *Ironman* magazine. He trains professional and Olympic athletes on an ongoing basis.

Contributing Authors

Robert S. Bray, M.D., is a neurosurgeon who specializes in minimally invasive surgery and has extensive experience in this area. His help in developing innovative approaches for preservation of ligamentous structures has resulted in reduced blood loss, operation time, and recovery time. He has contributed to the field of spinal surgery by developing new instrumentation and codeveloping laser disk decompression instrumentation. In addition, he is part of a multicenter teaching research team for percutaneous discectomy. After receiving his medical degree from Baylor College of Medicine, Dr. Bray completed his internship and neurosurgical residency at Baylor affiliated hospitals. He was the chief of neurosurgery at David Grant Medical Center, the largest referral center for the United States Air Force on the West Coast. Bray still serves as a major in the United States Air Force Reserve. A diplomate of the American Board of Neurologic Surgeons, Bray is also a member of many organizations, including the American Medical Association, the California Medical Association, the Los Angeles County Medical Association, the Congress of Neurologic Surgeons, the Association of Military Surgeons, and the Society of Clinical Air Force Surgeons. Bray is currently chief of spine surgery at Cedars-Sinai Hospital in Los Angeles, California.

G. Douglas Andersen, D.C., currently serves as the director of sports medicine for the Association of Volleyball Professionals. Andersen is a diplomate of the American Chiropractic Board of Sports Physicians and a certified clinical nutritionist; in addition, he is certified for manipulation under anesthesia. Andersen is the author of a monthly column on clinical and sports nutrition for *Dynamic Chiropractic*, the most widely read publication in his profession. He is also the team nutritionist for the Los Angeles Kings and Long Beach Ice Dogs. Andersen has lectured to professional athletes on a wide variety of subjects (including dehydration) and has had a high degree of success managing difficult cases of hydration and nutritional needs. He is also on the medical staff of the Association of Surfing Professionals and Ballet Pacifica (professional ballet). Andersen is a member of the American Chiropractic Association (ACA) Sports Council, the ACA Nutrition Council, and the International and American Association of Clinical Nutritionists. He has also won awards for the best abstract at the 1997 and 1998 Chiropractic Sports Sciences Symposia.

Ian I. T. Armstrong, M.D., received his medical degree at Baylor College of Medicine. His residency included oncological, pediatric, and traumatic neurosurgery, and he is a fellowship-trained specialist in neurosurgery, microsurgery, and spinal instrumentation. His fellowship specialty training included work at the University of Marseilles Hospital de Concepcion in Marseilles, France, and was completed at the University of South Florida. Armstrong is the chief of neurosurgery at Century City Hospital in Los Angeles, California, and is director of the Southern California Spine Institute. He is also on staff at Cedars-Sinai Medical Center, Daniel Freeman Memorial Hospital, and Centinela Hospital. He is active in teaching neurosurgical residents and in neurosurgical research. The National Institute of Health awarded him a fellowship grant for research in spinal cord trauma. Armstrong is a neurosurgical consultant to the Long Beach Ice Dogs.

A. Patric Cohen, D.D.S., studied biology at Stanford University and dentistry at the University of Southern California. Following dental school, Cohen pursued a two-year program in advanced treatment of the temporomandibular joint (TMJ) and full-mouth rehabilitation through the Foundation for Advanced Continuing Education in Northern California. He has presented papers on topics including "mouth guard protection" and "on-site treatment of mandibular trauma," and he is currently writing a book on TMJ and its relationship to headaches. He is the team dentist for the Long Beach Ice Dogs and served on the medical staff at the 1995 U.S. Tae Kwon Do Junior Olympic Championships. He is a member of the American Dental Association, the Academy of Sports Dentistry, the Academy of General Dentistry, the American Academy of Cosmetic Dentistry, and the American College of Implantology.